Feminism and Men

Feminism and Men

Reconstructing Gender Relations

EDITED BY

Steven P. Schacht and Doris W. Ewing

New York University Press

NEW YORK AND LONDON

NEW YORK UNIVERSITY PRESS
New York and London

Library of Congress Cataloging-in-Publication Data
Feminism and men : reconstructing gender relations / edited by
Steven P. Schacht and Doris W. Ewing.
p.   cm.
Includes index.
ISBN 0-8147-8077-6 (clothbound : acid-free paper)
ISBN 0-8147-8084-9 (pbk. : acid-free paper)
1. Feminism—United States.   2. Masculinity—United States.   3. Sex
role—United States.   4. Men—United States—Psychology.   5.
Men—United States—Attitudes.   6. Men—United States—Sexual
behavior.   I. Schacht, Steven P.   II. Ewing, Doris W., 1939–
HQ1426 .F44 1998
305.3—ddc21   98-19689
CIP

Manufactured in the United States of America

10 9 8 7 6 5 4 3 2 1

To my mother, Jaci (1939–1980), for sharing her vision of a feminist future with me.
—SPS

To my son, Quintin, in hopes that he and other young men of his generation will bring about a feminist future
—DWE

Contents

    on the Movement from Gender Identity to
    Moral Identity   146
    John Stoltenberg

9. A Good Man Is Hard to Bash: Confessions of an
    Ex-Man-Hater   161
    Kay Leigh Hagan

PART III: Reconstructing Gender Relations

10. Feminism, Men, and the Study of Masculinity:
    Which Way Now?   173
    Matthew Shepherd

11. Feminism and Masculinity: Reconceptualizing the
    Dichotomy of Reason and Emotion   183
    Christine A. James

12. The Multiple Genders of the Court: Issues of Identity
    and Performance in a Drag Setting   202
    Steven P. Schacht

13. Gender Politics for Men   225
    R. W. Connell

14. Sex, Gender, and Transformation: From Scoring
    to Caring   237
    Riane Eisler

15. Men: Comrades in Struggle   265
    bell hooks

PART IV: Profeminist Men's Groups Working toward
    Meaningful Change   281

    Contributors   305
    Permissions   309

Preface

Shortly after we met, over six years ago, we began what has become an ongoing dialogue on men's possible relationships to feminism. This led us to organize a session on feminism and men for the Midwest Sociological Society in the spring of 1993, guest coedit a special issue on feminism and men for the *International Journal of Sociology and Social Policy,* and write several articles on this topic for various publications. The ideas we explored in these forums moved us to propose and edit this anthology.

The first part of the book examines men's past relationships to feminism and how they influence both individual and societal gender politics in the present. Part 2 offers some individual perspectives on the importance of realizing a feminist future. The third part proposes different ways of viewing and constructing gender that could be more conducive to realizing gender equality. Finally, part 4 provides short descriptions of a sampling of existing profeminist/feminist men's groups. We believe that this anthology offers a diversity of voices that all point to the possibilities and promise of men helping create larger feminist realities in the present and future.

We sincerely thank all the contributors to this anthology, without whom it would not have been possible to publish this volume. We also thank the reviewers of our original proposal for their sage advice on what sort of pieces would best be included in an anthology on feminism and men. Special thanks are due Michael Rose, editorial assistant at New York University Press, for his helpful feedback in preparing final copy of the text, and Timothy Bartlett for his support throughout this project.

Chapter One

Introduction

Doris W. Ewing and Steven P. Schacht

Many men are sympathetic to issues of gender equity and supportive of feminist goals, but see feminism as basically irrelevant to their interests. They may be engaged in research, teaching, community activities, and/or personal activities that advance feminist objectives, but never examine their efforts in a feminist framework. Too often feminism has been seen as a "woman-only" arena or defined in competitive terms of male versus female privilege, rather than a cooperative effort to improve the quality of life for everyone. The few men who have attempted to embrace a feminist worldview often have been marginalized by women who view them with suspicion and by men who see them as gender traitors (or as a friend says, "The worm in the sperm").[1] The goal of this anthology is to expand the definition of feminism to include cooperative ventures between men and women working together to bring about positive social change.

As Riane Eisler has written, "male dominance, male violence, and authoritarianism are not inevitable, eternal givens . . . rather than being just a 'utopian dream,' a more peaceful and equalitarian world is a real possibility for our future" (1987, 73). Ancient societies in the Middle East were based on partnership models; power and decision making were shared between men and women. Many of the Native American nations were also based on cooperation and gender equality. In fact, the utopian views of the nineteenth-century American feminists often were based on practices of the Iroquois and Cherokee. Our past and present provide numerous examples of cultural arrangements and individual actions that are not based on male dominance, control, and violence. While it is our firm belief that the modern world order contains within it the seeds of its own destruction, we also believe that it contains the seeds of its rebirth into a life-affirming world order based on acceptance, equality, and liberation for all people.

Clearly, if this rebirth is to occur, we will have to reexamine and change the most basic values, purposes, and forms of social organization and relational interaction on which patriarchy is based. Rationality will have to be tempered with emotion, materialism with spirituality, competition with cooperation. Individual interest will have to be transformed and reinvested in the larger good of the community. The powerful, instrumental "male" energy associated with the father will have to be balanced with the nurturing, life-sustaining "female" energy associated with the mother if humankind is to survive on this planet. This is feminism in its most basic sense, ultimately neither female nor male in orientation, but a joint pursuit of human interests. Feminist goals cannot be realized until men and women come together to eliminate the shared harm of present patriarchal realities and to promote alternative ways of being that are beneficial to everyone.

Unfortunately, much of what is being written by those in both women's studies and men's studies seems to have increasingly become bogged down in theoretical abstractions that are of intellectual interest to academics but offer little to those working to make changes in the everyday world. Further, much of the scholarly work in this area (especially in men's studies) often fails to take into account the relational nature of gender. What it means to be a man can be understood only in relation to women and femininity, just as what it means to be a woman can be understood only in relation to culturally constructed notions of men and masculinity. We believe that trying to explain gender issues by focusing on only one gender is a form of intellectual masturbation: such an approach feels personally gratifying, but it is unlikely to bring about significant social change.

The primary purpose of our introduction to this anthology is to outline what we see as the key epistemological assumptions underlying a more positive working relationship between feminism and men. We will critically examine individual assumptions and actions that reflect and support preexisting societal structures and the interrelationship between the individual and society. By questioning the present oppressive and limiting relations between men and women, we encourage the search for peaceful, egalitarian alternatives. Rather than presenting a clear vision or definitive statement on this subject, we hope to begin a dialogue that will lead to sociocultural transformations.

Some Epistemological Assumptions

What Is Gender?

Most if not all people understand gender in terms of two discrete categories, male and female. As a society we use dichotomous characteristics, based on sex, psychological states, and interpersonal ways of being, to illustrate polarized differences. At birth each of us is given one of only two possible labels, girl or boy, which subsequently determines how others treat us and how we are expected to act. When we initially meet someone, this label is the first and, perhaps, most important assessment we will make, whether consciously or unconsciously, and it directly determines our expectations and treatment of the other person. Individuals who fail or refuse to live up to these two essentially prescribed social states of being are met with "ostracism, punishment, and violence" (Butler 1991, 24). Social forces demand that we accept one of only two possible states of being, and our attitudes and actions reflect and sustain that gender designation. *gender norm based from society*

The dichotomy of male and female also provides an important ontological blueprint for preexisting hierarchical inequalities. To many the values, characteristics, and ways of being associated with men and the masculine are seen as dominant and inherently superior to those associated with women and the feminine. Accordingly, men are seen as the rightful leaders of society while women are seen as natural subordinates. Although in recent years people pay lip service to equally valued and complementary gender traits, many people still react in emotional ways that strongly suggest that these traits are not viewed as equal. This either/or societal design is also found in an array of other social categorizations such as white/black, rich/poor, straight/gay, which also call for the sorting of all people into corresponding dominant and subordinate statuses. When woven together, these intersecting matrices of existence simultaneously enable, constrain, and almost entirely determine one's life choices and experiences.

While male dominance and female subordination are by far the most firmly established and formally mandated social categories of being, they are far from the only approaches to being in our world. Cross-cultural and historical evidence strongly suggests that male dominance and gender dimorphism are anything but immutable givens and instead vary considerably in meaning and application within a culture, between cultures, and over time (Eisler 1987, 1995; Herdt 1994). Not only do cultures have an infinitely diverse array of gendered expectations, but some also formally recognize more than just two genders. Gender diversity, and the highly indeterminate ways this is expressed, would seem more the "norm" than any essential definitions of male and female accepted by our contemporary society. ⟩ *Cultural difference /def of gender*

Most of what is so neatly conceived of as male or female (or other discrete binary states of being) often is quite paradoxical in application (Lorber 1994) and can be fully defined only in relation to what it supposedly is not (Connell 1995; Schacht 1996a; Stoltenberg 1996; West and Zimmerman 1987). To understand what it means to be a woman or a man, as previously noted, is to understand its apparent opposite. Thus, in everyday interactions we may hear condemning statements like "quit acting like a girl" or "she wears the pants in their marriage" that demarcate what are seen as inappropriate ways of acting for a person of a given gender. Controlling comments like these enforce conformity to societal gender norms and emphasize differences between genders.

Since a great deal of what society considers male and female is about learning appropriate ways of acting in relation to others, it is also quite appropriate to view gender as a form of imitation and performance (Butler 1990; Garber 1992; Schacht 1997). The same can be said about other social statuses such as race, class, and sexual orientation (Butler 1991; Lemons 1996; Schacht 1996b; Willie 1995; Winant 1994). Men and women who most convincingly appear and act masculine (superior) and feminine (subordinate) are rewarded—albeit differentially—for their gendered accomplishments. Of course, this is situationally determined and often tempered by other social statuses. A great deal of our personal and social worth is based on how well we live up to and perform our assigned gender in relation to audiences of gendered others. Viewing gender in this manner suggests that female or male identities are extremely fluid, varying substantially over one's lifetime, and in one's daily interactions depending on situational expectations.

If all definitions of gender are in fact socially constructed, then exploring what it means to be female or male is a quest not for absolute "truth" but for social consequence: how do our definitions of male and female affect us and those with whom we interact? Thus, in this anthology we are concerned not with "discovering the truth about gender" but with exploring the practical implications of the available (and potential) socially constructed gender frameworks. Some ways of formulating gender are conducive to cooperative efforts between men and women and lead to the construction of egalitarian realities, while others do not. The next three sections will further discuss the ramifications of present gendered relations and suggest some nonoppressive replacements.

Assessing the Personal Realities and Consequences of Current Gender Relations

The gendered scripts discussed thus far obviously have had very different consequences for women and men. Until recently most young women have been taught at an early age that they will "catch more flies with honey than with vinegar" and that to succeed as a woman means "being sweet." Like slaves or indentured servants, women have been expected to study men's moods, anticipate their needs, avert their eyes, and try to never directly threaten the male ego. Becoming handmaidens in their own oppression, women learned to take on the actions of the powerless: to control information, manipulate behind the scenes, play on the master's emotions, and make themselves indispensable. Today these messages are more subtle and veiled, but they still exist. Women intuitively know that they are far more likely to be "rescued" from male tyranny if they appear helpless than if they act like competent adult women. The constant threat of "indiscriminate" male brutality serves to keep all women in their place, even when not consciously recognized. A deep fear of male power makes many women accept a pretense of inferiority, a farce that in time turns to self-hatred and anger.

Young men, on the other hand, are most typically taught that manhood is synonymous with domination and the control of others. Clearly, this is not possible on a sustained basis since much of life is uncontrollable and there is always someone stronger, richer, younger, more powerful. The consequence is a killing stress, being "other-driven," living with performance anxiety and an assiduous fear of impotency; ultimately being in a constant state of terror of becoming the other (e.g., women and powerless men). Men feel deep anger because, in spite of all their efforts to "get it right," success is fleeting, so their rage turns inward, often resulting in self-destructive behaviors and depression. Men's frustration leads them to inflict pain on others, frequently those who they supposedly care about most. Deep denial is required to keep functioning. To do otherwise would mean recognizing the destructive basis of their actions for others and even themselves. They blindly become addicted to the competitive, often destructive nature of the process, making true intimacy with either women or men nearly impossible.

Because of these gendered outcomes, those in men's studies (Hearn and Morgan 1990; Kaufman 1993; Kimmel and Messner 1995; Connell 1995) and other feminist-oriented men (Snodgrass 1977; Rowan 1987; Stoltenberg 1990, 1993) have rightfully concluded that patriarchy is harmful to both women and men. Unfortunately, however, when most men become aware of the oppressive nature of present gender practices, they merely seek to modify or reform the social system so that they can still reap the rewards without suffering the negative consequences. One of the criticisms of competitive sports for young boys is that not all are athletically accomplished, leaving some feeling like failures. The desire to expand the definition of manliness is so that other accomplishments can qualify for male privilege, not to reduce status differences between men and women. In truth, oppression always harms the oppressor regardless of how manipulatively subtle or veiled its form; the only way to escape the pain is to relinquish the power and privilege.

Many young people today are in a profound state of denial about the oppressive nature of gender. Acutely aware that the realities of modern life are inconsistent with old scripts, they recognize that the fairy-tale promise of "living happily ever after" is an empty vessel. They look sadly at the mistakes of their parents and vow to do things differently. Sexism and racism are seen as things of the past while they are free to be anything that they want to be without gender or racial restrictions; everyone is seen as competing on a level playing field. Young women, like other minority group members, desperately want to believe in the pretense of sameness—the liberal idea that we are all just people—that underlies the notion that sexism and racism are dead because of "a longing to possess the reality of other" (hooks 1995, 32). By attempting to imitate the values, speech, and habits of the dominant other, women hope and believe they will equally receive societal rewards. Young men readily pay lip service to beliefs of sameness so that when women fail they can be individually blamed for their own shortcomings and victimization. This simultaneously relieves men of any accountability for their oppressive actions: the playing field is now level, so it is women's fault when they do not measure up.

Nevertheless, young women continue to experience the terror associated with male violence as they quickly hang up on an obscene telephone caller, hear the loud hoots and whistles as they pass the fraternity house or construction site, or comfort a friend who has been raped. What results is a schizophrenic existence of verbalized sameness and repressed experiences of terror, resulting in naïveté and denial, a deadly combination that inevitably produces victimization. While verbalizing liberal or even feminist attitudes, young men still "know" they are the superior gender, destined for power and privilege. On Saturday night they want to "score" and often are willing to use their power and physical strength to fulfill this wish. Under the mantle of sameness, the old system of sexism is merely a shape-shifter reappearing in an altered form. Things often have to change an awful lot—sometimes quite quickly—to stay the same. Differences that lead to disparate experiences and expected ways of acting, whether or not they are socially constructed, are still differences.

In this time of rapid social change and accompanying problems and uncertainties, many people live with a deep anxiety and pessimism about the future. Some seek comfort in romanticized, more conservative ideals of the past. Members of the Promise Keepers and participants of the Million Man March promote a return to yesterday's values and gender roles. Yet others, perhaps the vast majority of people in our country today, pursue solace in cynical consumerism and the shallow search for immediate pleasures and narrowly defined self-interest. In such an outlook an individual's worth is measured in terms of what they own and what sorts of gratifying experiences they can purchase, often with little or no concern for the effect their actions have on others. Disillusioned by old ideologies and social institutions, many people refuse to make a commitment to any new causes or beliefs.

But current social change cannot be stopped with archaic ideologies incompatible with newly emerging interpersonal arrangements and economic realities. Two-paycheck and single-parent families are here to stay, women are entering traditionally male professions in increasing numbers, men are taking a more active role in their families and often refusing to be "married to their jobs," and young women everywhere are demanding equal opportunities and benefits (Gerson 1993). In a world of finite resources and an ever-growing population, the immediate gratification associated with rampant consumerism and its all too frequent resultant waste will have to become a thing of the past. The challenge is to be ready with a vision of positive and cooperative change that will guide us on our individual journeys into the next millennium. We believe that feminism is best posed to provide us with meaningful directions for the future.

The Promise of a Feminist Future

Feminism, like gender itself, can be viewed from an array of historical, cross-cultural, interactional, and experiential standpoints (Smith 1987; Haraway 1988; Offen 1988). There is no one feminism but rather an extensive assortment of feminisms; there are liberal feminists, cultural feminists, radical feminists, radical lesbian separatist feminists, socialist feminists, radical women of color, black feminists, multiracial feminists, womanists, radical feminist men, and socialist feminist men (Collins 1991; Dworkin 1987; Eisenstein 1979, 1983; Johnson 1987; Moraga and Anzaldúa 1983; Walker 1983; Baca Zinn and Dill 1996).[2]

Instead of blindly aligning ourselves with any one of these theoretical perspectives, we believe that a far more meaningful approach is to ask the question, What kind of new feminisms will be needed for the twenty-first century? Fortunately in answering this question we have some clues from current developments. Feeling overwhelmed by the large-scale, out of control nature of many social issues, some people are turning to their communities and asking themselves, What small things can I do here and now to make a positive difference in the place where I live? As the slogan goes, "Think globally, act locally." Feminism must be ready with answers on how this could be accomplished. Individual commitment and moral responsibility hinge on the belief that one can make a difference. People seek small practical changes today, not large-scale, radically transforming ideologies. Demonstrated success is a necessary requisite for continued commitment. As feminists, we need to be ready to provide an agenda for achievable community change.

Individuals are situationally located in a mass of social arrangements and roles that result in a hyphenated identity (e.g., poor-white-gay-woman-with-a-disability). We need feminisms that are sensitive to this diversity so that many choices and levels of involvement will be available. Much of contemporary feminism has demonized men as the oppressive other, refusing to give its energy to men's issues and concerns, substituting female power and imagery for that of men. As a consequence, it assumes a dichotomy of two discrete categories, each hopelessly alienated from the other. Framing gender relations in such a manner makes cooperative ventures nearly impossible. Whites of European descent will become a numerical minority in this country in the twenty-first century and, correspondingly, white middle-class feminism will become a minority choice. Definitions of "how to do feminism correctly" must be expanded to include everyone—men and women of all races, classes, and orientations. The new feminisms must be inclusive and based on respect for all people, have an explicit awareness of relational connectedness, and always recognize that inequality anywhere harms us all.

The twenty-first century may bring into question the very term "feminism" as it is equated with exclusivity, dichotomy, and mistrust. Even now numerous women and men who believe in many of the basic tenets of feminism refuse to identify themselves as feminists. In all likelihood, it will be easier to embrace new terminology than to erase the negativity associated with this term. This is dangerous, since much of the opposition to the word "feminism" is based on denial of the continued existence of basic inequalities. Those wishing to move ahead to a new inclusive feminism will be confused with those wishing to stay behind in the old liberalism of sameness and universal subjectivity. Others, wishing to protect academic turf, which has brought them status and prestige, will also resist change. But real change will take place in people's daily lives, in spite of any debate over terminology or proprietorship, and the larger cause will move forward.

What is presently needed is a new feminist outlook that will provide a sustaining ideology for equality as inevitable societal changes continue to occur. Economic realities presently cause most wives with children to work, and this has forced changes in the family. AIDS has caused changes in the gay community, the repeal of the draft forced the military to accommodate more women in its ranks, and the labor shortage during World War II forced opportunities for Rosie the Riveter. True, these are viewed as temporary inconveniences unless a supporting ideology is developed; not surprisingly, after the war Rosie was retired to the homemaker role in the fifties. But things were never quite the same because by example Rosie had proven that women "could do it" and that her subordinate role was only a function of male privilege and gender oppression. Rosie lay dormant until the 1970s, when her daughters once again pushed open these gates. When there are changes in what people do, what they think changes too.

What, then, are the basic assumptions of a new feminism and what promise does it offer for shaping a more life-affirming future? A beginning definition is offered by Karen Offen:

> I would consider as feminists any persons, female or male, whose ideas and actions (insofar as they can be documented) show them to meet three criteria: (1) they recognize the validity of women's own interpretations of their lived experience and needs and acknowledge the values women claim publicly as their own (as distinct from an aesthetic ideal of womanhood invented by men) in assessing their status in society relative to men; (2) they exhibit consciousness of, discomfort at, or even anger over institutionalized injustice (or inequity) toward women as a group by men as a group in a given society; (3) they advocate the elimination of that injustice by challenging, through efforts to alter prevailing ideas and/or social institutions and practices, the coercive power, force, or authority that upholds male prerogatives in that particular culture. (1988, 152)

To her emphasis on gender in particular, we would add that the recognition of the validity of experience, anger over injustice, and confronting prevailing ideas and practices must also be equally extended to oppressive realities experienced in race relations, class relations, sexual orientation issues, and other categorical forms of inequality. Since we believe all forms of oppression are interconnected and experientially related (Young 1988), the feminism we are suggesting challenges all forms of dominance and resulting inequalities. For true equality to ever exist, all forms of subjugation must be questioned and eliminated.

We call for new and different approaches not only to our everyday existence but also to the ways individuals and groups interact. Present relations between feminism, men, and all people in general will have to be reconstructed in such a manner that they promote egalitarian ways of being and acting. Current interpretations of reality that are sexist, racist, classist, and homophobic in meaning and practice will have to take on fundamentally new forms. What specific worldviews and ways of acting might be conducive to this?

Feminist Values and Ways of Acting for Men

Once something is dismantled, such as the oppressive "nature" of gender, something must be offered in its place. Otherwise, at best, old forms will manifest themselves in new ways to fill these voids, or at worst, total chaos will reign. Since the creation of nonoppressive realities will require all people—men and women—to join together in cooperative partnership, we will have to envision a new social order. The following feminist values and ways of acting for men are offered as necessary considerations for constructing an equalitarian future. As change occurs, other values will also need to be incorporated.

As reflected in the subtitle of this anthology, constructing positive/affirming/feminist associations between men and women requires a radical reconstruction of gender relations. On the surface, this may sound like an overwhelming, maybe even impossible task. However, since feminist values are ultimately human values, such ideals and ways of acting are perhaps commonsensical and not all that unconventional, even for men. In fact, we suggest that to varying degrees, all of us as young children were taught the following "traditional values," values that are also quite feminist in meaning and potential application:

- It is better to help than hurt people, especially those less fortunate, such as the poor, the elderly, the sick, and children.
- People are more important than things. Everyone should be treated with respect and never as a thing or an object.
- Violence is never an acceptable way to solve problems.
- Getting along with others, cooperation, working together, and sharing are better than competition, conflict, and trying to get and keep everything for yourself.
- Everybody should get a turn, equally have a say in decisions, and get their fair share.
- We should try to make the community where we live and the world in general a better place to live for everyone.
- We should treat the land with reverence and act kindly toward nature.
- Equality, fairness, and justice for all are morally right, while dominance, exploitation, and oppression are morally wrong.

Unfortunately, as young boys grow older they are taught that traditional/feminist values do not apply to the "real world"; long before puberty they are forced to learn what are seen as more practical, instrumental ways of being (such as those previously discussed). On the other hand, girls and other apparently lesser beings (the poor and people of color) are expected to continue holding these admirable traditional/feminist values into adulthood, their very "naïvté" seen as charming, attractive, entertaining, and necessary for applying the healing bandages to the damage wrought by men's rational actions.

The second wave of feminism correctly identified how these insidious beliefs were used to maintain women's subordination and oppression. The truly powerless have always been taught to focus on relationships, to emphasize emotional and intuitive qualities of being, and to have lower career aspirations. Women formed consciousness-raising groups, rejected their childhood socialization, and took assertiveness training to learn to think and act more like men. It was hoped that if women—especially white, educated, middle-class ones—could learn to successfully operate in the competitive male world, they would equally share in the privileges and benefits categorically but differentially afforded to men. A few women have individually benefited as a result of these strategies, but there has been little change in the social structure. Women who advance by learning to think and act like men are unlikely to be strong proponents for feminist change.

Clearly, what is required is that men (and perhaps some women) give up masculine privilege and ways of being in relation to others and instead learn to think and act more like women. Men must reaffirm those traditional values we were all taught as children. They must demand that institutions be more responsive to human needs and use their power and privilege to bring about structural change to this end. What is needed is coalition politics: the coming together and joining of men and women who share traditional values so that each can contribute to constructing and living such a worldview where they can individually make a difference in a manner that benefits everyone. We then become fellow travelers in the search for social justice and more humane, life-affirming ways of living.

Already we can see examples of this happening. The success of the Green movement in Europe and the environmental movement in the United States indicates that large numbers of people are recognizing that unlimited growth and technological advancement in the search for ever greater profits lead to environmental destruction. Many men are no longer willing to sell their souls to the corporation for material gain (Gerson 1993). The destructiveness of modern warfare makes it an unacceptable solution to most international problems. As a nation, almost everyone in the United States abhors the violence and chaos in our cities, the moral decay and loss of meaning, and the social isolation we feel from our communities. People are ready for change.

However, we cannot genuinely change society by using the same old patriarchal strategies and ways of doing things. As Audre Lorde insightfully stated nearly twenty years ago, "the master's tools will never dismantle the master's house." Feminism is much more than just an awareness of injustice and the affirmation of humanistic values. It is a style of working together where cooperation replaces competition, a way of being that welcomes and respects a diversity of nonoppressive perspectives, and a value system that rewards efforts for the common good over individual self-interest. Since most people shape their behaviors to the expectations of the existing reward system, there must be real change in how benefits are distributed. It is not enough to recognize the shrinking rewards given for conformity in the present patriarchal system. Men and other dominant members of society will be willing to give up privilege and power only when they see that dominance, control, and exploitation are no longer viable options and that more equitable ways of being are positively rewarded.

It is for this reason that groups such as the men's organizations listed in the end of this book are so vitally important. Each, in some specific arena, involves men talking with other men about the negative consequences of patriarchal assumptions and behaviors, and each offers positive, feminist-based alternatives. The truth is that feminist/traditional styles of thinking and acting simply work better for self and community. These groups provide resocialization to teach men to think and act more like women, not to be passive and powerless, but to use the personal power each of us has for the general good of all people.

When rational/instrumental values are not balanced with more traditional/feminist values, then materialism, competitive individualism, runaway technology, and exploitation for narrow definitions of profit that benefit the few eat away at and destroy the social fabric of our families, communities, society, and world. The new feminism we are suggesting, inclusive of men and all people, seeks to bring about a balance, and to return to those traditional values most people were taught as young children, but many of us have sadly forgotten as we have grown older. This will ultimately require us all, but especially men, to relearn how to view and relate to others.

This new social order must be based on the recognition that it is not possible to reap the benefits of dominance and privilege without also being a potential victim. Winners are only made possible by losers and, in hierarchical social orders where almost all are marginalized on some criteria, we inevitably share in the losing. Men must recognize that their pain, both physical and mental, is the result of patriarchal values and that they too would benefit from change.

Social institutions reward aggressive/competitive behavior, and men fear being discounted and "treated like women" if they fail to successfully compete. Most implicitly know that it is a patriarchal lie that wealth and power inherently bring happiness, but they also recognize that as long as oppression exists, it is better to exploit than be exploited. Active steps to change the values and rewards on which our basic institutions operate are obviously required.

A famous feminist slogan is "the personal is political." Today, in this time of political disillusionment and apathy, a perhaps better slogan would be "the political is personal." No longer can we hide from the pain of patriarchy by pretending that what happens outside our immediate social networks is irrelevant. We must work together to bring about systemic change. We passionately believe that traditional/feminist values and ways of being are the only ones that can reverse the cataclysmic direction we presently are traveling in as we enter the next millennium.

Realizing a Feminist Future

Any meaningful feminist agenda will have to be rooted in an awareness of the hitherto invisible ways patriarchal and corresponding gender assumptions have dominated our thinking and prevented us from recognizing viable choices for social change. This work will have to be done by both women and men, separately and together, if we are to ever move beyond the narrow range of options that can be seen through patriarchal lenses. We believe that the time has come for us to reject these priggish patriarchal boundaries and begin to rethink old problems in new ways.

The creation of nonoppressive realities will ultimately involve all people cooperatively joining together in new partnerships to seek radically new ways of envisioning and acting in relationships. This will require a belief that things can be different, a vision of what this should be, and a commitment to making these changes happen. It also requires a change in what behavior is rewarded. Such positive social change will require each of us, but especially men, to relearn those traditional—perhaps ultimately feminist—values we were taught as children.

This book is very much like an aerial photograph of a largely uncharted territory. Each of the essays in this anthology attempts to map out small pieces of this vast landscape. We hope that this anthology will contribute to illuminating this frontier and will lead others to join in this ongoing dialogue and exploration. Present ways of doing things must change before we destroy ourselves and the planet. The time has come for us to start working together instead of slowly but all too surely suffocating under the oppressive weight of divisive, individualistic patriarchal realities. Drawing on the strength of our individual threads that each of us travels on, when woven together in an all-encompassing, nonoppressive manner, a brilliant tapestry emerges that radiates with the potential beauty of everyone's center.

PARABLE

Spider knows
    each strand of Her web

and when Her callers
break away
destroying her weaving as they go
She does not die
but spins again
the pattern
of her life

no fool is She
no more a fool than I
    for traveling on
    a single thread
because she knows
having often seen
    what comes from the center
    can never be
forever broken.
           —Jaci (1939–1980)[3]

REFERENCES

Baca Zinn, Maxine, and Bonnie Thorton Dill. 1996. "Theorizing Difference from Multiracial Feminism." *Feminist Studies* 22:321–31.
Butler, Judith. 1990. *Gender Trouble: Feminism and Subversion of Identity.* New York: Routledge.

Butler, Judith. 1991. "Imitation and Gender Insubordination." In *Inside/Out: Lesbian Theories, Gay Theories*, edited by Diana Fuss, 13–31. New York: Routledge.

Collins, Patricia Hill. 1991. *Black Feminist Thought: Knowledge, Consciousness, and the Politics of Empowerment*. New York: Routledge.

Connell, R. W. 1995. *Masculinities: Knowledge, Power, and Social Change*. Berkeley: University of California Press.

Dworkin, Andrea. 1987. *Intercourse*. New York: Free Press.

Eisenstein, Hester. 1983. *Contemporary Feminist Thought*. Boston: G. K. Hall.

Eisenstein, Zillah R., ed. 1979. *Capitalist Patriarchy and the Case for Socialist Feminism*. New York: Monthly Review Press.

Eisler, Riane. 1987. *The Chalice and the Blade: Our History, Our Future*. San Francisco: Harper & Row.

———. 1995. *Sacred Pleasure: Sex, Myth, and the Politics of the Body*. San Francisco: Harper San Francisco.

Garber, Marjorie. 1992. *Vested Interests: Cross-Dressing and Cultural Anxiety*. New York: Routledge.

Gerson, Kathleen. 1993. *No Man's Land: Men's Changing Commitments to Family and Work*. New York: Basic Books.

Haraway, Donna. 1988. "Situated Knowledges: The Science Question in Feminism and the Privilege of Partial Perspective." *Feminist Studies* 14:575–99.

Hearn, Jeff, and David Morgan. 1990. *Men, Masculinities, and Social Theory*. London: Unwin Hyman.

Herdt, Gilbert. 1994. *Third Sex, Third Gender: Beyond Sexual Dimorphism in Culture and History*. New York: Zone Books.

hooks, bell. 1995. *Killing Rage: Ending Racism*. New York: Henry Holt.

Johnson, Sonia. 1987. *Going Out of Our Minds: The Metaphysics of Liberation*. Freedom, CA: Crossing Press.

Kaufman, Michael. 1993. *Cracking the Armor: Power, Pain, and the Lives of Men*. Toronto: Penguin.

Kimmel, Michael, and Michael Messner, eds. 1995. *Men's Lives*. 3d ed. Boston: Allyn and Bacon.

Lemons, Gary L. 1996. "Young Man, Tell Our Stories of How We Made It Over: Beyond the Politics of Identity." In *Teaching What You're Not: Identity Politics in Higher Education*, edited by Katherine J. Mayberry, 259–84. New York: New York University Press.

Lorber, Judith. 1994. *Paradoxes of Gender*. New Haven: Yale University Press.

Moraga, Cherrie, and Gloria Anzaldúa, eds. 1983. *This Bridge Called My Back: Writings by Radical Women of Color*. New York: Kitchen Table: Women of Color Press.

Offen, Karen. 1988. "Defining Feminism: A Comparative Historical Approach." *Signs: Journal of Women in Culture and Society* 14:119–57.

Rowan, John. 1987. *The Horned God: Feminism and Men as Wounding and Healing*. London: Routledge.

Schacht, Steven P. 1996a. "Misogyny on and off the 'Pitch': The Gendered World of Male Rugby Players." *Gender & Society* 10:550–65.

———. 1996b. *"Paris Is Burning:* How Society's Stratification Systems Make Drag Queens of Us All." Paper presented at the annual meeting of the American Sociological Association, New York.

———. 1997. "Female Impersonators and the Social Construction of 'Other': Toward a Situational Understanding of Gender and Power." Paper presented at the annual meeting of the American Sociological Association, Toronto.

Smith, Dorothy E. 1987. *The Everyday World as Problematic: A Feminist Sociology*. Boston: Northeastern University Press.

Snodgrass, Jon, ed. 1977. *For Men against Sexism*. Albion, CA: Times Change Press.

Stoltenberg, John. 1990. *Refusing to Be a Man: Essays on Sex and Justice*. New York: Penguin.

———. 1993. *The End of Manhood: A Book for Men of Conscience*. New York: Dutton.

———. 1996. "How Power Makes Men: The Grammar of Gender Identity." Unpublished manuscript.

Walker, Alice. 1983. *In Search of Our Mothers' Gardens*. New York: Harcourt Brace Jovanovich.

West, Candace, and Don H. Zimmerman. 1987. "Doing Gender." *Gender & Society* 1:125–51.

Willie, Sarah Susannah. 1995. "Blackness: From Social Construction to Performance." Paper presented at the annual meeting of the American Sociological Association, Washington, DC.

Winant, Howard. 1994. *Racial Conditions: Politics, Theory, Comparisons*. Minneapolis: University of Minnesota Press.

Young, Iris. 1988. "Five Faces of Oppression." *Philosophical Forum* 19:270–90.

NOTES

1. We thank Nancy Schwartz for this insightful observation.

2. Please see Michael Messner's essay included in this anthology for a more detailed discussion of radical and socialist feminist men.

3. This poem was written by Steve's mother, now deceased. We believe its sentiments are strongly reflected in this introduction and anthology.

Part I

Relational Examples from Our Past and Present

Chapter Two

From "Conscience and Common Sense" to "Feminism for Men"
Pro-Feminist Men's Rhetorics of Support for Women's Equality

Michael S. Kimmel

The true degradation and disgrace rests not with the
victim but with the oppressors.
—Henry Brown Blackwell to Lucy Stone,
22 December 1854

Feminism is going to make it possible for the first time
for men to be free.
—Floyd Dell, "Feminism for Men" (1914)

Since the late eighteenth century American men have supported women's
equality (see Kimmel and Mosmiller 1992).[1] Even before the first
Woman's Rights Convention at Seneca Falls, New York, heralded the
birth of the organized women's movement in 1848, American men had
begun to argue in favor of women's rights. That celebrated radical, Thomas Paine, for example, mused in 1775 that any formal declaration of
independence from England should include women, since women have,
as he put it, "an equal right to virtue" (Paine [1775] 1992, 63–66). Other
reformers, like Benjamin Rush and John Neal, articulated claims for
women's entry into schools and public life. Charles Brockden Brown,
America's first professional novelist, penned a passionate plea for
women's equality in *Alcuin* (1798).

By the middle of the nineteenth century profeminist men were active in every arena that women had identified as significant. The founders of the first women's colleges and the pioneers of coeducation were champions of a gender equality that would come from equal educational opportunities. By the mid-nineteenth century, many noted abolitionists had made a connection between the juridical enslavement of blacks and the subjection of women. Several mid-nineteenth-century communal experiments were organized by men who challenged traditional marriage as a form of slavery.

By the turn of the century there were new ways for American men to support feminism. In the first few decades of the new century, men organized voluntary associations to press their case and began to integrate feminist ideas into their personal lives. Many men began to support feminism not only because women had "an equal right to virtue," but because they, as men, would be transformed by women's equality.

The evolution of profeminist men's rhetorical strategies through the last century and into the present one roughly paralleled the history of feminism. Although this was not a fully sequential pattern, in which one form superseded the other, three distinct patterns of profeminist male rhetoric emerged during this period, and each one defined the profeminist male discourse of its time. Nor do they conform to any discrete historical periods. Rather, I intend to show how they illustrate shifting emphases in the prevailing arguments of the time.

The first rhetorical strategy urged women's incorporation into the body politic as a moral act, based on abstract conceptions of justice and fairness: if the franchise was to be extended to slaves, or, later, to ex-slaves, it ought to be extended to women on the same grounds. Women were equal individuals, possessed of equal mind, equal soul, and equal rights to virtue.

The second strategy was inspired by women's participation in the social reform movements of the end of the century; it cast women's participation less as moral and more as *moralizing*. Women's entry into the public arena would soothe men's battered egos, purify and cleanse a system that had grown impure from the indulgences of male vice, and serve as a balm on a painful national existence. This argument extended women's role as the guardians of the home to include the national home and hearth. If woman could tame the wild beast at home, perhaps she could also team up with her sisters to clean up the national household.

The third strategy stressed the positive influences that feminism would have on men. Women's demands for sexual freedom and reproductive rights (birth control) had the potential to free men from restrictive gender roles and introduced the possibility of sexual relations among equals. Feminism might mean more than incorporation into a preexisting system; rather, it might signal an opportunity to develop new forms of masculinity.

That men developed these three rhetorical strategies of argument does not mean, as one recent author argued, that "men are essential, often the leading figures, in the history of feminism to date" (Meyer 1987, 38). In my view, during this period men neither made nor led feminism, nor was their participation integral to its successes. Profeminist men's rhetorical strategies were, in themselves, reactive to the shifting ideological strategies of feminist women, who often used an alloy of moral principles, social reformism, and political expediency as the basis for their discursive claims.

Yet men were present. Men supported feminist demands, organized other men around those demands, and attempted to integrate feminist principles into their lives. In this chapter, I will explore the various ways men were involved in feminist struggles during the nineteenth century and through the beginning of the twentieth. I will argue that each rhetorical strategy corresponds not only with a different stage of feminist activism, but also with a different perception of the possibilities for men. Prior to the 1880s men held an expansionist ideal of masculine potential, and believed that women's incorporation would simply expand those possibilities. After the 1880s profeminist male discourse articulated an effort to reconstitute American masculinity, which was of growing cultural concern as being in "crisis." Men continued to refer to abstract conceptions of justice and morality, to be sure, but now they also sought to use feminism as a vehicle for reforming men. By the first few decades of the new century, that social vision of feminism's transformative potential was extended to include more than national morality; it now included men's individual, personal lives. Feminism could provide the antidote to the crisis of masculinity. Feminism promised men's liberation.

Profeminist Men before 1880: "Good" Men and "Good" Works

For most of the nineteenth century, men's support of feminism revolved around three issues: the extension of the franchise, equal education, and personal autonomy for women in communal experiments. Much of the discourse by profeminist men claims a natural equality for women, based on a presumed equality at birth. Such a discourse drew on Christian theologians, medical discourse, and liberal political theory that stressed the inherent rights of each individual. Each individual was a sacred entity, not subject to involuntary dependency or unwanted claims from society. Such arguments depended less on the qualities of women as women than on the qualities of women as human beings.

Transcendentalist thinkers like Ralph Waldo Emerson and Henry David Thoreau supported woman suffrage because the boundaries of the individual could not be compromised by political dependency and exclusion. In "Woman," a lecture at the Woman's Rights Convention in 1855, Emerson explained that human society is "made up of partialities. Each citizen has an interest and a view of his own, which, if followed out to the extreme, would leave no room for any other citizen." Thus, to bring all these biases together ensures that "something is done in favor of them all" (Emerson [1855] 1883, 10:352). Equality before the law, Emerson reasoned, will allow women to participate as individuals and therefore determine "whether they wish a voice in making the laws that are to govern them" (354).

These sentiments were echoed by many abolitionists, who extended their arguments about slavery to the position of women as disenfranchised individuals. A number of prominent men—among them William Lloyd Garrison, Frederick Douglass, Thomas Wentworth Higginson, Theodore Weld, Wendell Phillips, James Mott, Parker Pillsbury, Theodore Tilton, James Birney, and Samuel Gridley Howe—actively supported woman suffrage. Mott chaired the convention at Seneca Falls in 1848, and the resolution calling for woman suffrage, the only resolution not passed unanimously, was approved only after an impassioned speech by Douglass. "We hold women to be equally entitled to all we claim for man. We go farther, and express our conviction that all political rights which it is expedient for man to exercise, it is equally so for women," he argued from the convention floor (Douglass, 28 July 1848, 1).

What grounded his convictions was, as Douglass put it, "conscience and common sense." Political equality derived from natural equality between women and men. At a woman's rights convention in Rochester, New York, in 1848, it was reported that Douglass said that "the only true basis of rights was the capacity of individuals, and as for himself, he dared not claim a right which he would not concede to women" (editorial in the *North Star*, 11 August 1848, 1). Douglass argued that the failure to incorporate women and blacks into the political community had graver consequences than "the perpetuation of a great injustice"; it implied "the maiming and repudiation of one-half of the moral and intellectual power of the government of the world." Seeing, he continued, "that the male governments of the world have failed, it can do no harm to try the experiment of a government by man and woman united" (1881, 480). Who was to blame for women's subservience? Of course, some men argued that women themselves were to blame, while other men defensively suggested that though women's condition be subordinate, men had not made it so intentionally. It was, they said, not their fault. Douglass was not convinced, nor was he reluctant to blame men for the condition of women, insisting that to do otherwise would have been to blame the victim for her diminished condition. As he wrote in the *North Star*, "By nature she is fitted to occupy a position as elevated and dignified as her self-created master. And though she is often treated by him as his drudge, or a convenient piece of household furniture, 'tis but a striking evidence of his mental imbecility and moral depravity" (26 May 1848).

In this sentiment Douglass was joined by Garrison, who explicitly rejected arguments that suggested that women's inferior condition was either their own fault or at least the shared responsibility of women and men. At the Fourth Woman's Rights Convention in Cleveland in 1853, Garrison made a strong case for male responsibility for women's oppression. Believing in "sin, therefore in a sinner; in theft, therefore in a thief; in slavery, therefore in a slaveholder; in wrong, therefore in a wrongdoer," he argued that "unless the men of this nation are made by women to see that they have been guilty of usurpation, and cruel usurpation, I believe very little progress will be made." Nor did Garrison believe that men's oppression of women was accidental or the result of ignorance:

> To say all this has been done without thinking, without calculation, without design, by mere accident, by a want of light; can anybody believe this who is familiar with all the facts in this case? . . . There is such a thing as intelligent wickedness, a design on the part of those who have the light to quench it, and to do the wrong to gratify their own propensities, and to further their own interests. So then I believe that as man has monopolized for generations all the rights which belong to women, it has not been accidental, not through ignorance on his part; but I believe that man has done this through calculation, actuated by a spirit of pride, a desire for domination

which has made him degrade woman in her own eyes, and thereby tend to make her a mere vassal.

It seems to me, therefore that we are to deal with the consciences of men. . . . The men of this nation, and the men of all nations, have no just respect for woman. They have tyrannized over her deliberately, they have not sinned through ignorance, but theirs is not the knowledge that saves.

Women, Garrison concluded, "are the victims in this land, as the women of all lands are, to the tyrannical power and godless ambition of man" (1853, in Kimmel and Mosmiller 1992, 212–14).

Other abolitionists were equally articulate in making the claim that women's natural equality with men entitled them to political equality. "Woman is a human being; and it is a self-evident truth that whatever right belongs to man by virtue of his membership in the human family, belongs to her by the same tenure," wrote Henry C. Wright in a letter of support to the Woman's Rights Convention in Akron in 1851 (*Woman's Rights Convention* 1851, 44; SL).[2] A decade later, Wendell Phillips fused Lockean notions of property in the person with Protestant theology to repudiate putative biological differences as the basis for the denial of suffrage; at the Tenth Woman's Rights Convention in New York, he proclaimed that

I believe . . . in woman having the right to her brain, to her hands, to her toil, to her ballot. The tools to him that can use them and let God settle the rest. If He made it just that we should have democratic institutions, then He made it just that everybody who is to suffer under the law should have a voice in making it; and if it is indelicate for women to vote, then let Him stop making women, because republicanism and such women are inconsistent. ([1851], 1891, 127)

Such theological arguments for woman suffrage were echoed from pulpits around the country. Many of the abolitionists were ministers, and many profeminist statements originated as sermons. For example, Samuel J. May's sermon "The Rights and Condition of Woman," delivered in Syracuse in 1846, was an articulate pre–Seneca Falls statement of individualist Protestantism's search for the spiritual grounding of feminism. May began his argument from a presumed moral equality: men and women are "equal in rank, alike rational and moral beings." Thus, the disenfranchisement of women "is as unjust as the disenfranchisement of the males would be; for there is nothing in their moral, mental, or physical nature that disqualifies them to understand correctly the true interests of the community, or to act wisely on reference to them" (1846, 5, 4; SL). Since men and women are equals before God, May argued, we may "with no more propriety assume to govern women than they might assume to govern us." And, he continued, "never will the nations of the earth be well governed until both sexes, as well as all parties, are fairly represented, and have an influence, a voice, and, if they wish, a hand in the enactment and administration of the laws" (1846, 6).

Many of this first wave of profeminist men also campaigned for women's equality in education. Many of the men who were the founders and early presidents of women's colleges saw their efforts as facilitating women's equality by providing equal quality education. Women's education was promoted by men who found the idea of exclusion anachronistic or offensive to individualist sensibilities. A poem in *Littell's Living Age* in 1869 (578) posed the question

> Ye fusty old fogies, Professors by name,
> A deed you've been doing, of sorrow and shame;
> Though placed in your chairs to spread knowledge abroad,
> Against half of mankind you would shut up the road.
> The fair sex from science you seek to withdraw
> By enforcing against them a strict Salic law:
> Is it fear? is it envy? or, what can it be?
> And why should a woman not get a degree?[3]

Why, indeed? There was no reason at all, according to Matthew Vassar and Milo Jewett at Vassar, William Allan Nielson and Joseph Taylor at Smith, and Henry Durant at Wellesley, each of whom expressed articulate claims for women's right to education. Durant claimed that the real meaning of higher education for women was "revolt." "We revolt against the slavery in which women are held by the customs of society—the broken health, the aimless lives, the subordinate position, the helpless dependence, the dishonesties and shams of so-called education," he wrote. "The Higher Education of Women . . . is the cry of the oppressed slave. It is the assertion of absolute equality" (1877, in Kimmel and Mosmiller 1992, 132).

Perhaps no one better synthesized the positions of this first wave of profeminist men than Thomas Wentworth Higginson. Long a fierce abolitionist, Higginson was also a strong advocate of woman suffrage and women's education. His series of essays, "Woman and the Alphabet," was published in *Atlantic Monthly* even though its editor, James Russell Lowell, had earlier considered them "too radical" for the magazine (Mary Higginson 1914, 156). In these articles Higginson developed an articulate rationale for suffrage and equal education, and pierced the veneer of woman's presumed moral superiority as the basis for her oppression. (In this, he also evidenced a striking empathy for women's anger):

> I do not see how any woman can avoid a thrill of indignation when she first opens her eyes to the fact that it is really contempt, not reverence, that has so long kept her sex from an equal share of legal, political and educational rights. In spite of the duty paid to individual women as mothers, in spite of the reverence paid by the Greeks and the Germanic races to certain women as priestesses and sibyls, the fact remains that this sex has been generally recognized, in past ages of the human race, as stamped by hopeless inferiority, not by angelic superiority. (1859, 304, in Kimmel and Mosmiller 1992, 111–14)

Higginson was careful not to advocate feminist ideas because of women's supposed moral superiority, a claim advanced by antifeminists who suggested that women's superior morality ought to "exempt" them from the tawdry worlds of commerce and politics. "It is a plausible and tempting argument, to claim suffrage for woman on the ground that she is an angel," he wrote, "but I think it prove wiser, in the end, to claim it for her as being human" (1862, 285). Higginson countered both anti- and profeminist arguments of woman's moral superiority with arguments about complementarity and coeducation; woman needs equal rights, he reasoned,

> not because she is man's better half, but because she is his other half. She needs them, not as an angel, but as a fraction of humanity. Her political education will not merely help man, but it will help herself. She will sometimes be right in her opinions, and sometimes be altogether wrong; but she will learn, as man learns, by her own blunders. The demand in her behalf is that she shall have the opportunity to make mistakes, since it is by this means she must become wise. (1862, 84)

Fallibility, to Higginson, led him to argue that "in politics, as in every other sphere, the joint action of the sexes will be better and wiser than that of either singly"(1862, 285).[4]

For these first-wave profeminist men, women's participation in the public sphere simply extended individual rights—whether experienced in the state of nature, or through Divine Plan, or simply by human existence in civil society—in analogy to the ways that they also urged it for black slaves. Suffrage was, as Wendell Phillips put it (1891, 129), "not alone woman's right, but woman's duty," and men's support of women's rights was a matter, in the words of Frederick Douglass, of "[c]onscience and common sense" (1848, 1).

The Crisis of Masculinity at the Turn of the Century and Profeminist Men's New Rhetorical Strategies

In the last two decades of the nineteenth century, profeminist men continued their reference to abstract conceptions of justice and morality, but also developed new rhetorical strategies to justify their support of women's struggles. Now profeminist male discourse became embedded in a larger context of American men's responses to feminism, which were the product of structural transformations that had undermined the traditional definitions of masculinity. Thus feminism and masculinity became intertwined in the late nineteenth century in a way that they had not been entangled before. Masculinity was widely perceived as in "crisis"; men were confused about the meanings of masculinity in a rapidly industrializing, postbellum economy. The traditional moorings on which a stable and secure antebellum masculinity had been anchored—independent control over one's work, expansive geographic boundaries at whose edges masculinity could be tested and proved—were fast disappearing in the consolidation of the postbellum industrial order, and men struggled to redefine masculinity. The closing of the frontier, rapid industrialization, the decline of the individual farmer and small shopkeeper, and the concomitant rapid rise of mass production and the factory system served to unhinge masculinity. Prior to the Civil War, nine of every ten American men were farmers or self-employed businessmen; by 1870 that figure had dropped to two of every three, and by 1910 less than one-third of all American men were independently employed. The transformation of the household and gender relations, in part augured by women's entry into the public spheres of work and education, and the contemporaneous articulation of feminist demands also put pressure on men to resolve the crisis.[5]

Structural changes provided the backdrop against which the dramatic renegotiations of gender relations were taking place. Women's entry into the public sphere was buttressed by changes in the organization of the family—shrinking family size, increasing nuclearization of the family structure, and a clearer demarcation between workplace and households as separate zones of production and consumption, respectively. The articulation of claims by women for increased participation in the public sphere (education, professional training, suffrage, labor force participation) seemed to threaten the entire structure of gender relations.

American men evidenced several different reactions to the claims articulated by women at the turn of the century. For some, feminism was an ill-advised movement that would cause serious social and physiological harms. To these antifeminists, women were biologically ill suited for public life and should return to the private sphere where, it was argued, they belonged. Health reformer Horace Bushnell and Harvard education professor Edward C. Clarke argued that women would grow larger and heavier brains and lose their uniquely feminine mannerisms were they to vote or attend college (Bushnell 1870; Clarke 1873). "I think the great danger of our day is forcing the intellect of woman beyond what her physical organization will possibly bear," wrote the Reverend John Todd (1867, 23).

For others, feminism was a symptom of a general feminization of American culture, through which American manhood had been enervated. For these masculinists, women's participation in the public sphere was not problematic, as long as separate institutions remained all-male preserves and men could dislodge women from their monopoly over child rearing. Masculinists advocated separate educations and recreational outlets for males and females; keeping the sexes separate would retain manhood and maintain "the mystic attraction of the other sex," that is, serve as a hedge against homosexuality (see Beveridge 1905; McKeever 1913; Macfadden 1900).

Finally, profeminist men suggested that feminist claims represented deep democratic impulses, and equal rights ought to be extended to women. Some men followed the lead of social reformers and argued that feminism would redeem a society bathed in male vice; at the least it should allow women and men to wallow equally in the mire.[6] This represented a shift in the rhetorical strategies used by profeminist men in their efforts to support equal rights for women.

Woman as Moralizer: Profeminist Rhetorics of Redemption

The last few decades of the nineteenth century witnessed a new discourse on women's equality, a discourse that took discussions about male responsibility for women's oppression and the moral imperative of political incorporation in new directions. As women became involved in social reform movements, such as temperance and Social Purity, they were cast as the moral reformers of male vice, the cure for contemporary social ills. Women's political participation was justified on the grounds that it would provide greater degrees of morality, purity, and beauty in the world. Supporters of women's education, for example, argued that equal education was necessary to combat the degeneracy and vice that had seeped into American culture. Joseph Sayers argued that "a liberal, literary, moral and virtuous female education [was] the only detergent remedy for vice, crime, and immorality" (1856, iv). Coeducation was to be supported because through it, men would be refined and women empowered and "inspired with a higher, nobler ambition" (Buchanan 1851, 49).

Advocates of woman suffrage began to resort to arguments that stressed women as a moralizing force, instead of the more simple and abstract morality of individual rights that had marked earlier discourse. Clifford Howard, for example, argued that "woman should have the ballot, not only for her own benefit, but for the benefit of you and me and every other man who stands for good government and public cleanliness and purity" (Howard 1890, 3). Howard and other pamphleteers co-opted the antifeminist argument about separate spheres and yoked it to a contention that women's participation was imperative precisely because women's sphere was the home. "The woman's place is the home," Howard wrote, "but today would she serve the home she must go beyond the house. No longer is the home compassed by four walls. Many of its most important duties lie now involved in the bigger family of the city and state" (7). Edward Ward facetiously asserted the separate sphere argument when he wrote that "[w]omen should mind their own business. That is, they would vote in the modern government, for this is their proper sphere, except in its destructive, anti-social, military expression" (Ward 1900, 7). If woman were to exercise her natural role as the guardian of the home, "she must of necessity interest herself in public affairs and take a part in their management" (Howard 1890, 8).

Frederic C. Howe argued that social reforms would be possible only when women's proper sphere was extended into the public realm. In "What the Ballot Will Do for Women and for Men," he cast suffrage as the redemption from "the muddle we have made of politics," alone capable of ending poverty, hunger, diseases, and suffering. In a lyrical romanticization of women's civic participation, he wrote,

I want to live in a world that thinks of its people rather than of business; of consumers rather than producers; of users rather than makers; of tenants rather than owners; in a world where life is more important than property, and human labor more valuable than privilege.

As women are consumers, users, and tenants rather than producers, makers, and owners, I have hope for a society in which women have and use the ballot.

I want woman suffrage because I believe women will correct many of these law-made wrongs that man has made. For women will vote in terms of human life rather than in terms of special privilege. (Howe, 1905, 7–8)

Finally, men who participated in the Social Purity Movement and supporters of temperance also promoted women's public participation as the social extension of their natural role as guardian of the home. It was women's role to save men from the cruelties and excesses that accompanied masculinity in crisis.

Feminism as Men's Liberation

Finally, a small group of profeminist men embraced feminist ideas as much for their potential to liberate men as their importance to the liberation of women. In the first two decades of the century, among the Bohemian subculture in New York's Greenwich Village, a group of men were actively linked to feminist causes because the liberation of women implied the demolition, not the beautification, of industrial capitalism. As inspired by Freud as much as by Marx, many of these profeminist men were as actively concerned with social questions of women's sexual autonomy as they were with political enfranchisement. They sought to organize other men around feminist issues and attempted to lead lives that were consistent with their beliefs. In this, they embraced a new kind of feminism that emerged in the 1910s and 1920s, a feminism that was in a sense "a reaction against an emphasis in the woman movement itself, the stress in nurturant service and moral uplift" (Cott 1987, 37). The woman's movement had promoted social reform as women's duties; these new feminists promoted women's rights and sexual autonomy as their entitlement. To the writer Floyd Dell, feminism was more than "a revolt of women against conditions which hamper their activities; it is also a revolt of women and men against the type of woman created by those conditions" (1921, 349).

The Bohemian radicals who clustered in Greenwich Village attempted to create new relationships while they promoted feminist causes. In this "moral health resort," as Dell called it (cited in O'Neill 1978, 29), they confronted issues of monogamy and sexual fidelity, women's sexual autonomy, and women's rights to birth control and abortion. Feminism had created a new type of woman; as writer Randolph Bourne put it,

> They are all social workers, or magazine writers in a small way. They are decidedly emancipated and advanced, and so thoroughly healthy and zestful, or at least it seems so to my unsophisticated masculine sense. They shock you constantly. . . . They have an amazing combination of wisdom and youthfulness, of humor and ability, and innocence and self-reliance, which absolutely belies everything you will read in the story books or any other description of womankind. They are of course all self-supporting and independent, and they enjoy the adventure of life; the full, reliant, audacious way in which they go about makes you wonder if the New Woman isn't to be a very splendid sort of person. . . . They talk much about the "Human Sex," which they claim to have invented, and which is simply a generic name for those whose masculine brutalities and egotisms and feminine pettiness and stupidities have been purged away so that there is left stuff for a genuine comradeship and healthy frank regard and understanding. (Cited in Cott 1987, 34–35; see also Abrahams 1981)

Such New Women needed "new men," men who could thrill to women's sexual autonomy, who were outraged at economic and political discrimination, and who worked in both public and private arenas to bring about a system of sexual equality and gender justice.

Men like the young Max Eastman, Floyd Dell, Hutchins Hapgood, William Sanger, and Randolph Bourne. Eastman, the editor of *The Masses* and secretary and organizer of the Men's League for Woman Suffrage was (in his early years) an exemplary character, organizing other men around feminist issues and struggling toward equality in his personal life. Eastman and his wife, Ida Rauh, caused a scandal when they posted Rauh's full name on their mailbox in 1911. Their mailman refused to deliver their mail, and they were forced to go to court to change the law, starting a Village tradition of both names on mailboxes. Eastman wrote that he wanted his wife to be "entirely independent of men in every way—to be as free as she was before we were married" (cited in Stricker 1974, 88). Eastman linked his support for feminism with his understanding of masculinity. "There was nothing harder for a man who had my mama's boy complex to do than stand up and be counted as a male suffragette," he wrote in the first volume of his autobiography. "It meant not only that I had asserted my manhood, but that I had passed beyond the need of asserting it" (Eastman 1936, 316).

To be sure, men continued to support feminism because it "is just and right and . . . men want to deal fairly and justly by women," as one pamphlet from upstate New York concluded (*Why New York Men Should Give Women the Vote* 1915, 4). A pamphlet from San Francisco that same year drew a similar conclusion, that there was "no good reason why our women should be treated with less justice" (*The San Francisco Man: A Fable* 1915, 4). Prominent members of the Men's League for Woman Suffrage, the nation's first explicitly profeminist men's organization, relied on such abstract conceptions of morality and justice. An editorial in *La Follette's* from May 1911 praised the eighty-five "courageous and convinced men" who marched in one recent demonstration; one marcher counted being "booed and hissed down the Avenue a very thrilling experience" and indicated his determination that "if I can help to that end, there shall be a thousand men in line next year." And he wasn't far off target. An editorial in the *New York Times* predicted that eight hundred men would march the next day in a suffrage demonstration, although Eastman counted far more marchers. "Even when the Men's League occupied five blocks, four abreast," he wrote,"the press could see only a grudging thousand of them" (1936, 351).

For this generation of profeminist men, as Eastman put it, it was neither "justice as a theoretic ideal, nor feminine virtue as a cure for politics" that animated their support for feminism. They did "not look to women's votes for the purification and moral elevation of the body politic." It was, instead, "democratic government as the practical method of human happiness" that motivated them (Eastman 1912, 8, 2). Many of this generation of profeminist men saw the social revolution offered by feminist demands for personal autonomy as the complement to the socialist revolution that they also hoped to accomplish. Woman's assertion of her freedom was a necessary fulfillment of social change, and they believed that women would be the leaders in the revolution.

Such personal autonomy required sexual freedom, and profeminist men supported women's struggles for birth control. William Sanger was arrested in 1915 for distributing his wife, Margaret's, pamphlet *Family Limitation*. At home he was equally supportive. "You go ahead and finish your writing," she quotes him as saying, "and I'll get the dinner and wash the dishes." (Margaret did draw the curtains to their first-floor kitchen when he did so, lest passersby notice this emasculating gender reversal [Forster 1985, 252; Reed 1977, 136].) Women's sexual autonomy was vital, perhaps even more central than the vote, as Floyd Dell explained in his volume *Women as World Builders*:

> Her development, her freedom, her independence, must come from and through herself. First, by asserting herself as a personality, and not as a sex commodity. Second by refusing the right to anyone over her body; by refusing to bear children unless she wants them; by refusing to be a servant to God, the State, society, the husband, the family, etc.; by making her life simpler, but deeper and richer. That is, by trying to learn the meaning and substance of life in all its complexities, by freeing herself from the fear of public opinion and public condemnation. Only that, and not the ballot, will set woman free, will make her a force hitherto unknown in the world, a force for real love, for peace, for harmony; a force of divine fire, of life giving; a creator of free men and women. (1913, 61–62)

Both Dell and Eastman sought to join Marx and Freud, to link their socialist political economy with feminist critiques of sexual repression. Thus did Dell argue, in "Feminism for Men," that capitalism opposed feminism because "it wants men with wives and children who are dependent on them for support." But feminism—and only feminism—will allow men to rediscover women as equals, which means to discover women all over again. That could happen only in the public sphere; the home was "a little dull":

> When you have got a woman in a box, and you pay rent on the box, her relationship to you insensibly changes character. It loses the fine excitement of democracy. It ceases to be companionship, for companionship is only possible in a democracy. It is no longer a sharing of life together—it is a breaking of life apart. Half a life—cooking, clothes, and children; half a life—business, politics, and baseball. . . . It is in the great world that a man finds his sweetheart, and in that narrow little box outside of the world that he loses her. When she has left that box and gone back into the great world, a citizen and a worker, then with surprise and delight he will discover her again and never let her go. (Dell 1914, 20)

Eastman claimed a similar motive for supporting feminism, an "unqualified liking for women with brains, character, and independence" (1936, 315), and was equally certain that feminism held important messages for men as well as women. In a vignette from *The Masses* in 1914, Eastman recounts a (possibly apocryphal) conversation with the magazine's new stenographer:

"Are you a feminist?" we asked the stenographer.
   She said she was.
"What do you mean by feminism?"
"Being like men," she answered.
"Now you are joking!"
"No, I'm not. I mean real independence. And emotional independence
too—living in relation to the universe rather than in relation to some other
person."
"All men are not like that," we said sadly.
"Then they should join the feminist movement!" (Eastman 1914, 7)

Feminism was the culmination of the revolutionary impulse of the first
few decades of the century, worth supporting precisely because of the
extent of that revolution. Women, Dell wrote,

> will not exchange one place for another, nor give up one right to pay for
> another, but they will achieve all rights to which their bodies and brains
> give them an implicit title. They will have a larger political life, a larger
> motherhood, a larger social service, a larger love, and they will reconstruct
> or destroy institutions to that end as it becomes necessary. They will not
> be content with any concession or any triumph until they have conquered
> all experience. (1913, 51)

Men now understood that feminism would "make it possible for the first
time for men to be free" (Dell 1914, 19).

   Such were the vicissitudes of profeminist men's discourses from the
mid-nineteenth century to the first decades of the twentieth. Each strain
of profeminist male rhetoric remains visible today. Of course, the ethical
imperative based on individual rights remains the single largest rhetorical
foundation of support for women's equality. In campaigns for the ERA,
women's right to choose, opposition to workplace sexual harassment, and
the admission of women to all-male military colleges, men's support of
feminism is framed in a rhetoric of women's individual rights. Much of
this support is based on the assumption of similarity between women and
men, the assumption that observable differences between the genders are
less significant and more highly variable than antifeminists might suggest.
Women are more like men than they are different, this line of reasoning
goes; therefore, women should not be prevented from achieving their full
individual potential.

   Some contemporary profeminist male rhetoric, however, embraces the
moralizing rhetoric of the previous century, especially in the debates

about sexuality. Male support for feminist-inspired campaigns against prostitution and pornography is particularly illustrative of this rhetorical strategy. Such campaigns often characterize men as impulsive, uncontrolled predators, whose every behavior is saturated with signifiers of male domination. Against this, women's "natural" virtue, if it can remain uncorrupted by male supremacist ideology, is the only possible salve. Women are animated, they argue, by a different ethical code of conduct (an ethic of care) or a different framework for language and its deployment ("genderlects"), contemporary moralizing rhetoric exaggerates the differences between women and men as a political strategy to gain power for women and to protect them from men.

Neither the rhetoric of individual rights nor the moralizing rhetoric of difference requires that men change as a result of supporting feminism. If women receive individual rights, they will claim the rights already enjoyed by men. Moralizing women will protect the victims of male excess and constrain men from acting on their violent, rapacious impulses—but the men will remain, in essence, unchanged. To a small number of contemporary profeminist men, however, feminism offers men both the ethical imperative to change and the political opportunity to be changed. In this model, earlier rhetorical strategies ultimately converge: to the extent that women and men are the same, there can be no logical justification for political discrimination; to the extent that women and men are different, one could not possibly expect men to represent women adequately, and thus, women must have their equal rights.

To this last group, the women-as-moralizer model of feminist sexual reform and antipornography campaigns freezes men in a position of self-denial. Men simply *are* the rapacious beasts, sexual predators, and woman-hating monsters that the reformers depict. They are incapable of change; their best hope is to renounce masculinity, to refuse to be men at all.[7] Not only is this a rather dubious strategy for political organizing—social movement participation based on self-renunciation and self-hatred—but it fails logically to address men's capacity for transformation in the first place. Such a position is often overly dismissive of men's ability to change and unforgiving of men's clumsy and inconsistent efforts to do so.

And the rhetoric of individual rights presents what we might call the "Field of Dreams Fallacy," after the recent movie, whose recurring theme was the line "If you build it, he will come." Individualists seem to suggest that if equal opportunities can be provided, "they"—meaning women—

will come and be equal. In so doing, they will act precisely as other "individuals"—namely, men—have always acted. "They" will act just like "us," so that "we" do not have to do anything but move over slightly. However, when women do actually enter the public arena, they enter both as women and as individuals; "they" will not necessarily become just like "us." That fact will, of course, require that men change—a requirement that is currently provoking fierce resistance in workplaces and universities across the nation as new standards of harassment and new codes of sexual etiquette are being articulated.

Feminism is about transformation, both for women and for men. Feminism offers to women a political agenda and a philosophical position that address both women's public sphere experience of discrimination and exclusion and their private experience of powerlessness, pain, and thwarted personal vision. To men it offers the ethical imperative to change as well as the opportunity to change. Men can retheorize past behaviors so that, for example, our earlier models of "dating etiquette" or "office behavior" can be relabeled date rape or sexual harassment, our earlier ideals about family life can be revisioned as the disempowerment and negation of the visions of our wives or partners. Feminism requires such public pronouncements of support for political participation—a process long, difficult, and potentially painful. And feminism requires a personal commitment to engage in that equally long, equally difficult, and equally painful process of personal transformation, to personalize the political even as we politicize the personal. Feminism promises the transformation of the relations between women and men: as it will set women free, it cannot help but liberate men.

If today's profeminist men inherit all three rhetorical strategies of support for feminism, we inherit a mixed legacy of modest successes and inspired failures. Persistent inequalities make struggles for public participation and personal freedom necessary, but we remain hopeful that men can and will support women's claims to a vision of sexual equality and gender justice.

BIBLIOGRAPHY

BECHSL (Buffalo and Erie County Historical Society Library)
CSHL (California State Historical Library), manuscripts division

SL (Arthur and Elizabeth Schlesinger Library on the History of Women in America), Radcliffe College, Women's Rights Collection.

Abrahams, Edward. "Randolph Bourne on Feminism and Feminists." *Historian* 43 (3),1981.
Beveridge, Albert. *The Young Man and the World*. New York: Appleton, 1905.
Buchanan, Joseph R. "The Sphere of Woman." In *Proceedings of the Woman's Rights Convention*. Cincinnati: n.p., 1851.
Bushnell, Horace. *Woman Suffrage: The Reforms against Nature*. New York: Scribners, 1870.
Case, Carl. *The Masculine in Religion*. New York: n.p., 1906.
Clarke, Edward C. *Sex in Education, or: A Fair Chance for the Girls*. Boston: James Osgood, 1873.
Conant, R. W. *The Manly Christ: A New View*. Chicago: n.p., 1904.
Cott, Nancy. *The Grounding of Modern Feminism*. New Haven: Yale University Press, 1987.
Dell, Floyd. *Women as World Builders*. Chicago: Forbes, 1913.
———. "Feminism for Men." *The Masses*, July 1914, 19–20.
———. "Feminism and Socialism." *The New Masses*, October 1921.
Doane, Rev. William Croswell. "Why Women Do Not Want the Ballot." *North American Review* 162 (466), September 1895.
Douglas, Ann. *The Feminization of American Culture*. New York. Knopf, 1977.
Douglass, Frederick. Editorial. *North Star*, 26 May 1848.
———. Editorial. *North Star*, 28 July 1848.
———. *The Life and Times of Frederick Douglass*. Hartford, 1881.
Dubbert, Joe. *A Man's Place: Masculinity in Transition*. Englewood Cliffs: Prentice Hall, 1979.
Eastman, Max. *Is Woman Suffrage Important?* New York: Men's League for Woman Suffrage, 1912.
———. "What Do You Know about This?" *The Masses*, March 1914.
———. *The Enjoyment of Living*. New York: Harper and Bros., 1936.
Ehrenreich, Barbara, and Deirdre English. *For Her Own Good*. New York: Anchor, 1979.
Emerson, Ralph Waldo. *Complete Works*. Vol. 10, *Miscellanies*. Boston: Houghton Mifflin, 1883.
Forster, Margaret. *Significant Sisters: The Grassroots of Modern Feminism*. New York: Knopf, 1985.
Frothingham, O. B. *Woman Suffrage: Unnatural and Inexpedient*. Boston: privately printed, 1894.
Hall, G. Stanley. "The Awkward Age." *Appleton's Magazine*, August 1900.
———. *Adolescence*. New York: Appleton, 1904.

Hertwig, John George. *Woman Suffrage*. Washington, DC: Eckler, 1883.

Higginson, Mary Thatcher. *Thomas Wentworth Higginson: The Story of His Life*. Boston: Houghton Mifflin, 1914.

Higginson, Thomas Wentworth. *Woman and the Alphabet*. Boston: Houghton Mifflin, 1862.

Howard, Clifford. *Why Man Needs Woman's Ballot*. New York: National American Woman's Suffrage Association, 1890.

Howe, Frederic C. *What the Ballot Will Do for Women and for Men*. New York: National American Woman Suffrage Association, 1905.

Kimmel, Michael S. "Men's Responses to Feminism at the Turn of the Century." *Gender & Society* 1 (3), 1987.

————. *Manhood in America: A Cultural History*. New York: Free Press, 1995.

Kimmel, Michael S., and Thomas Mosmiller, eds. *Against the Tide: Pro-feminist Men in the United States: A Documentary History*. Boston: Beacon, 1992.

La Follette's. May 1911.

Littell's Living Age, vol. C, 1869.

Macfadden, Bernarr. *The Virile Powers of Superb Manhood*. New York: Physical Culture Publishing Company, 1900.

May, Samuel J. *The Rights and Conditions of Woman Considered in the Church of the Messiah*. Syracuse: Stoddard and Babcock, 1846.

McKeever, William. *Training the Boy*. New York: Macmillan, 1913.

Meyer, Donald. Letter to the editor. *New York Times Book Review*, 29 November 1987.

North Star, 11 August 1848.

O'Donnell, Edward. "Women as Bread Winners: The Error of the Age." *American Federationist*, October 1897.

O'Neill, William. *The Last Romantic: A Life of Max Eastman*. New York: Oxford University Press, 1978.

Paine, Thomas. "An Occasional Letter on the Female Sex" [1775]. Reprinted in *Against the Tide: Pro-Feminist Men in the United States, A Documentary History*, edited by Michael Kimmel and Thomas Mosmiller. Boston: Beacon, 1992.

Phillips, Wendell. "Suffrage for Woman." In *Speeches, Lectures and Letters*. Boston: Lee and Shepard, 1891.

Pierce, Jason Noble. *The Masculine Power of Christ; or, Christ Measured as a Man*. Boston: Pilgrim Press, 1912.

Reed, James. *From Private Vice to Public Virtue*. New York: Basic Books, 1977.

Rosenthal, Michael. *Building Character in the American Boy: The Boy Scouts, YMCA, and Their Forerunners, 1870–1920*. Madison: University of Wisconsin Press, 1983.

San Francisco Man: A Fable. San Francisco: California Equal Suffrage Association, 1915. CSHL.

Sayers, Joseph. *Women's Rights: or, a Treatise on the Inalienable Rights of Women, Carefully Investigated and Inscribed to the Female Community of the U.S. of America.* Cincinnati: Applegate, 1856.

Stanton, Elizabeth Cady, and Susan B. Anthony. "The Just and Equal Rights of Woman." *Frederick Douglass's Paper*, 25 November 1853.

Stoltenberg, John. *Refusing to Be a Man: Essays on Sex and Justice.* Portland, OR: Breitenbush Books, 1989.

———. *The End of Manhood: A Handbook for Men of Conscience.* New York: Dutton, 1993.

Stricker, Frank. "Socialism, Feminism and the New Morality: The Separate Freedoms of Max Eastman, William English Walling and Floyd Dell, 1910–1930." Ph.D. diss., Princeton University, 1974.

Thompson, Maurice. "Vigorous Men, A Vigorous Nation." *Independent*, 1 September 1898.

Todd, Rev. John. *Woman's Rights.* Boston: Lee and Shepard, 1867.

Ward, Edward. *Women Should Mind Their Own Business.* New York: National American Woman Suffrage Association, 1900.

Why New York Men Should Give Women the Vote. New York: Empire State Campaign Committee, 1915. BECHSL.

"The Woman Peril." *Educational Review*, 47, February 1914.

The Woman's Rights Convention. Akron, 1851.

Woody, Thomas. *A History of Women's Education in the United States.* 2 vols. New York: Science Press, 1929.

NOTES

1. This essay is based on the archival research for Kimmel and Mosmiller, eds., *Against the Tide* (1992), which documents the existence of profeminist men.

2. Many of these documents can be found in the Women's Rights Collection at the Arthur and Elizabeth Schlesinger Library on the History of Women, Radcliffe College.

3. This poem is also reprinted in Woody 1929, 1:114.

4. In one letter, Higginson did seem to indicate a belief in women's moral superiority: "I do go for rights of women as far as an equal education and an equal share in government goes . . . I think it a monstrous absurdity to talk of a democratic government and universal suffrage and yet exclude one-half the inhabitants without any ground of incapacity to plead." He goes on to argue that women's participation is not only right and just, but would infuse the political process with morality (cited in Mary Higginson 1914, 73).

5. I develop this idea of crisis of masculinity at the turn of the century at greater length in Kimmel 1995, chaps. 3–6.

6. I develop my analysis more fully in Kimmel 1987 and 1995.

7. I refer here, of course, to the two works of John Stoltenberg (1989, 1993), who is perhaps the most visible and articulate purveyor of this rhetoric of support.

Chapter Three

To Be Black, Male, and Feminist
Making Womanist Space for Black Men on the Eve of a New Millennium

Gary Lemons

> Womanist. . . . A black feminist or feminist of color. . . .
> Committed to survival and wholeness of entire people,
> male *and* female.
> —Alice Walker, *In Search of Our Mothers' Gardens*

> If black men and women take seriously Malcolm [X]'s
> charge that we must work for our liberation "by any
> means necessary," then we must be willing to explore
> the way feminism as a critique of sexism, as a movement
> to end sexism and sexist oppression, could aid our strug-
> gle to be self-determining.
> —bell hooks, "Reconstructing Black Masculinity"

To know that one is not alone in a time of struggle is a knowledge to be cherished. When I recently came to know and interact with young black men at Morehouse College who had founded the organization Black Men for the Eradication of Sexism, I found myself struggling to understand the historical importance of that moment. On the weekend of September 28 and 29, 1996, a year after the Million Man March, they (we) made history. At the conference entitled "Black, Male and Feminist/Womanist," devoted entirely to the subject of *black* men's relation to feminism/womanism, African American men had organized to declare publicly their commitment to the eradication of sexism. In their mission statement they proclaim,

> We believe that sexism is a global form of oppression of no less importance than any other form of oppression. All forms of oppression, including sexism, racism, classism, homophobia are interconnected and support each other. *For too long the struggle for the liberation of African people in the united states [sic] has been centered on the liberation of black men.* This male-centered analysis inhibits us from fully confronting the oppression we constantly face and perpetuate within and without the black community. The struggle against sexism must become an issue of primary importance if we are to advance as a people. (Emphasis added)

Declaring that the struggle for black self-determination in the United States has for "too long . . . been centered on the liberation of black men," BMES calls for an end to a "male-centered analysis" of our oppression. It contends—and rightly so—that a dismissal of the struggle against sexism jeopardizes the welfare of an entire people.

Contemplating the meaning of black liberation struggle in the twenty-first century, I focus in this essay on what it means to be a black male feminist on the eve of the new millennium. My primary aim is to examine the meaning(s) of black manhood and masculinity in relationship to the issue of sexism, thinking about its impact on black people's struggle for self-determination in the United States under white supremacist patriarchy. I will examine the interrelation of female oppression to racism and the role we, as black men, play in the perpetuation of women's subjugation—particularly that experienced by black women. Black feminist analysis of gender oppression in the contemporary period has shown that sexism in black communities is a problem that basically we, as black men, still do not take seriously. We continue to believe that the struggle against white supremacy supersedes all others, as if racism is the only form of oppression experienced by black people.

The work of Black Men for the Eradication of Sexism suggests the possibility for the emergence of a movement of antisexist black men. Recognizing the necessity of a critique of black sexism, BMES establishes a critical standpoint that strikes at the core of the problem:

> We believe that sexist oppression against women pervades every aspect of our communities and must be eradicated. . . . Although it has often been said that black women are held in high regard by the black community, the reality is that black women are either denigrated as whores and enemies or

placed on a confining pedestal as superwoman. The humanity of our sisters is lost in these classifications which only succeed in further dividing our people and preventing us from dealing with other forms of oppression. *Sexism is a radical problem that requires a radical solution. . . . We support feminism/womanism and all efforts to eradicate sexist oppression. We ultimately demand a complete and fundamental revolutionary change that eradicates oppression based on sex, race, class, and sexual orientation, both within and without.* (Emphasis added)

Naming the dehumanizing effects of sexism on the lives of black women, this statement calls for a radical revision of black liberation struggle as we know it. "Demand[ing] a complete and fundamental revolutionary change," BMES has laid the groundwork for a feminist/womanist transformation of black manhood that strategically links the liberation of women to other resistance struggles across the boundaries of race, class, and sexuality. In the *revolutionary* spirit of the new work this organization has begun—in light of the history of profeminist/womanist activism of men like Frederick Douglass, W. E. B. Du Bois, and others like them—I argue for a coalition politics in black liberation struggle that honors the tradition of black women and men's fight for race and gender rights. As black men speak, write, and act out our support for antisexist work allied with struggles against racism, classism, and homophobia, we resist the power of patriarchy that would have us believe we are more powerful because we can exercise power over women. Such male supremacist thinking is particularly dangerous for black men precisely because our history in the United States has been about the racist obliteration of our manhood. Is our attainment of patriarchal power through the oppression of women any less insidious than racist white people's perpetuation of a system of racial oppression to dehumanize us? Many of us have become so obsessed with fighting racism as a battle for the right to be patriarchal men that we have been willing to deploy the same strategies to disempower black women as white supremacists have employed to institutionalize racism.

In light of the current success of certain black women writers, who have received unprecedented media attention over the last thirty years, and as more and more black women writers have begun to write back to the power of patriarchy, black men have begun to think about the impact of feminism on the gender relations of black men and women. bell hooks says in "Reconstructing Black Masculinity" that "[c]ollectively we can break the life threatening choke-hold patriarchal masculinity imposes on black men and create life sustaining visions of a reconstructed black masculinity that can provide black men ways to save their lives and the lives of their brothers and sisters in struggle" (1990, 113). To work toward the political reunification of the genders in black communities today, black men must acknowledge and begin to confront the existence of sexism as one of the chief obstacles to black liberation struggle. Making womanist space for black men to participate in feminist movement to oppose the oppression of women means that black men must go against the grain of the racist and sexist mythology of black manhood and masculinity in the United States. Its underlying premise, rooted in white supremacist patriarchal ideology, continues to foster the idea that we pose a racial and sexual threat to American society such that our bodies exist to be feared, brutalized, imprisoned, annihilated—made invisible.

The fear of emasculation originates in the history of black male lynching; the power of white (male) supremacy performed itself in the ritual act of castration (the violent sexual *dismembering* of our bodies) as a tool "to put/keep us in our place"—expressly because we were *black* and male—to "feminize" us. Thus, it is the fear of feminization in the minds of many black men that has led us to overdetermine our sexuality, believing that our identity as men resides only in the power of our penises. Against the inhumanity of our past, we must create a place/space to make ourselves over again in our own image. This place/space must not reconstruct the very mythology that sexually demonized our bodies as the scourge of white womanhood; rather, it must free us *to be black* in the most radically revolutionary manner, *to be male* in the most nonoppressive, antisexist way, *to be feminist* in the most supportive, nonpatriarchal way to bring about an end to the domination, subordination, and mistreatment of women because they are women.

In part, this essay also works to oppose black male antifeminist contempt and mistrust of contemporary black women writers, and to recover and reaffirm the history of black men in profeminist alliance with black and white women begun in the woman suffrage movement. Moreover, it functions to assert the idea that black feminist critique of sexism in black communities is not about "black male bashing," but about black women confronting the reality of patriarchy acted out by black men. Such an attitude only perpetuates popular media sensationalism grounded in the myth of a black gender war. Creating space for progressive dialogues on the prevalence of black sexism need not be governed by male supremacist thinking as if the black male ego remains too fragile for the rigor of critique, even as black women labor under the myth of the matriarch, the castrating "superwoman." Recovering black men's prowomanist past acts to engender a politic of intervention whereby black men (and women) come to understand the necessity of feminist critique in liberation struggle as a critical means to empower all black people.

Black Women Writing to Liberate Themselves: Breaking a Tradition of Silence

If the first wave of American feminism in the nineteenth century represented the struggle of black women to be recognized as "women," the second movement for women's liberation set the stage for a renaissance of black women writers who employed literature as a vehicle for self-empowerment. As I have already noted, the liberatory writings of black women have misguidedly become the targets of black male antifeminists precisely because many believe that the sole aim of black female writers is to bash them. When black women have written or spoken out in critique of black male status, privilege, and/or sexism, black men have accused them of perpetuating white supremacist emasculation of the black male. In the contemporary period, feminist black women writers continue to be the "object" of antifeminist rhetoric. In a 1979 *Black Scholar* essay, which initiated the debate on black sexism, Robert Staples's critique of black feminist writings by Michele Wallace and Ntozake Shange foreshadowed subsequent attacks in the 1980s and 1990s on Alice Walker, Gayl Jones, Gloria Naylor, Toni Morrison, and Paule Marshall, among others, as well as the onslaught of black male criticism against the film version of Terry McMillan's recent novel *Waiting to Exhale*.

The antiwomanist response by many black men against the film echoed the negative reaction expressed toward the cinematic representation of *The Color Purple*, Alice Walker's epistolary novel of black female search for self-empowerment. Scoring big at the box office during the first weeks it played, *Waiting to Exhale* generated significant dialogue among black women and men on the current state of gender relations in black communities. Yet many black men contested male representation in the film, asserting that once again a black woman had misrepresented them and focused on negative images. Viewing it as nothing more than black male bashing, they saw no redeeming value to "airing the dirty laundry of black people." Listening to a radio program in which callers discussed their

Maybe not ... became a devote feminist but accept feminist viewpoint and became conscious of the and to accept both about reality that hinder the black females

views of the film, I found myself wondering why every male caller lambasted McMillan for having "(mis)treated black men in such stereotypical ways." A couple of weeks earlier I had encountered a black man who came on the bus equipped with a copy of *Waiting to Exhale*, ranting to black female passengers that he *had* to read "another male-bashing book by a sister." Rather than challenge my black "brother" to rethink his misguided notion of black women writers, I sat in silence, remembering the outspoken manner in which I had defended the book and film version of *The Color Purple* more than a decade ago.

Critical dialogue during and since the debate has centered on what black male detractors of feminism consider the emasculation of black men by "angry black feminists," as Staples calls Wallace and Shange. Black men opposed to feminism, such as Ishmael Reed, have accused black women writers of complicity with white women feminists toward the racist castration of all black men. Black women writers are repeatedly accused of breaking faith with a standing agreement with their male counterparts, and their representation of black men is said to be counterproductive to African American struggle against racist oppression. Yet few of their critics are willing to acknowledge the reality of sexism in black communities. In "Family Plots: Black Women Writers Reclaim the Past," Thulani Davis articulates the perceived attack this way: "Contemporary [women] writers are being accused of pillorying black men, promoting homosexuality, ignoring sociological overviews of black oppression—and they're often pegged as the first black writers to commit such sins" (1987, 14). To the extent that black women have embraced feminism, many black antifeminists believe it has led them into acts of betrayal through the misrepresentation of black men. The price black women writers pay is expulsion from the tradition of "racial uplift" writing dominated by African American writers. According to Mel Watkins in "Sexism, Racism and Black Women Writers," "Those black women writers who have chosen black men as a target have set themselves outside a tradition that is nearly as old as black American literature itself. They have, in effect, put themselves at odds with what seems to be an unspoken but almost universally accepted covenant among black writers" (1986, 36).

The "unspoken covenant" to which Watkins refers is a myth. Black writers have never had such an unstated agreement. In African American literary history, prescriptive notions of representation have traditionally met opposition. To suggest (as Watkins does later in his article) that the Harlem Renaissance was a period during which "the earliest fiction by

American blacks, produced by the Talented Tenth school of writers . . . [was] characterized by [its] emphasis on establishing humane, positive images of blacks" (36) reveals his limited knowledge of the period's literary crisis regarding the representation of blacks in fiction. He completely ignores the many black female *and male* writers who contested the provincialism, sexism, and homophobia of the black middle class. Watkins's claim that contemporary African American women writers initiated a trend toward negative images of black men ignores those less than positive portrayals created by a number of male writers. Like Watkins, Robert Staples would have us believe Shange and Wallace were the first "angry black feminists." How would black men like Mel Watkins and Robert Staples read the feminist writings of Frederick Douglass and W. E. B. Du Bois? Would they be called "angry black feminists"? Apparently, contemporary black men who oppose feminism have no knowledge of Shange and Wallace's historical black male womanist counterparts.

Black Men Speaking and Writing in Feminist Alliance: (Re)Constructing a Womanist History

In 1925 Amy Jacques Garvey, editor of the "Women's Page" of the *Negro World* (and wife of Marcus Garvey), declared,

> We are tired of hearing Negro men say, "There is a better day coming" while they do nothing to usher in the day. We are becoming so impatient that we are getting in the front ranks and serve notice that we will brush aside the halting, cowardly Negro leaders. . . . Mr. Black Man watch your step! . . . Strengthen your shaking knees and move forward, or we will displace you and lead on to victory and glory. (Quoted in Giddings 1984, 195)

Exhorting black men to act more aggressively toward racial progress or be "displace[d]" by more radically mobilized black women, Amy Garvey wrote without regard to the disposition of the black male ego. From the rise of black feminism in the second half of the nineteenth century and the fervor of its movement in the 1920s through its reemergence in the writings of contemporary black women novelists, critics, poets, theorists, and academics, black women feminists have determined for themselves a course of action often against the grain of black racial and gender party lines. Always having to weigh their actions with regard to notions of race solidarity and the defense of themselves as women, black feminists share a history of liberation struggle cultivated in a political interrelation of racism and sexism.

In the text above, Amy Jacques Garvey authoritatively calls into question black male power (without compromising the movement for racial liberation). *Rewriting* the destiny of black women in liberation struggle, she proclaims the power of black female agency. The emergence of a black female intelligentsia in the last decade of the nineteenth century was preceded by the rise of Douglass as one of the century's most recognized black intellectuals, and followed by Du Bois as the major arbiter of the intellectual and artistic movement known as the Harlem Renaissance. In the African American literary tradition these men stand as acknowledged leaders of the "race," but each in his own right commanded more than one discursive field in which he spoke and wrote on the subject of women's rights. To view Douglass and Du Bois only as race leaders obscures and diminishes their distinguished careers as advocates of the rights of women. To overlook their active participation in the developing stage of black women's intellectual and political enterprise (from which African American feminist movement emerged) represents a grave oversight. Frances Ellen Harper, Pauline Hopkins, Anna Julia Cooper, and Ida B. Wells, among others, constituted a feminist intellectual body of which Frederick Douglass and W. E. B. Du Bois were an integral part.

As prowoman speakers and writers, these men belonged to the black feminist tradition at the incisive juncture of black women's political and social activism, characterized in the writings of the "Woman's Era." I assert the importance of the prowoman position Douglass and Du Bois held partly to counter the phallocentric identification of blackness, though at times both men represented themselves in rather traditionally patriarchal ways. Recovering the women's rights discourse of Douglass and Du Bois as a model of black male profeminism enables its employment as a counterposition to contemporary black male antifeminist sentiment. My argument is that the vision of liberation struggle these men constructed around a race/gender coalition politic holds transformative possibilities for black liberation movement today. The liberatory nature of feminist writings by Douglass and Du Bois rests precisely on the conjoinment of gender and race issues. This way of thinking is representative of the ideals early coalition strategists conceived in linking abolitionism to feminism. Douglass, Elizabeth Cady Stanton, and Susan B. Anthony among others viewed gender and race oppression in coterminous relation. Therefore, a movement to oppose gender and race oppression could constitute a much more politically viable and powerful location from which to strategize black enfranchisement and the political freedom of women.

(Black) Men in (or out of?) Feminism: Theorizing Womanist Black Men as Profeminist Comrades

Womanist is to feminist as purple to lavender.
— Alice Walker, *In Search of Our Mothers' Gardens*

(I believe womanism, as Alice Walker conceived it, to be a liberatory location for remaking black manhood into a male identity that transgresses the boundaries of patriarchy, freeing us from the oppressive racist/ sexist, sexually "othered" space we occupied in the past.) Theorizing a womanist space for black men means focusing on the historical impact castration and lynching have had on the black male psyche and on ways we construct our identity as men. It may begin to tell us why many black men have internalized the racist sexual myths of black manhood and masculinity such that images of "black macho" and the supersexual "buck/stud" have prevailed in black communities as legitimate representations of black male power. hooks maintains that "black men who are most worried about castration and emasculation are those who have completely absorbed white supremacist patriarchal definitions of masculinity" (1992, 93). The black buck stereotype, conceived in the white racist imagination during the period of slavery, signified that every black male (who did not fit the "Uncle Tom," older, nonsexualized type) stood as the symbol of the sexually brutalizing phallus operating always already as a sexual threat to the purity of white womanhood—thus the need for castration.

As controlling images in the contemporary period, phallic representations of black masculinity in the Black Power movement of the 1960s manifested themselves in popular culture via the performance of hypermasculinity as witnessed in the popularity of blaxploitation films in the 1970s (a genre made famous by the movie *Shaft* and a host of others featuring the "superfly" or the hypercool black male stereotype). Yet the mythology of black machismo remains grounded in the image of the black man as supersexual savage, an image created to control black men during slavery.[1] The reproduction and perpetuation of a hypersexualized, hard black manhood/masculinity in white supremacist capitalist media is fed by stereotypical portrayals of black males. The very sexually over-determined images that have "essentially" typed us through history are played out repeatedly on the contemporary scene in the arena of popular culture, where the "dick-clutching" posture of many black male rappers has obtained as a status symbol of male power in hip-hop.

I defy the notion that black manhood and masculinity are about a "dick thing." Progressive black men who renounce sexist, misogynist, and patriarchal practice against women—which is the taproot of the "dick thing" mentality—begin to mediate the painful historical memory of our own dehumanization. Challenging the white supremacist stereotype of the "super dick" (that so many black men have internalized as the symbol of black male power) means resisting the racist/sexist sexual mythology created to control us. It would have us believe that we are no more than one big collective "walking, brutalizing phallus." When we begin to interrogate its oppressive power over us, we start to perceive the interrelated ways racism and male supremacist privilege work together to dehumanize all black men. Understanding the link between white privilege and male privilege—realizing that empowered images of black manhood do not rest in the reclamation of lost phallic power (the preeminent fallacy of manhood thinking in general)—black men come to experience transformative, liberatory power as men. When we begin to claim our bodies as our own—beyond the bounds of white supremacist capitalist patriarchal control—we no longer have to fear that our penises will be cut off as punishment for being black and male. When we fully realize this, we confront the psychic/sexual wound/violation that castration/lynching represents, discovering that our quest for power in the myth of the "big black buck" is a self-dehumanizing act—physically, psychologically, and spiritually. Black men who come to feminist consciousness signify a radical departure from the racist/sexist ideology of black manhood/masculinity that has consumed many of us. Black men who move to reclaim our womanist/feminist past contest the power of the phallus in our lives and the lives of women, and move toward truly liberatory meanings of manhood.

The absence of a large-scale presence of black men in support of antisexist activism suggests that in the contemporary period something called "black male feminism" is invisible. And in many ways, being black and male in feminist alliance means being an "invisible (wo)man"—not passing as a woman, but not acting like a man in traditional phallocentric terms, either. Without oversimplifying this condition, perhaps, it is a kind of gender/race ambiguity that informs the idea of black male feminism. But, as stated earlier, it is the idea of feminism connected to a perverse notion of the feminine that in the historical memory of black men conjures up images of feminization, castration, and ultimately death, which may partly account for contemporary black male antifeminism. Thus, in white supremacist patriarchal culture, to many black men feminism represents a threat to their vision of black masculinity and manhood—familial and cultural authority, responsibility, nationhood, and "manliness." Many view feminism as synonymous to white supremacy that attempts to reenact the sexual "unmanning" of black men as the prime spectacle of lynching. Is it any wonder we remain mistrustful of feminism?

While the history of joint movement against racism and sexism in the United States is a record of uncertainty, as a feminist I believe progressive feminism (founded on the liberation of all people, female and male) remains a crucial site in which to foster a coalition politics, linking political resistance to gender, race, class, and sexual oppression. I believe the infusion of coalition politics, informed by feminist thinking, in black people's movement for liberation would transform the dynamics of gender relations in black communities such that no one—regardless of sex, sexual preference, and/or class—is excluded from the battle for black people to live as whole beings. In the process, black men interrogating meanings of manhood (beyond white supremacist patriarchal denial of black male humanity) come to view feminism as a life-sustaining way of thinking that enhances rather than threatens our lives. As woman suffragists and advocates of women's rights, Frederick Douglass and W. E. B. Du Bois have much to offer us as black male feminists.

Considering the effect of race on the relationship between black men and feminism, I analyze black male feminism in the light of African American male participation in the woman suffrage movement. This analysis forms the basis for theorizing womanism as a site of resistance to antifeminist thinking and a location for gender solidarity, where transformative ideas of black manhood and masculinity in support of women's rights work against the ideology of male supremacy. Contesting black male attacks on black feminists—from Michele Wallace and Ntozake Shange in the late 1970s to Alice Walker and Terry McMillan in the following decades—black men understanding the long-standing relationship between black women and men in coalition struggle for woman suffrage disrupt the contemporary myth that all black men are antifeminists. (Re)establishing a black men's womanist history represents an important step toward ending the myth that feminism is an alienating force in black lives.

On the one hand, in the racial imperatives articulated in the framework of race and cultural nationalism since the 1960s—during the rise of the Black Power movement and most recently in the call for black male repatriarchalization by Louis Farrakhan with the Million Man March— "blackness" has become synonymous with "maleness," reinscribing a male-centered view of race that always already ignores issues of sexism. On the other, in the 1960s, issues of gender equality and women's rights led the agenda of the women's liberation movement, principally dominated by middle-class white women. And for many white women feminists still, the relation of men to feminism continues to be articulated in terms of gender alone, excluding the impact race has had and continues to have on gender relations in the United States. By the end of the Black Power movement, just as racial injustice had come to be identified mostly with the plight of the black male, so at the height of the women's liberation movement the oppression of women had come to be associated with women who were white and middle-class.

Reflecting on the race and gender politics of the 1960s, I have come to view the Black Power movement and the second wave of feminism as important clarifying moments in my evolution as a black male feminist teacher in the 1990s. But like black women feminists advocating the struggle against racism, black men supporting women against sexism find ourselves on the margins of both black liberation and women's movements. Often having to confront the question, Are you "black" first or "feminist"? we find ourselves walking a race/gender tightrope, always having to negotiate a position of split allegiance. For black women feminists, emphasis on their status as women has been equated in many black communities with a betrayal of race solidarity and lesbianism (as if heterosexual affiliation alone should determine one's affinity to blackness).

In the 1980s male feminism was debated in *Men in Feminism* (1987), edited by Alice Jardine and Paul Smith. Centering on the theoretical problematics of male feminism, essays in the anthology focused on issue of men's relation (or nonrelation) to feminist theory. Given the ever-increasing presence of male critical and theoretical discourse on women, a volume such as *Men in Feminism* possessed the potential to be crucially important to a continuing dialogue on where men stand in relation to feminism. But it woefully failed. Where are the folks of color? The volume includes not one essay by a woman or man of color. For the most part, there are no substantive discussions of race and sexuality, and references to black men and women are only incidental. In other words, in this book we remain at the margin of white feminist discourse, invisible at nearly every level of discussion. Men of color's relation to feminism is never addressed, as if white men are the only men questioning whether there exists a place for them "in" feminism. Not only is *race* not seriously dealt with in this volume, its heterosexist bias looms large. Only one essay (written by a white gay man) overtly engages the relationship of men to feminism in the context of male sexuality. While I, as a man of African descent, literally occupy no discursive or theoretical space in *Men in Feminism*, it is important for me to state here that my thinking about male feminism is not invested in a version of theory disconnected from practice.

Jardine and Smith blame the virtual absence of nonwhite and gay perspectives on their "trouble locating intellectuals, who, having shown interest in the question, would offer . . . a gay or black perspective on the problem." Rather than simply confess to the failure of their search, they point to academia's lack of institutional commitment to diversity in its hiring practices (vii-viii). I seriously question how extensively the editors looked for the "other" perspective, when by 1987 bell hooks had already written on the relationship of men of color to feminism in *Feminist Theory: From Margin to Center* (1984). In spite of its glaring silence on the subject of black men and feminism, conceptually *Men in Feminism* raises a fundamental question as to whether male feminists can work to empower women in nonpatriarchal ways. In "Male Feminism," Stephen Heath addresses this question, asserting that "[m]en's relation to feminism is an impossible one . . . politically. Men have a necessary relation to feminism . . . and that relation is also necessarily one of a certain exclusion . . . no matter how 'sincere,' 'sympathetic' or whatever, we are always in a male position which brings with it all the implications of domination and appropriation" (1). The idea that men in feminist alliance with women cannot politically subvert the power of male supremacy is like saying that white people in antiracist solidarity with black people cannot divest themselves of white supremacist thinking.

Considering the institutionalization of women's studies in the academy and the proliferation of feminist scholarship by men (mostly white), I too am suspicious of male presence in this arena, particularly when so much of it appears appropriative, motivated by professional advancement. Yet male feminism situated in activist relation to feminist movement demonstrates a necessary engagement in theory and practice. Otherwise, the *in* space that feminist men construct is always already patriarchal—characterized by control, penetration, and violation. Discovering and writing about the lives of Douglass and Du Bois as woman suffragists has helped me free myself from the kind of paralyzing male-feminist, theorizing trap that Stephen Heath sets up. If all feminist men concluded as he does that our relation to feminism is indeed an impossible one, we would never get on with the task at hand—to end sexism and the oppression of women. The history of black male profeminist relation to women's movement against sexism shows that despite the patriarchal baggage all men carry, we can be men without being oppressors of women. Relying on black feminists theorizing race, gender, and class as interlocking systems of oppression, I draw on the history of black women and men in feminist movement to clarify the dual positions Douglass and Du Bois occupied as race spokesmen and advocates of women's rights. Grasping the strategy Douglass and Du Bois conceived to advance the struggle of black people enables contemporary black men to reconceptualize a movement in resistance to white supremacy that encompasses strategies to oppose the oppression of women.

Women can no longer afford to theorize men on the margin of feminism when sexist practice impacts the daily lives of women as its victims and men as its perpetrators. Women's acceptance of progressive men as feminist allies will end the stigma of feminist movement as a separatist enterprise. While such thinking may free women from the presence of men, it does not eradicate sexism in the society at large. Instead, it mirrors the very sexist behavior feminist women seek to end. As the 1960s brought forth with it a renaissance of black women writers, so it gave birth to a new generation of black female scholar/critics who would become the architects of a black feminist theory and criticism. From the reemergence of feminism in black communities in the 1960s came some of today's most outspoken black feminists. Of them, bell hooks, more than any other, has addressed the necessity of black men in feminist movement. "Men: Comrades in Struggle" (in *Feminist Theory: From Margin to Center* [1984]) critically addressed the need for men's political engagement in feminism. In one of her most radical essays on the subject, "Feminist Focus on Men" (from *Talking Back: Thinking Feminist, Thinking Black* [1989]), she calls for women scholars to begin writing on men: "Now we [women] can acknowledge that the reconstruction and transformation of male behavior, of masculinity, is a necessary and essential part of feminist revolution. . . . While it is critical that male scholars committed to feminist struggle do scholarship that focuses on men, it is equally important that women scholars focus on men" (127, 132). Putting into practice that which she advocates, hooks works in the tradition of nineteenth- and early twentieth-century black feminist coalition struggle. *Yearning: Race, Gender, and Cultural Politics* (1990) includes "Black Women and Men: Partnership in the 1990s," a dialogue with Cornel West. *Breaking Bread: Insurgent Black Intellectual Life* (1991), coauthored with West, opens with that essay as the basis for a book-length continuation of the conversation the two began earlier. As intellectual partners discussing the challenge of integrating radical intellectualism into the struggle against racism, sexism, and the economic and cultural exploitation of African Americans, they become comrades of the mind, negotiating "the point of connection between black women and men [that is the] space of recognition and understanding, where we know one another so well, our histories, that we can take the bits and pieces, the fragments of who we are, and put them back together, re-member them" (19). In "re-member[ing]" black women and men's histories, hooks and West remember the legacy of those gone before them, who fought for the liberation of black people. That hooks and West would frame their coming together in the tradition of African American intellectualism brings a new, even more lucid understanding of a historic exchange between black women and men. Well-known dialogues have been recorded between Frederick Douglass and Sojourner Truth, Frances Harper, and Ida B. Wells-Barnett, among others. Dialogues have been documented between W. E. B. Du Bois and Mary Church Terrell, Anna Julia Cooper, and Jessie Fauset, as well as a number of other black female thinkers of his day. *Breaking Bread* is about maintaining and preserving the historical continuity of intellectual life. In the company of Douglass and Du Bois, bell hooks and Cornel West find their dialogue solidly grounded in a long history of black female/male "partnership" in feminist movement.

(Black) male feminism as a politics of intervention (opposing sexism in black communities) represents a crucial step toward educating men on the ill effects of male domination. The struggle against sexist oppression will be most successfully fought, hooks believes, when men undergo feminist transformation—only when they are challenged by women to understand that the oppression of women is a form of self-oppression.

*"I" Declare: Teaching Feminism to "Re-member," from
Theory to Practice*

Today black men must begin remembering their feminist past, one in
which the fight against racist oppression was integrally linked to women's
liberation struggle. Comprehending the power of this crucial fact, we will
have to rethink the meaning of contemporary black liberation struggle.
Beyond the exclusionary politics of antiracist strategizing based solely on
a masculinist recuperation of manhood, black men must begin resisting
sexist propaganda that tells us wrongfully that to be fully empowered as
black men we should strive to "atone" for the loss of manhood. Progressive black people in the United States, calling out sexist and misogynist
practice perpetrated by black men, create counterhegemonic black male
and female space where locations of race, gender, and sexual healing are
created. Considering the fact that at this moment there exists an emerging
movement around the repatriarchalization of black masculinity, black
men need to recognize the vital link between the histories of feminist
movement and black liberation movement connected to womanist concerns. Only when we act to reconnect these struggles will black men
achieve a status of dignity and self-worth that is not bound to patriarchy.
In this manner, we construct an integrative, holistic movement against
the dehumanizing power of patriarchal thinking.

In a period when a new black manhood movement has emerged
around the patriarchal capitalist ideas of Louis Farrakhan, can a progressive coalition movement against domination be forged that transgresses
the borders of identity politics? Can the academy be a site of oppositional
struggle where progressive educators employ the classroom as a strategic
location for liberatory education practice? And what difference can a black
male feminist make toward a vision of "wholeness" in black communities,
where every individual woman, man, and child is valued and cared for?
Addressing these questions, I envision a political space where black men
can work to empower themselves in feminist solidarity, working in the
tradition and spirit of their womanist legacy.

I claim the feminist activism of Douglass and Du Bois as a critical
standpoint from which to call contemporary black men into renewed
dialogue with black women on the status of gender relations in black
communities. As a college professor teaching African American literature,
I teach courses that politically engender the antiracist/antisexist agenda

Douglass and Du Bois conceived. Committed to progressive feminist movement as articulated by bell hooks, I view my teaching as a process of remembering in which African American literary narratives become agents of social healing across the boundaries of race, gender, class, and sexuality (1996b, 259–84). Many students interested in ways these categories intersect come to my classes seeking an approach to understand the complex relation between them. I set up the political struggle of black Americans recounted in fiction, poetry, and/or essay form as a model for liberation politics.

Over the past five years, having developed a course repertory grounded in feminism, I apply a sociological perspective to the representation of black female/male gender relations rather than a strictly traditional "literary" method.[2] This approach illustrates the juncture where the personal, political, and pedagogical meet to establish the classroom as a space of feminist activism, where teaching black literature serves a liberatory purpose. It is, however, my use of an antiracist/feminist pedagogy in the classroom that distinguishes my teaching as a male feminist (Lemons 1996a, 158–70). Thinking about ways to contest male privilege, sexism, and patriarchal hegemony, and to affirm the power of the maternal in my life as a man, a husband, a father, and a teacher, I have come to draw on the style, attitudes, and critical thinking about life experience my mother passed on to me. For me, teaching as a male feminist in the classroom means tapping into the maternal as a transformative space in which to nurture the development of critical consciousness in my students. I work to achieve a relationship with them associated with a maternal posture rather than paternal, patriarchal, or traditionally masculine-identified interaction. I follow Sara Ruddick's progressive line of thought that "a man who engages in mothering to some extent takes on the female condition and risks identification with the feminine" (1989, 45).

In my pedagogy, the act of "mothering" is affirmed as a liberatory location to employ the maternal as a strategy of nurturance in opposition to the ways of the Father. I grew up in a patriarchal household where my father's experience as a military officer informed the masculine rigidity of its day-to-day operation. As an often withdrawn, timid little boy, I came to fear, despise, and later resist his notions of manhood, manliness, and masculinity. More than anything, my sympathies were aligned with my mother, who for a time served as a housekeeper/cook in the homes of elite white families. I often think about the powerlessness she must have felt, working tirelessly at the whims of her wealthy employers, always having to enter the back doors of their elegantly appointed homes to perform what they believed themselves unsuited to do. But it is my mother's sharp tongue, her resolute will to struggle, her critical understanding of the way race shaped her experience as a black, female, working-class mother and wife that have informed how and what I teach. When I teach students (male students in particular) to resist the antifeminist idea that men embracing feminism necessarily means a loss of a masculinity, Ruddick's idea of the maternal man comes to me:

> The fear of becoming "feminine" . . . is a motivating force behind the drive to master women and whatever is "womanly." . . . [G]rown men should confront the political meaning of "femininity" and their own fear of the feminine. *A man does not, by becoming a mother, give up his male body or any part of it. To be sure, by becoming a mother he will, in many social groups, challenge the ideology of masculinity.* (45; emphasis added)

It stands to reason that men who embrace feminist thinking risk having their masculinity called into question; this is the point exactly. For a man, advocating and teaching feminism means taking risks, breaking through barriers of manhood and masculinity inscribed in patriarchy, which devalues the qualities of nurturance and mothering. The maternal, as Ruddick insists, possesses *transgendered* capabilities.

Since my first course in feminism nearly ten years ago in graduate school, when I read *Feminist Theory: From Margin to Center* for the first time, hooks's progressive vision of feminist movement against all forms of domination has shaped and guided my vision of the classroom as a space for liberatory education practice. But feminism itself remains a contested ideology in and outside the classroom not only because it subverts patriarchal power but also because it is bound up in complicated issues of race, class, and sexuality. For any teacher—whether female or male, black or not, gay or straight—employing progressive feminist politics to teach against white supremacy and male domination represents a transgressive act. Antiracist feminist practice in the classroom requires risk-taking by the teacher and student. Often it means speaking from the personal, a space loaded with ideological baggage in need of exposure and examination.

When I tell students I am a feminist, they always react in complex ways, depending on their race, gender, and sexual affiliations. But a feminist black man in (or outside) the classroom is always already an oddity. First of all, I am at odds with many white students' fear of black men and racist attitudes about black people in general. Second, I am at odds with many black students whose rage against and contempt for all white people blind them to the possibilities of progressive coalition movement across racial boundaries in resistance to racism, when we begin to de-essentialize blackness. I am also at odds with male students especially (of color and not) who buy into male supremacist ideas of manhood and masculinity. They view me as a traitor to mankind, a misanthrope of the worst kind!

As a black man teaching feminism as a strategy to combat racism, I take risks in the classroom that pose a particular challenge to essentialized meanings of black liberation and racial solidarity linked to narrow ideas of black manhood and masculinity. Like black women feminists, I find that my commitment to black struggle against racism is called into question by students of color (always few in number) who argue that "feminism is a white woman's thing." As a black man teaching in a predominantly white, private institution who advocates an end to male privilege, sexism, and misogyny from a particularly "black" feminist perspective, I realize that my color and gender pose problems for white students in my classes. While white male presence in them is rare, those white men they do attract are often in the process of coming to grips with their fear of "blackness"—especially that personified in negative stereotypes of black men. Similarly, white women in my classes, whether feminist or not, respond to me in ways that suggest they too are working to figure out their own relationship to a "feminist black man." Feminist students who are female (of color and not), suspicious of men's motives for teaching and claiming feminist alliance, often display attitudes of distrust toward the notion of a male feminist.

Generally, in the minds of both white students and students of color, I represent an image of black manhood and masculinity out of sync with the racist and sexual mythologies inscripted on the black male body over the course of time. I am not a Sambo, an Uncle Tom, a buck, a rapist, or a dope-dealer. But I must downplay the fact of my tallness (6'4") and my "loud" voice (I have been told by white females in my classes that these aspects of my identity frighten them) because I am specifically "black" and "male."

By the same token, I disclaim a patriarchal nationalist black masculinity, as represented by the ideas of Farrakhan and dramatically played out in the Million Man March. Many black male students view me as having sold out not only my blackness but my manhood as well because I opposed the march and most of its mission statement.[3] I maintain that a major contributing factor to the failure of black liberation movement in the 1960s was its overemphasis on issues relating to the needs of black men that excluded those of black women. The inability of the movement to sustain a successful oppositional stance and resistance to white supremacy and white supremacist capitalist patriarchal exploitation of black culture resided in the fact that many black men who participated in the movement viewed the struggle against racism solely in male-identified terms, as I have already argued.

Black students in my classes (often because they feel threatened by implicit and explicit acts of racism perpetrated by white administrators, faculty members, and staff persons in a predominantly white university setting) resist my claim that antiracist ideology must be affected through a number of radical strategies, beyond the limited perspective of black male identity politics. In accord with bell hooks's liberatory vision of "education as the practice of freedom," I claim a pedagogical strategy rooted in the politics of progressive feminist movement against all forms of domination, where teachers committed to coalition building cross race, gender, class, and sexual borders to teach students ways to oppose the dehumanization of all people.

Contemporary black men who actively call into question male supremacy represent a potentially powerful impetus for rethinking black masculinity. Transformative strategies of black liberation linked to a liberatory vision of black manhood and masculinity reflect a critically oppositional view of black men's racial oppression and the power we possess to oppress women precisely because we are men. When black men begin to construct a large-scale movement against racism and sexism, we embark on a new path of struggle—one of feminist reclamation, not patriarchal atonement. Accepting our past as black men fighting racism as we waged the battle for gender rights with women, we claim a destiny beyond the bounds of patriarchy.

We can no longer use the myth that feminism is a racist ploy to emasculate black men while we assert our power as men to oppress women. Progressive black men, whether or not we advocate feminism, ought to begin divesting ourselves of male privilege in support of black women. Opposing sexism and misogyny, we embrace our history of profeminist alliance in women's rights struggle. Confronting the fear of the feminine that feminism represents to many men, black men can begin to formulate effective, liberatory strategies of gender empowerment in black communities that affirm the rights of all women. Moreover, as we insist on our right to be treated with dignity and respect in this society, we do so not because we are men but because we are human beings. Black men need to know that feminism—as a belief rooted in the right of women to lead nonoppressive, nonobjectified lives—is not inherently racist, sexist, or classist. We must vigorously denounce black male antifeminist rhetoric that reduces the feminism of black women to a diatribe against black men.

If black women feminists are "angry" with black men (to use Robert Staples's terms), then we need to ask why—without the cloak of self-pity that so many of us wear as we hide behind the wall of sexist denial to defend our oppressive behavior and misogynist ways. We can no longer construct ourselves as innocent victims of racism, castrated by "our" women who have no sympathy for the battle we wage against the (white) "Man" who refuses us a bigger slice of patriarchal pie. Black men in the woman suffrage movement, speaking and writing in feminist alliance, rejected the "black-man-as-victim" status as they fought to obtain social, economic, and political rights for black men and women—while working to secure certain rights for women particularly based on the condition of gender oppression across the boundaries of race. Why can't we?

Black men who take responsibility for ending male supremacy, acknowledging the ways it systematically undermines black women's place in the struggle against racism, create womanist space for us to do antisexist work. Thus, opposing the race and sexual oppression of women means that men of color must be traitors to patriarchy—refusing to bond with men at the expense of women's subjugation. In other words, it means that we must denounce the phallacy of patriarchy. In spite of the structural inequalities of racism we experience as black men, patriarchal thinking would lead us to believe that male supremacist power is rightfully ours as a form of racial justice. That black nationalist men have made the struggle against racism the same as a struggle for manhood rights in the current "black power movement" led by Farrakhan suggests that we are experiencing a serious backlash against black feminism. Regardless of class, men of color who are male supremacist believe that we are just as powerful as white men when we move to exert manhood privilege to "keep women in their place"—physically, sexually, economically, mentally, and otherwise. Male supremacist black men have failed to understand the mechanics of domination. For example, the history of black male experience in the United States necessitates an analysis of the interrelation of race and sex oppression. Yet comprehending the extent to which white male patriarchal power operates to promote the myth that black men pose a racial and sexual threat to the country without fully understanding the ways racism and sexism combine to render black women completely powerless is unequivocally wrongheaded. In racist, capitalist culture, just as our bodies are socially constructed to be feared, brutalized, exploited, annihilated, made invisible because of our race and gender, so black women have been made to endure even more in a culture of patriarchy.

My argument in this essay has been that when we black men oppress women through male supremacy, we reenact the very same strategies that the white supremacist employs to dehumanize us. Given the enormity of the toll sexism exacted on the political and communal effectiveness of black liberation strategy during the 1960s, it stands to reason that we would not want to repeat the failures of our past. Be assured that black women's call for recognition and equality in the struggle for black self-determination will not cease simply because they have been told to stay home while their partners, husbands, brothers, fathers, and uncles go off to claim their manhood. Patriarchal "atonement" can never be a substitute for the freedom autonomous black women have claimed as a fundamental right of their existence—the right to determine the course of one's own destiny. Surely, given the history of our struggle to survive as black men, shouldn't we understand this more than anyone and be compelled to serve in the cause of justice for the liberation of black women? This will be among the preeminent questions facing black people in the twenty-first century.

REFERENCES

Cleaver, Eldridge. 1968. *Soul on Ice.* New York: Dell.

Davis, Thulani. 1987. "Family Plots: Black Women Reclaim the Past." *Voice Literary Supplement,* March, 14–17.

Giddings, Paula. 1984. *When and Where I Enter: The Impact of Black Women on Race and Sex in America.* New York: Bantam.

Hernton, Calvin. 1965. *Sex and Racism in America.* New York: Grove.

hooks, bell. 1984. *Feminist Theory: From Margin to Center.* Boston: South End Press.

———. 1989. *Talking Back: Thinking Feminist, Thinking Black.* Boston: South End Press.

————. 1990. *Yearning: Race, Gender, and Cultural Politics*. Boston: South End Press.

————. 1992. *Black Looks: Race and Representation*. Boston: South End Press.

hooks, bell, and Cornel West. 1991. *Breaking Bread: Insurgent Black Intellectual Life*. Boston: South End Press.

Jardine, Alice, and Paul Smith, eds. 1987. *Men in Feminism*. New York: Routledge.

Lemons, Gary. 1996a. "Teaching the (Bi)Racial Space That Has No Name: Reflections of a Black Male Feminist Teacher." In *Everyday Acts against Racism: Raising Children in a Multiracial World*, edited by Maureen T. Reddy, 158–70. Seattle: Seal Press.

————. 1996b. " 'Young Man, Tell Our Stories of How We Made It Over': Beyond the Politics of Identity." In *Teaching What You're Not: Identity Politics in Higher Education*, edited by Katherine J. Mayberry, 259–284. New York: New York University Press.

Ruddick, Sara. 1989. *Maternal Thinking: Toward a Politics of Peace*. New York: Ballantine.

Staples, Robert. 1979. "The Myth of Black Macho: A Response to Angry Black Feminists." *Black Scholar*, March–April, 24–32.

Walker, Alice. 1983. *In Search of Our Mothers' Gardens*. San Diego: Harcourt Brace Jovanovich.

Watkins, Mel. 1986. "Sexism, Racism and Black Women Writers." *New York Times Book Review*, June, 36.

NOTES

For their sound advice in the evolution of this essay, I would like to thank the editors, Steven Schacht and Doris Ewing in particular. Ewing's suggestion for the rearrangement of certain sections in this version made for more coherent reading. My special gratitude extends to my partner, Fanni Green, who pushed me to write with needed candor.

1. In *Soul on Ice* and *Sex and Racism in America*, respectively, Eldridge Cleaver and Calvin Hernton offer provocative versions of U.S. race, gender, and sexual hierarchy in which the racist sexualization of the black male operates.

2. For example, students in a course I teach called Black Female Representation in the Harlem Renaissance focus on the politics of gender and race in the United States during the 1920s. They study fictional accounts of "mixed-race" women in the African American literary genre known as the "novel of passing." Examining the impact of miscegenation on the female body, students call into question "race" as an inherently natural category while analyzing the interrelated

ways white supremacy, male privilege, classism, and homophobia function to shape the destiny of "biracial" women. Female and male students reading, discussing, and writing about the dilemma of "the tragic mulatta" come to understand the value of progressive feminist critique to engage the multiple oppressions she experiences. Interrogating the fallibility of racial categorizing and the fallacy of whiteness, they comprehend the oppression of women as bound up in a complex matrix of competing power relations. Moreover, they come to understand that all forms of domination are interconnected. I suggest to them that for individuals concerned with issues of social justice, coalition politics rooted in feminist movement can be a powerful force toward mobilizing people across borders. For me, the classroom serves as a viable site for the development of critical consciousness that values coalition building and resists the dehumanization of all people. Teaching in the spirit of feminist black men like Frederick Douglass and W. E. B. Du Bois, I put into practice the antiracist-feminist legacy they created.

3. Calling black men to begin taking control of our own social, economic, political, spiritual, and personal destinies speaks powerfully to the urgent necessity for a dialogue between black men and women toward a rethinking of black manhood and masculinity in black communities. Yet even as it acknowledges the existence of black sexism, there is no questioning of the heterosexism and homophobia it promotes in order to repatriarchalize black men.

Chapter Four

Radical Feminist and Socialist Feminist Men's Movements in the United States

Michael A. Messner

Many men have said that their male hurt and their male pain would be tempered if only men would learn to cry more, or feel more, or trust other men more, or have better sex. Many such men would prefer to make self-interested emotional accommodations rather than moral commitment. . . . But I believe that there are a few genital males who are persuaded that what is wrong with the culture is its sexist injustice and that what is wrong with their lives is their complicity in it.

—John Stoltenberg, 1977

For socialist men especially, it is necessary to challenge a prevailing left-wing sectarianism which relegates questions of personal and family life to peripheral status—as "women's issues." Feminists and gays have themselves criticized the chauvinism on the left. . . . Both groups have initiated a far-reaching debate with a male-dominated socialist tradition. It is vital that "men against sexism" begin to take a constructive position within this debate—supporting the attention to personal experience, and the critique of socialist dogmatism. . . . The challenge to socialist men is to understand masculinity as a social problem—and thus to work together for a non-sexist socialist society.

—Andrew Tolson, 1977

In the early 1970s, as the women's liberation movement was exploding on to the social scene, most men responded with either hostility or stunned silence. But from the very first, mostly centered around colleges and universities, some men were starting to consciously engage themselves with feminist ideas and politics, and to ask a potentially subversive question: what does this all have to do with us? One of U.S. men's first organized responses to the reemergence of feminism in the early 1970s was the origination of "men's liberation" consciousness-raising groups and newsletters. As early as 1970 women's liberation gatherings, such as the March 8 teach-in at Northeastern University, were including workshops on the "Male Liberation Movement" (Sawyer 1970). Soon, the first book-length men's liberation texts appeared (Farrell 1974; Fasteau 1974; Nichols 1975).

From the beginning, men's liberation was a welter of contradictory political discourses and practices. The main divisions were between liberals, who sought to highlight the "costs of masculinity" to men, and radicals, who sought to emphasize the ways all men benefited from the systematic patriarchal oppression of women. In the early days the boundary lines between these two tendencies were not clearly drawn at all, but they were evident. For instance, in the spring of 1971 a collective of four radical men in Berkeley, California, put out the first issue of *Brother: A Male Liberation Newspaper*. By the fall of 1971 the third issue of *Brother* had a different subtitle: *A Forum for Men against Sexism*. As I have discussed elsewhere, by the late 1970s a major fraction of the men's liberation movement had given rise to a conservative, antifeminist men's rights movement (Messner 1997; Messner, in press). But there were other men— such as the *Brother* collective in Berkeley—who were less impressed with the liberal, middle-class feminism of Betty Friedan, Warren Farrell, and NOW than with radical feminism and the radical impulses in the fledgling gay and lesbian liberation movement.

Radical Feminist Men

Early radical feminist men did focus on the emotional costs of masculinity to men, but they attempted to do so in the context of a critique of patriarchy. For example, in 1971 one of the first expressions of this new men's consciousness was published in a sixty-page book called *Unbecoming Men*, a product of a profeminist men's consciousness-raising group. The men in the group critically examined their own lives in light of the feminist dictum that "the personal is political." As a result, the book was startlingly personal: for instance, the men in the book discussed their masturbation habits and the pain of having been considered a "sissy" as an adolescent. The personal level of this discourse was a major contribution of early men's groups, especially when it is seen in light of many New Left "radical" men's tendency to revel in theoretical and rhetorical debates that abstracted away from the personal, thus enabling them to ignore their own gender (and other) privileges in their own progressive and revolutionary organizations. On the other hand, the lack of an analytical framework within which to discuss these personal feelings tended to leave much of the early men's radical profeminist discourse at the level of guilty personal interrogation rather than critical social analysis.

By the early to mid-1970s feminist women (e.g., Hanisch 1975) had begun to criticize men's liberation, especially for its tendency to posit a symmetry between women's and men's "oppression." Radical profeminist men responded to this criticism by moving their discourse much more clearly in the direction of de-emphasizing the costs of masculinity and emphasizing the ways all men derive power and privilege in patriarchal society, a shift that had been foreshadowed earlier by the 1971 change in the subtitle of *Brother*. By the mid-1970s radical men's profeminism had begun to take organizational form, as indicated in the formation of the East Bay Men's Center in Berkeley. An excerpt from the EBMC's "Statement on Rape" illustrates how far the radicals' antipatriarchal discourse had parted from the sex role symmetry of men's liberation discourse: "Sexism is a system where one sex has power and privilege over another. In a society, such as ours, where men dominate women, this system can be called male supremacy. We believe violent rape to be the extreme form of sexism and male supremacy" (in Snodgrass 1977, 137). The EBMC's statement contains three themes that came to characterize radical feminist men's discourse. First, sexism is seen as a *system* of male supremacy—patriarchy—rather than simply a set of attitudes or values that can be unlearned. Second, in this system "men as a group" *dominate* women. In other words, men are viewed as a category of people who systematically oppress—and benefit from the oppression of—another category of people, women. And third, rape and other forms of sexual violence are viewed as "the extreme form" and the major locus of male domination of women. This perspective was presented in a clear and analytically sophisticated way for the first time in a 1977 collection called *For Men against Sexism*, edited by Jon Snodgrass. Several articles in the book soundly criticized the men's liberation movement; in the essay "Warren the Success Object," Don Andersen wrote that while reading Warren Farrell's book *The Liberated Man*, "I sometimes got the feeling that businessmen are finally reacting to the threat of the women's movement, and that Farrell is here to take the bite out of it and to demonstrate how women can be compromised" (Andersen 1977, 147). In place of men's liberation, these radical men posited a men's politics of "antisexist practice," focused mainly on sexual violence issues. In particular, Jack Litewka's article "The Socialized Penis," a powerful synthesis of critical self-reflection and radical feminist analysis of the social construction of patriarchal heterosexuality, eventually became one of the most widely reprinted and discussed articles on male sexuality. Litewka began by describing three troubling recent experiences when he had difficulty getting, or keeping, an erection when making love with a woman. Instead of seeing this purely as his own "personal trouble," Litewka examined his experiences in light of the social construction of the patriarchal male heterosexual script. This three-part sexual script, which boys and men learn from the media (especially from pornography) and from other males, essentially trains men to relate to women—and to their own bodies—in prescribed ways that are oppressive to women and ultimately dehumanizing to men:

1. *Objectification:* From a very young age, males are taught by everyone to objectify females (except Mom?). They generalize the female, in an almost platonic sense. This generalized woman is a concept, a lump sum, a thing, an object, a non-individualized category. The female is always "other," ...

2. *Fixation:* Part of the male sexual initiation is learning to fixate on portions of the female's anatomy: at first, breasts, and later, that hidden unknown quantity, the vagina. . . . Because of the way we are socialized, erection follows fixation or occurs in a situation in which fixation plays a role. . . . We learn that we can *will* an erection without a woman being near us. And since it is pleasurable (and, at first, astounding), since it gives us assurance that we are male, we create erections out of our imagination, by merely objectifying a female of our choice [and] fixating on the parts of her body that excite. . . .

3. *Conquest:* To conquer is a highly valued skill in our society. We are taught to alter the enemy into nothingness, to convert the bear into a stuffed head or rug, to gain power and rule. . . . In sexual matters,

the male conquers when he succeeds in reducing the female from a being to a thing and achieves some level of sexual gratification. . . . Conquest logically (ahem) follows Objectification and Fixation. (Litewka 1977, 23–24)

Through this three-stage process, Litewka argues, men learn to relate to women as objects to be fixated on and conquered, rather than as full human beings. The line between this form of "normal sex" and rape is pretty thin. And the way this process intertwines erotic pleasure with power and conquest over a devalued female object also alienates men from their own bodily pleasures. As a result, according to Litewka, men like himself often experience "sexual dysfunctions" when their anxieties are raised by being confronted by a female sexual partner who demands to be seen and treated as a fully human, empowered subject (rather than a fragmented, disempowered object).

Snodgrass's collection of works by men against sexism was also one of the first places where the work of John Stoltenberg was made more widely available. Heavily influenced by the ideas of Andrea Dworkin and other radical feminists, Stoltenberg utilized a powerfully moving speaking style and insightful analytic capacity to become a major leader in radical feminist men's politics. Stoltenberg founded Men Against Pornography in New York City, and was chair of the NOMAS Task Group on Pornography. The titles of his books, such as *Refusing to Be a Man* (1989), speak to the radical feminist politics of renunciation: this is no move to *reform* masculinity, but to do away with gender distinction (and thus, inequality) altogether. Stoltenberg's categorical view of men as oppressors and women as the oppressed, and his nearly constant focus on male sexuality and sexual violence as the major locus of patriarchal oppression reveal the major strengths and the limitations of radical feminist men's discourse and politics.

First, viewing men as categorically privileged at women's expense and viewing one cluster of issues (sexuality, sexual violence) as the major link in patriarchy provide an analytic simplicity through which an otherwise complicated politics of antisexist practice might be concretely forged. Buttressed with this analysis, profeminist men began to link up with feminist women's antirape, antipornography, and battered women's movements to attempt to stop these problems at their sources: men's violence. In the United States, radical feminist men organized mostly at a local level: in 1979 RAVEN (Rape and Violence Ends Now) was organized in St. Louis,

Missouri, and EMERGE: A Men's Counseling Service on Domestic Violence was formed in Boston. In California, also in 1979, the Oakland Men's Project was launched with the slogan "Men's Work: To Stop Male Violence" (Kivel 1992). These groups still exist, and have inspired and germinated groups in other cities that engage in antiviolence education and offer therapeutic interventions with men who batter. In Canada, men's antiviolence efforts have had a more national impact, especially with the impressive success of the White Ribbon Campaign (Kaufman 1993). Begun in response to the 1989 murder of women at the University of Montreal, the campaign gained the support of a large number of Canadian men who were (at least symbolically, by wearing a white ribbon on the anniversary of the massacre) stating a commitment to ending violence against women. Through the campaign, discussions of violence against women, and moves by men to contribute to ending the violence, have broadened far beyond what the antisexist men's movement in the United States has been able to imagine possible.

But the sense of clarity and focus that radical feminist male discourse gives to political organizing is also its major limiting factor as well, for two reasons. First, focusing almost entirely on men's shared privileges and largely discounting the costs of masculinity contribute to a politics of guilt in which men's major reason for challenging patriarchy might appear to be altruism toward women. As Connell (1995, 221) puts it, although this may be a noble reason for activism, "How can a politics whose main theme is anger towards men serve to mobilize men broadly?" Second, although the universalizing claims about "male power" make for moving oratory that arouses a passion for justice among a few men who commit themselves to work to stop violence against women, a discourse that posits gender as the fundamental dividing line of power in the world does not accurately reflect the complexity of the real world. Social class, racial/ethnic, sexual, and other systems of power intersect with gender in ways that make progressive political organizing a tremendously complex reality. Just as the universalization of "women" tends to obliterate the differences, power differentials, and inequities among women (Baca Zinn et al. 1986; Segal 1987), so too does the radical feminist universalization of "men" create a context in which a profeminist men's movement obliterates the different (and perhaps at times, opposing) experiences, views, and interests of poor men, blue-collar men, and men of color (Brod 1983–84). Radical feminist men's discourse has not entirely obliterated the recognition of difference among men. In fact, the "gay-straight" binary has been fundamental to the development of radical thought on men and masculinity. But through this lens, "gay issues" are, first and foremost, examined in terms of radical feminist *women's* standpoint. For example, many gay men have been openly opposed to the feminist antipornography movement, due to the fact that they have experienced gay porn as a liberating medium in a heterosexist society that has denied them pleasure, community, and identity (Clark 1990; Tucker 1990). In response to this, John Stoltenberg (1988) argues that gay porn is simply another part of the oppressive apparatus that eroticizes violence. Gays who are "in the pro-pornography movement" are not advocating freedom, Stoltenberg asserts; to the contrary, they are merely "having the hots for sex discrimination." This refusal to adopt (even tentatively) the different standpoints of oppressed groups of men and put them into play with feminist standpoints leads to the near impossibility of radical feminist men's discourse and practice leading to coalition-building politics.

A final, related limitation of radical feminist men's discourse is its reductionist focus on "male sexual violence" as the locus of men's oppression over women. The analysis of male sexuality borders on a categorical essentialism that often leads to a politics of individual guilt. And the focus on sexual violence as *the* issue tends to lead activists away from engagement with structured inequalities in social institutions such as workplaces, families, and the state. The irony in this, as Segal (1987, 1994) and others have argued, is that in the search for an issue (like pornography) that links all women, radical feminists have ignored or marginalized issues like pay equity, day care, parental leave, and welfare reform—issues that are often the major concerns of working women, mothers, poor women, and women of color. Radical feminist men have followed suit, thus leading to a politics of disengagement with issues that have the greatest potential for coalition building.

Socialist Feminist Men

Socialist feminism, which began to develop in the mid-1970's as a blending of some radical feminist and Marxist concepts and strategies (Eisenstein 1979; Hartmann 1976, 1981), informed some impressive attempts at antisexist organizing efforts in workplaces in Australia (Gray 1987) and Britain (Tolson 1977). In the United States, despite some efforts by socialist feminists to organize women workers (Hansen 1986; Sealander and

Smith 1986), and despite a highly influential presence in organizations such as the Democratic Socialists of America (DSA), socialist feminism never developed a significant activist base outside academia (Hansen and Philipson 1990). Despite this limited base, socialist feminists have been an important presence in much of the U.S. profeminist men's movement (especially NOMAS), and in its academic wing, the Men's Studies Association, which sponsors a scholarly journal called *masculinities*. As a result, the curriculum of a growing number of college courses on men and masculinities is highly influenced by socialist feminist thought (Brod 1987; Kimmel 1987; Kimmel and Messner 1989, 1995).

The discourse of socialist feminism, highly influenced by Marxist structuralism, parted dramatically from the psychologism and individualism of men's liberationism. Socialist feminists viewed masculinity not as a personal style or internalized attitude, but as part of a structure of power. But socialist feminism also parted significantly from radical feminism, in that class inequalities were given at least as much analytic importance as gender inequalities. Thus, socialist feminists were among the first to call for an examination of inequalities *among* men, rather than relying on a simplistic and falsely universalized definition of "men" as an undifferentiated sex class. This was (and still is) a very difficult and tricky task, but socialist feminists set about attempting to strike a balance between an analysis of the ways patriarchy benefits all men and an acknowledgment of the ways social class inequalities benefit some men at the expense of other men and women.

Andrew Tolson's 1977 book, *The Limits of Masculinity*, was among the first attempts to grapple with these ideas. Tolson made several important contributions to the emerging sociology of masculinities. First, he pressed socialist men to confront feminist insights concerning the importance of personal life and sexual relations. But he refused to define "masculinity" entirely—or even mainly—in terms of sexuality, as many radical feminists appeared to be doing. Instead, Tolson illuminated the importance of work as central to men's identities and positions in industrial capitalism. And, importantly, Tolson began to delineate how men's different experiences and interests, grounded in their different—often oppositional—positions in workplaces and in the larger political economy, led to the social construction of a "working-class masculinity" that was in some ways distinct from "middle-class masculinity." Working from examples in his native Britain, where class distinctions have been more acknowledged than in the United States, Tolson (1977, 81) argues that working-class and middle-class men both "have inherited the patriarchal culture of the past and both experience the erosion of patriarchal privilege by capitalist expansion." But for working-class men, the breadwinner role offers a "paradox of masculinity." On the one hand, the wage bolsters a man's "public presence" and gives him a material basis for power in his family. On the other hand, the daily experience of work "poses a constant threat to masculinity" (48), due to the fact that every day, the manual worker faces an "immediate alienation (his product is 'objectified' against him) and a direct, personal humiliation (constant confrontation with authority)" (58–59). In short, waged work *simultaneously supports and undermines* working-class men's masculine status. This paradox leads to two interrelated outcomes. First, in a context of a lack of institutional power, exaggerated styles of masculine bravado become more pronounced. Second, "because of the often brutal and unpredictable nature of the work, the worker is directly dependent on 'masculine' compensations, and in some situations, patriarchal aspects of working-class culture may even be potentially subversive. A male chauvinism of the shop-floor is a way of asserting collective control, and sometimes, sabotaging the production process itself" (Tolson 1977, 59). In short, one common way that male manual workers bond together is to talk and joke about their male managers in disparaging ways: the managers are positioned as feminized "paper pushers" who do not do "real men's work." Through this process, the men on the shop floor utilize misogyny and homophobia to position themselves as the "real men." This sort of masculine posturing and bonding may result in feelings of masculine power in a context where these men have very little institutional power (see Collinson 1988; Peña 1991). In effect, however, this kind of masculinity (relying as it does on an assertion of superiority over women and over feminized males) serves as a "cultural bribe," where the working-class man's "social commitment is won at the price of his independence—for which he is offered the empty promise of 'manhood' " (Tolson 1977, 46).

Middle-class men, according to Tolson, face different paradoxes in their relationship to work and families. Until fairly recently, professional/ managerial-class work for men involved a moral commitment to a career and an "ethic of service" to "Empire, the Nation, or at a local level, the 'community,' 'civic pride' " (Tolson 1977, 82). But in the post–World War II era, the rise of large bureaucracies and an increasingly insecure and shifting economy has "stripped away the idealistic cloak surrounding middle-class work and has revealed, for the first time, its naked insecurity" (86). The resulting alienation and "crisis of confidence" among middle-class men have led to two distinct reactions. One pattern is the development of a "cynically detached business personality." Here, professional/managerial-class men who lack any moral foundation for their work simply decide to pursue their work as a game in which the goal is gaining status, power, and wealth. This sort of masculine cynicism seemed to reach a new level in the 1980s, as some yuppies got rich quick by selling illegal junk bonds and drove new BMWs with bumper stickers that read, "He Who Dies with the Most Toys Wins!" A second response to the middle-class crisis of confidence, according to Tolson, was the development of "the myth of domesticity." In short, many middle-aged, professional-class men became disillusioned with their work and turned to family life:

> For the disillusioned male careerist, this myth of "domesticity" has become his last remaining source of support. Against the anxiety of his professional "crisis of confidence" he will still make domestic plans, direct operations, project himself into the future. As husband and father, he is the *subject* of an ideology to which his wife and children are the *objects*—of his concern, his protection, his authority. And his focal position is maintained by his continuing *economic* power. (95)

Tolson points out that a major strain in professional men's retreat to domesticity as a haven, as a place where they could revive their sense of patriarchal authority, was the fact that this is a time in history when middle-class *women* are moving into the public world of higher education and careers. In both a symbolic sense and in a very concrete way, men who are returning to the home in hopes of having their masculinity affirmed may be literally passing their wives who are going out the door into public life.

Tolson's socialist feminist approach offered new and increasingly complex ways to think about masculinity, not as a singular "male sex role" (as men's liberationists thought of it) or as a singular dominant "sex class" (as radical feminists saw it). Rather, masculinity began to appear as a multiple reality that is constructed in relation to women *and* in relation to men's varying and opposing class positions vis-à-vis other men. In the next decade, and largely influenced by Tolson and other socialist feminists, scholars such as R. W. Connell (1987), Harry Brod (1987), and Lynne Segal (1990) began to posit the now widely accepted notion that at any given time there are multiple masculini*ties*—some hegemonic, some marginalized, some subordinated. In short, socialist feminist examinations of gender were among the first to part with the universalizing tendencies of men's liberationists, men's rights advocates, and radical feminist men. The feminist impulse demonstrated that men benefit, as a group, from patriarchy, but the socialist impulse insisted that class inequalities among men distribute patriarchy's benefits—and its costs—very unequally.

Socialist feminism involved far more than a deconstruction of "masculinity." Feminist insights led to a radical rethinking and expansion of several key Marxist concepts. For instance, narrow Marxian notions of "labor" were criticized as contributing to the invisibility of women's work, especially unpaid labor in the home. Socialist feminism's expansion of the concept of labor to include unpaid labor and its problematization of the gendered public/domestic split laid the potential groundwork for a new politics of work and family that simultaneously challenged the hegemony of capitalist rationality, the male family wage, housework and child care as privatized women's work, and sexualized power relations in workplaces. Concretely, in the United States, socialist feminism informed the rise of comparable worth as a collective strategy to overcome structured pay inequities, as opposed to affirmative action, a strategy that relies on individual mobility out of underpaid and undervalued occupational ghettoes (Blum 1991). And socialist feminist discourse has also contributed to the call for a government family policy—ideally similar to those of social democracies like Sweden—which, in effect, would involve the state in breaking down gendered divisions of labor in and between workplaces and families (Sidel 1986). It is in this emphasis on the necessity to change *institutions* like workplaces and the state, rather than simply appealing to individual men to change their sexist attitudes and practices, that socialist feminism makes its most important contribution (Segal 1990, 309).

Some of the problems and limitations of socialist feminism have always been internal to it as a troubled (and mostly theoretical) "marriage" between what some have claimed are only partially compatible feminist and Marxist concepts (Hartmann 1981). And there has always been the dangerous tendency of Marxist categories eclipsing feminist concepts, thus reverting back to a prefeminist era when "the woman question" was always relegated by male Marxist leaders to an issue that would be dealt with "after the revolution" (Stacey 1983). A final problem internal to socialist feminism is grounded in the Marxian tendency toward an economic reductionism that tends to view race as a superstructural manifestation of class relations, and sexuality as an invisible nonissue. Thus, in socialist feminist discourse, "inequalities among men" risk being reduced to *class* (not racial/ethnic, sexual, or other) inequalities among men, and the "costs of masculinity" risk being reduced to costs related to poverty and work alienation, but not to racism or homophobia.

Despite its internal limitations, through the early 1980s socialist feminist discourse demonstrated the greatest potential among feminist discourses to develop a balanced understanding of the structured privileges, costs, and inequalities among men. The inability of this theoretical discourse to translate into effective political action is related, in part, to the internal problems of socialist feminism that I have discussed above, but it probably also has at least as much to do with the political-economic context of the United States. In short, although socialist feminist theory informs a view of the state as an arena in which to fight for issues like pay equity, day care, and parental leave, the two-party system in the United States has always precluded the development of a radical base in national politics, and leaves little room for anything but the most limited liberal feminist discourse on individual rights. This stands in sharp contrast to parliamentary democracies like Australia, Canada, Britain, France, and the Scandinavian countries, which have institutional space within state politics for the articulation of labor, socialist, feminist, Green, and other progressive politics (Franzway, Court, and Connell 1989). Second, the proportion of U.S. workers—especially women workers—who are unionized is very low. Moreover, unions in the United States are fairly weak, and thus most are not in a position to push for radical reforms such as comparable worth or paid family leave (Sidel 1986).

These internal and external barriers may have relegated socialist feminism to the margins of politics in the United States, but socialist feminist discourse has had a broadening influence on internal debates within U.S. profeminist men's discourse and practice. Whereas liberal feminism tends to focus on the articulation of individual rights and individual "growth" (an articulation that tends disproportionately to benefit class-privileged women and men), and radical feminism tends to take the body, sexuality, and violence as central to its analysis of power, socialist feminism tends to focus more centrally on production, work relations, and work/family relations (Clatterbaugh 1990). As a result of this focus, socialist feminist men in organizations like NOMAS have raised issues related to the "class basis and bias" of the profeminist men's movement and the importance of examining men's varying experiences in workplaces and in the economy (Brod 1983–84).

Socialist feminist men have also brought important insights to the debates about men, pornography, and violence against women. For instance, Harry Brod has been the most systematic in employing and adapting Marxist categories to analyze issues raised first by radical feminists, including those related to sexuality and violence. Brod does not dispute the radical feminist claims concerning the links between pornography and violent male domination of women. But he adapts Marxian concepts to argue that men, as consumers of pornography, experience a bodily alienation and a loss of sexual subjectivity that result in a denial of satisfaction of men's human desires. In short, commercial pornography simultaneously benefits and hurts men (Brod 1984). Michael Kimmel, another profeminist activist highly influenced by socialist feminist thought, has also engaged in the pornography debates, and has come to somewhat different conclusions. Kimmel (1990) agrees that we should be critical of the eroticization of violence against women, but also argues that (1) there is no established empirical link between viewing pornography and committing acts of violence against women; sexual fantasy, in short, is not the same as reality; (2) sexual repression itself is dangerous and oppressive, and the antipornography movement may contribute to increased state repression not only of sexual minorities but also of sexual pleasure in general; (3) some groups, such as gay men, find pornography liberating. The differences between Brod's and Kimmel's perspectives (though perhaps not as wide as I have portrayed them) raise a key question for all profeminist men: *with which feminism shall we ally ourselves?* The "feminism" in Brod's socialist feminist analysis of pornography leans toward the radical feminist antipornography views of Andrea Dworkin and John Stoltenberg, whereas the "feminism" in Kimmel's perspective is more clearly linked to the socialist feminist "pro-erotica, anticensorship" perspective of feminists like Ellen Willis (1983), Lynne Segal (1994), and Ann Snitow (1983). Whether one agrees with the antiporn feminists or the pro-erotica feminists on the centrality of pornography and rape in men's overall power over women, it seems clear that radical feminists tend to *reduce* women's oppression to this issue, while socialist feminists tend to *connect* women's need for sexual empowerment and safety to issues of larger institutional struggle. As British socialist feminist Lynne Segal (1987, 244) put it, struggles in and around the state and work around trade unions . . . are of equal importance to sexual politics and ideology if only because they are inevitably linked: economically independent women find it easier to make choices, to leave brutal men, assert a lesbian lifestyle if they want to, and decide if, when and how they wish to mother.

Socialist feminism, then, promises to broaden the terms of feminist debates about men and masculinity beyond individualistic discussions of sexual politics to more broadly political discussions of collective movements, made up of women and men who are working together to transform existing social institutions.

Radical and Socialist Feminist Contributions and Possibilities

Men's contributions to radical, antipatriarchal politics in the United States have been minimal, to say the least. But to the extent that they have been actively involved, a relatively small network of radical feminist men have had an impressive impact. As I have discussed, radical feminist discourse tends toward categorical views of "women" and "men" as, respectively, oppressed and oppressor sex classes. These categorical views are often grounded in a nearly exclusive focus on bodily oppressions, with sexuality being seen as the major nexus of men's bodily oppression of women. The view that bodies—particularly sexual bodies—are the locus of patriarchal oppression provides radical feminist politics with a singular focus for antipatriarchal actions. Moreover, the focus on extremes of bodily abuse, violence, and oppression (such as rape, violent pornography, wife beating, etc.) provides a powerfully emotional moral basis and impetus for action. As a result, a relatively small number of radical feminist men have been moved to focus their energies on antirape, antipornography, and anti–wife-beating education and counseling, in addition to supporting feminist efforts to change or enact laws that aim to empower women to avoid and resist men's violence. In short, given their small numbers, radical feminist men have had a disproportionately large impact in the communities in which they work. And given the often singular moral basis from which they work, their discourse has had a powerful impact on debates within the larger antisexist men's movement.

   Radical feminist politics of masculinity has its limits, though. First, its categorical focus on "men" tends to falsely universalize men's experiences. This categoricalism obliterates an understanding of how other systems of inequality such as social class, race, and sexuality intersect with gender in ways that limit and constrain marginalized and subordinated groups of men's ability to "cash in" on the "patriarchal dividend" (Connell 1995). Second, the radical feminist focus on "male sexuality" as an embodiment of power and "female sexuality" as an embodiment of women's subordination borders on an essentialist view of gender difference that undercuts social constructionist views of gender and sexuality. At its extreme, this view tends to present "male sexuality" as some essential will among men to eroticize violence and domination of women. To renounce it appears to be to renounce sexual pleasure altogether. This antisexual position created the impression among many that radical feminist activists had entered into a seemingly bizarre alliance in the 1980s with the antipornography Moral Majority/religious right. Though opposing pornography for somewhat different reasons, both the antiporn feminists and the antiporn conservatives shared a view of sexuality as a realm of danger for women, rather than (or even rather than in addition to) a realm of pleasure or empowerment for women (Segal 1994). And both tended to hold neo-Victorian assumptions that at the heart of male sexuality there is an *essentially* aggressive, violent, and dominating impulse that must be renounced for the good of civilization. This position severely limits radical feminism's appeal to men in general and to progressive gay men in particular. In addition, the radical feminist view of men as a relatively undifferentiated privileged sex class is likely to fall on deaf ears among men who are oppressed within racialized, class, and sexualized systems of oppression. In short, radical feminist action among men— especially its powerful moral appeal to stop sexual violence against women—has very likely led to some changes in some individual men that have made the world a somewhat safer place for a few individual women. But radical feminist discourse and organization among men have built-in limitations that make it very unlikely that radical feminist men will ever be in the forefront of forging progressive coalitions with gay men, poor and working-class people, and feminist women and men of color. And it is these sorts of coalitions that will be necessary if there is to be hope of bringing about fundamental institutional changes that are needed to confront the multiple systems of domination and oppression that are operating in the world today.

By contrast, because of the external and internal limitations discussed above, socialist feminist organizing among U.S. men has had, at best, a marginal impact on the ways people live their lives. In fact, by the mid-

1980s even some leftist academics were proclaiming the death of socialist feminism. But looking at it another way, we can see that many of the best ideas of socialist feminism have been picked up and adapted since the late 1980s through the 1990s by feminist women of color. In particular, Baca Zinn and Dill's (1996) concept of "multiracial feminism" can be seen as the direct descendent of socialist feminism. Multiracial feminism today occupies the center of what I have called "the terrain of progressive coalition-building" (Messner 1997). This terrain is the political territory occupied by groups who attempt to strike some balance in acknowledging men's structural power and privilege, the costs of masculinity, and the race, class, and gender inequalities among men (and among women). The closer a group's view is to a nuanced understanding of these three factors, the more complex—even contradictory—its internal debates about the social structure of power, inequality, and oppression are likely to be. But such a perspective also maximizes the potential for forging creative coalition building that can simultaneously confront men's structured power and privileges over women, in addition to confronting some men's structured power and privileges over subordinated and marginalized groups of men. And within multiracial feminism, a political assault on the privileges of hegemonic masculinity can be joined with the call for a healthy humanization of men that will eliminate the "costs of masculinity" to men.

There are currently several bridges being built that may link various movements into a multiracial feminist terrain of progressive coalition building. For instance, some African American men who have worked within a socialist framework, like Cornel West (1993) and Manning Marable (1994), appear to be formulating a feminist-informed critique of hegemonic masculinity within their race/class political program. Similarly, profeminist gay men continue to provide bridges between feminist women, gay liberation, and profeminist men's organizations. And especially, gay men of color (e.g., Almaguer 1991; Leong 1996; Mercer and Julien 1988) are in the forefront of attempts to integrate a critical understanding of the interrelationships between race, class, gender, and sexual systems of oppression. Thus, rather than proclaiming or mourning the "death" of the socialist feminism of the 1970s and 1980s, we should recognize and build on its potential as it is incorporated into the complex politics of the current historical moment.

REFERENCES

Almaguer, Tomas. 1991. "Chicano Men: A Cartography of Homosexual Identity and Behavior." *differences: A Journal of Feminist Cultural Studies* 3:75–100.

Andersen, Don. 1977. "Warren the Success Object." In Jon Snodgrass, ed., *For Men against Sexism*, 146–49. Albion, CA: Times Change Press.

Baca Zinn, Maxine, Lynn Weber Cannon, Elizabeth Higginbotham, and Bonnie Thornton Dill. 1986. "The Costs of Exclusionary Practices in Women's Studies." *Signs: Journal of Women in Culture and Society* 11:290–303.

Baca Zinn, Maxine, and Bonnie Thornton Dill. 1996. "Theorizing Difference from Multiracial Feminism." *Feminist Studies* 22: 321–31.

Blum, Linda. 1991. *Between Feminism and Labor: The Significance of the Comparable Worth Movement.* Berkeley: University of California Press.

Brod, Harry. 1983–84. "Work Clothes and Leisure Suits: The Class Basis and Bias of the Men's Movement." *M: Gentle Men for Gender Justice* 11:10–12, 38–40.

———. 1984. "Eros Thanatized: Pornography and Male Sexuality." *Humanities in Society* 7 (1&2).

———, ed. 1987. *The Making of Masculinities: The New Men's Studies.* Boston: Allen and Unwin.

Clark, Chris. 1990. "Pornography Without Power?" In Michael S. Kimmel, ed., *Men Confront Pornography*, 281–84. New York: Crown.

Clatterbaugh, Kenneth. 1990. *Contemporary Perspectives on Masculinity: Men, Women, and Politics in Modern Society.* Boulder: Westview.

Collinson, David L. 1988. " 'Engineering Humor': Masculinity, Joking, and Conflict in Shop-Floor Relations." *Organization Studies* 9:181–99.

Connell, R. W. 1987. *Gender and Power.* Stanford: Stanford University Press.

———. 1995. *Masculinities.* Berkeley: University of California Press.

Eisenstein, Zillah R., ed. 1979. *Capitalist Patriarchy and the Case for Socialist Feminism.* New York: Monthly Review Press.

Farrell, Warren. 1974. *The Liberated Man.* New York: Random House.

———. 1993. *The Myth of Male Power: Why Men Are the Disposable Sex.* New York: Simon and Schuster.

Fasteau, Marc Feigan. 1974. *The Male Machine.* New York: McGraw-Hill.

Franzway, Suzanne, Dianne Court, and R. W. Connell. 1989. *Staking a Claim: Feminism, Bureaucracy and the State.* Sydney: Allen and Unwin.

Gray, Stan. 1987. "Sharing the Shop Floor." In Michael Kaufman, ed., *Beyond Patriarchy: Essays by Men on Pleasure, Power, and Change.* New York: Oxford University Press.

Hanisch, Carol. 1975. "Men's Liberation." In Redstockings, eds., *Feminist Revolution*, 72–76. New York: Random House.

Hansen, Karen V. 1986. "Women's Unions and the Search for a Political Identity." *Socialist Review* 86:67–95.

Hansen, Karen V., and Ilene J. Philipson, eds. 1990. *Women, Class, and the Feminist Imagination: A Socialist-Feminist Reader.* Philadelphia: Temple University Press.

Hartmann, Heidi. 1976. "Capitalism, Patriarchy, and Job Segregation by Sex." *Signs: Journal of Women in Culture and Society* 1:137–69.

———. 1981. "The Unhappy Marriage of Marxism and Feminism." In L. Sargent, ed., *Women and Revolution.* Boston: South End Press.

Kaufman, Michael. 1993. *Cracking the Armour: Power, Pain and the Lives of Men.* Toronto: Viking.

Kimmel, Michael S. 1987. "Men's Responses to Feminism at the Turn of the Century." *Gender & Society* 1:261–283.

———. 1990. " 'Insult' or 'Injury': Sex, Pornography, and Sexism." In Michael S. Kimmel, ed., *Men Confront Pornography*, 305–19. New York: Crown.

Kimmel, Michael S., and Michael A. Messner, eds. 1989. *Men's Lives.* New York: Macmillan.

———. 1995. *Men's Lives.* 3d ed. Boston: Allyn and Bacon.

Kimmel, Michael S., and Thomas E. Mosmiller. 1992. *Against the Tide: Pro-Feminist Men in the United States, A Documentary History.* Boston: Beacon Press.

Kivel, Paul. 1992. *Men's Work: How to Stop the Violence That Tears Our Lives Apart.* Center City, MN: Hazelden.

Leong, Russell. 1996. "Introduction: Home Bodies and the Body Politic." In Russell Leong, ed., *Asian American Sexualities: Dimensions of the Gay and Lesbian Experience*, 1–18. London: Routledge.

Litewka, Jack. 1977. "The Socialized Penis." In Jon Snodgrass, ed., *For Men against Sexism*, 16–35. Albion, CA: Times Change Press.

Marable, Manning. 1994. "The Black Male: Searching beyond Stereotypes." In R. G. Majors and J. U. Gordon, eds., *The American Black Male.* Chicago: Nelson-Hall.

Men's Consciousness-Raising Group. 1971. *Unbecoming Men.* Albion, CA: Times Change Press.

Mercer, Kobena, and Isaac Julien. 1988. "Race, Sexual Politics and Black Masculinity: A Dossier." In Rowena Chapman and Jonathan Rutherford, eds., *Male Order*, 112. London: Lawrence and Wishart.

Messner, Michael A. 1997. *Politics of Masculinities: Men in Movements.* Thousand Oaks, CA: Sage.

———. In press. "The Limits of 'The Male Sex Role': A Discourse Analysis of the Men's Liberation Movement and the Men's Rights Movement." *Gender & Society.*

Nichols, Jack. 1975. *Men's Liberation: A New Definition of Masculinity*. New York: Penguin.

Peña, Manuel. 1991. "Class, Gender and Machismo: The 'Treacherous Woman' Folklore of Mexican Male Workers." *Gender & Society* 5:30–46.

Sawyer, Jack. 1970. "The Male Liberation Movement." Workshop presented at the Women's Liberation Teach-in, Northwestern University, March 8.

Sealander, Judith, and Dorothy Smith. 1986. "The Rise and Fall of Feminist Organizations in the 1970's: Dayton as a Case Study." *Feminist Studies* 12:321–41.

Segal, Lynne. 1987. *Is the Future Female? Troubled Thoughts on Contemporary Feminism*. New York: Peter Bedrick Books.

———. 1990. *Slow Motion: Changing Masculinities, Changing Men*. New Brunswick: Rutgers University Press.

———. 1994. *Straight Sex: Rethinking the Politics of Pleasure*. Berkeley: University of California Press.

Sidel, Ruth. 1986. *Women and Children Last: The Plight of Poor Women in Affluent America*. New York: Penguin.

Snitow, Ann, C. Stansell, and S. Thompson, eds. 1983. *Powers of Desire: The Politics of Sexuality*. New York: Monthly Review Press.

Snodgrass, Jon, ed. 1977. *For Men against Sexism*. Albion, CA: Times Change Press.

Stacey, Judith. 1983. *Patriarchy and Socialist Revolution in China*. Berkeley: University of California Press.

Stoltenberg, John. 1977. "Toward Gender Justice." In Jon Snodgrass, ed., *For Men against Sexism*, 74–83. Albion, CA: Times Change Press.

———. 1988. "Gays and the Pornography Movement: Having the Hots for Sex Discrimination." *Changing Men: Issues in Gender, Sex, and Politics* 19 (spring/summer).

———. 1989. *Refusing to Be a Man: Essays on Sex and Justice*. Portland, OR: Breitenbush Books.

Tolson, Andrew. 1977. *The Limits of Masculinity: Male Identity and Women's Liberation*. New York: Harper and Row.

Tucker, Scott. 1990. "Radical Feminism and Gay Male Porn." In Michael S. Kimmel, ed., *Men Confront Pornography*, 263–76. New York: Crown.

West, Cornel. 1993. *Race Matters*. Boston: Beacon Press.

Willis, Ellen. 1983. "Feminism, Moralism, and Pornography." In A. Snitow, C. Stansell, and S. Thompson, eds., *Powers of Desire: The Politics of Sexuality*, 460–67. New York: Monthly Review Press.

Part II

Some Personal Considerations

Chapter Five

"I Am Not a Rapist!"
Why College Guys Are Confronting Sexual Violence

John Stoltenberg

What follows is an emotionally charged conversation among members of a Duke University student organization called Men Acting for Change (MAC), one of many new men's groups at colleges and universities across the United States and Canada. Besides meeting regularly to talk personally, MAC members present programs about gender and sexuality, focusing on sexual violence and homophobia, to fraternities and other campus groups.

MAC came to national prominence in the United States when members appeared in a segment about pornography on the ABC newsmagazine program *20/20*. On January 28, 1993, millions of viewers heard these college-age males speak graphically about the negative effects of pornography, including *Playboy*, on their sex lives and their relationships with women.

A year earlier, Kate Wenner, an ABC producer, asked to pick my brains about how to do a pornography story that hadn't been done before. Over an amiable lunch at a café near Lincoln Center, I suggested she report how pornography has become a primary form of sex education for young men. She liked the idea and tracked down MAC. The resulting broadcast included footage of frank conversations among both female and male Duke students and was perhaps the most astute coverage of pornography's interpersonal effects yet to appear on network television.

After that *20/20* segment aired, MAC members were invited to appear on *Oprah, Donahue, Jerry Springer, Maury Povich*, and *Montel Williams*, but they declined to have their stories sensationalized. Meanwhile *Playboy* went ballistic and, in an apparent attempt at damage control, ridiculed them in print as "the pointy-headed, wet-behind-the-scrotum boys at Duke."

In January 1994, curious to know what makes MAC tick, I traveled to Durham, North Carolina, to attend the third annual Student Conference on Campus Sexual Violence, to be held at Duke. The brochure promised "focus on student activism and involvement in the anti-rape movement" and quoted Jason Schultz, a conference organizer and 20/20 participant: "Through our work against rape, we take control of our future and generate the skills and perspectives that we need to help make it a better, safer place for both women and men." The afternoon before the conference opened, Jason arranged a private conversation in his home among five MAC members. They understood that I would sit in, ask questions, and try to get an edited transcript of their conversation published where it could contribute to more accurate understanding of the student movement against sexual violence.

As I listened, I realized that these young men had taken the meaning of sexual violence to heart in some intensely personal and generationally specific new ways. Everyone in the group knew friends who had been sexually assaulted. At one point I asked them to estimate how many. One said that one in five of his friends had told him this. Another said fifty. Another said that among his twenty to twenty-five friends who had been sexually assaulted, he also knew the perpetrator in half the cases.

At another point one told something he had never before shared with his fellow MAC members: he himself had been sexually molested in his youth. That dramatic moment was generationally specific too, I realized. Such a disclosure would never have occurred among college-age males even a decade before. The vocabulary and sense of social safety would simply not have existed.

I came to understand that what these college-age males had to say is historically unprecedented: they had each become aware, through personal experience, of their own stake in confronting sexual violence.

There is a newsworthy story here, I thought to myself, a trend to be watched. An extraordinary new student-based social-change movement has begun; yet no major news-gathering medium has thought to listen in to the generationally specific experience represented by these five members of MAC.[1] Although they spoke as individuals and from particular viewpoints—the group was a mix of straight, bi, and gay; white and black—they also seemed at times to speak on behalf of many more male agemates than themselves. Quite matter-of-factly, without any prompting, they each described an experience now so common that it may define their generation more profoundly than any war ever has: how it feels to be perceived by female peers as a potential rapist.

Ever since the women's movement began to bring sexual violence to light in the early 1970s, the extent of rape and the extent of women's fears of it have been trivialized, refuted, and ridiculed by mainstream media. Today the aspirations of campus activists to radical gender egalitarianism and eroticized equality are similarly distorted in the popular press. For example, in the early 1990s students at Antioch College developed a comprehensive, nine-page policy spelling out the meaning of consent in sexual contact and conduct; defining and prohibiting a list of offenses that included rape, sexual assault, "sexual imposition," and nondisclosure of a known HIV-positive status; and detailing fair hearing procedures and remedies in case of violation. This path-breaking, gender-neutral, ethically acute initiative was widely sneered at by media commentators who had never read it, never talked to the students who drafted and implemented it. During the 1960s and early 1970s, many "with it" magazine and book editors reveled in the ribald romance of covering the radical student antiwar movement in depth and at length. By contrast, today's middle-age male media decision makers act as if their journalistic radar screens got stuck in time along with the anachronistic sexual politics of their youth. Nostalgic for the 1960s "sexual revolution" days before feminism made "no" even an option for women—when, in the hustle of the time, "Girls say yes to [sex with] boys who say no [to the military]"—today's middle-age male media decision makers package smug blather about "date-rape hysteria" (a *New York* magazine cover story) or "sexual correctness" (a *Newsweek* cover story) or "do-me feminism" (an *Esquire* cover story) and sign up execrably researched diatribes about "morning-after misgivings" (Katie Roiphe) or "the new Victorianism" (Rene Denfeld). Today's middle-age male media decision makers just don't get it.

What this conversation reveals, however, is that a significant subset of young males have started to get it. Typical of a brand-new kind of self-selected peer group, they voice values that do not much resemble the sexual politics of most men their fathers' age. Within their transcient, education-centered communities, the social and relational meaning of sexual violence to young women has become apparent to them as an everyday, lived reality. Never before have so many young males struggled to take this reality on board in their moral map of the world, and never before have so many known that others are doing so also.

In the student antiwar movement of the 1960s, many young women of conscience organized politically in behalf of young men whose bodies were then regarded as most at risk—deployable as cannon fodder in an immoral military operation. Today, more and more young men of conscience have begun to understand their vital role in the student movement against sexual violence, and this time it is they who have put their lives on the line in behalf of the women whose bodies are most at risk.

For older menfolk—especially those who hold jobs in academia and are therefore in a position to offer material support and substantive resources—this movement presents a classic challenge for teachers: to listen to and learn from students.

When student antiwar activists of the 1960s brought new ideals and values into their subsequent work, family, and civic lives, the cultural and political impact of that movement was felt throughout the larger society for decades. As I write, the president of the United States is a man who in his student days protested the Vietnam War. Who would have guessed back then that the fledgling youth counterculture, vibrantly antimilitarist, would not only help halt a war but one day inform this nation's governance at the highest level?

Today, too, it is easy not to reckon the profound cultural and political shift portended by the values and ideals of young people in the burgeoning campus antirape movement. But who knows? One day this country could elect a president who in her or his student days protested, and helped end, men's war against women.

Q: Why did you get involved in Men Acting for Change?

Warren Hedges (30, Ph.D. candidate in English)[2]: I got involved because of women I was close to and things they had survived. When I walk on campus at night and a woman in front of me sees I'm a man walking behind her, her shoulders tense up and she starts walking more quickly. Her keys come out of her pocket in case she needs them to defend herself from me. It wouldn't do any good to try and convince her I'm a nice guy or "enlightened." I'm perceived as something that doesn't fit with what I want to be, and the only way to change that is by changing the broader social structure—laws and economic relations and things like that.

In our culture having a penis is supposed to be a package deal: You're supposed to have specific desires (for women) and pursue them in specific ways (aggressively, competitively), identify with men instead of women, have specific—and usually boring—sexual practices. There's this broad cultural discourse saying, "This is who you should be if you happen to have this particular organ." I can't create a space where I can express myself and be more upfront about my desires and my identifications and my practices and so forth without trying to change the larger social structures.

Andy Moose (21, pre-law English major): My reason for doing this came through a slow process, especially with MAC meetings, of having the space to really reflect about how I felt about a lot of emotional and personal issues that I hadn't spent much time as a man thinking about before. I'm in a fraternity and have seen a lot of abuses that go on within that system. I want to stay in there and work to improve the situation so that my fraternity brothers get to that process as well. I've felt it could help them, and also stop a lot of the abuses that were going on to other friends. It's personal for me, rather than seeing a great deal of violence and wanting to work towards stopping that. That's a major concern, but the bigger driving force for me is the personal gains that I see possible for people in working with these issues.

Carlton Leftwich (25, premed): I'm twenty-five years old and I have come to the realization that I've never had a healthy relationship with a woman. There's a lot of issues here that make me reflect on my opinion of women and how I treat them, how I deal with them, and how I could develop a healthy relationship with one. Healthy to me is looking at them and not saying, "Oh, that's a *woman's* point of view"—making everything that she says or feels inferior. I'd like to get on an even keel when discussing something with a woman and not just look at her and say, "She's a totally different kind of thing."

Erick Fink (22, psych major and women's studies minor): I took this intro to women's studies class and it hit me that this feminist stuff made a lot of sense. Like, even though you've never raped anyone or even thought about it, other men are doing that in your name and they're hurting people that you love in your name. All the pressure that men feel to act a certain way and do a certain thing and fit a certain mold—maybe it *used* to work, but it's not working now. And now I'm here, and I'm going to try to do something about it. I feel like I and people with penises have something to gain from the women's movement, a lot to gain: being able to be exactly who you are without having to be "a man" in the traditional sense.

I've felt very limited by patriarchy. My sense of masculinity mostly came from where everybody else's does, TV—"If you do this, chicks will dig you." That was what was masculine for me—how to attract the opposite sex. But I didn't want to be this macho guy. It's not that I didn't want to be; I just wasn't.

Carlton: I never could identify with what straight was—this rugby-playing kind of rough-and-tumble guy, always having to prove that I was macho—so I just automatically thought that I had to be gay, because I was very sensitive and I loved classical music. I was not a quote unquote normal young man, because I never liked football. And I always heard, "Well, all guys like football—if you don't play football you're a sissy."

Jason Schultz (22, public policy major and women's studies minor): In high school I was one of the top ten in my class academically. The other nine were all girls. They were brilliant and they taught me—about math, physics, English. Learning from female peers really had a big influence. The culture tells you women are bimbos, don't know anything, and are ditzes, sex objects; but my reality was different. I had good relationships with women who were intellectual and spoke their mind and wouldn't let me get away with shit—in a very loving way. Not "Get the fuck out" but "You better change or *I'm* going to get the fuck out." When I got to college, the intelligent, assertive, self-confident women started calling themselves feminists, and these were the people I loved to hang out with—"Oh, sure I'll go to your meeting. Oh, that sounds like an interesting class"—and I started to get involved. But for me there was a piece missing. I went through fraternity rush, didn't find any men that I really liked to hang out with, and felt really stupid. Women in women's studies classes were focusing on women's experience, women's perspective—which made a lot of sense, because it's left out of traditional academia—but nothing was speaking to me on a first-person level. At that time there were a couple other men on campus who wanted the same thing, and it was framed as men interested in confronting sexual violence. It was this group that I felt could look at the other component, the part that I needed to match—not to feel isolated as much as I was sometimes, not to feel like I had to speak for men.

Q: How have you personally been affected by sexual violence?

Jason: My first year in college, a good friend of mine, a female friend, was avoiding me. We weren't communicating; we didn't have the intimacy I enjoyed so much. And I'm like, "What's up with you? what's bugging you? did you flunk some test or something?" I knew that she had gone out with this guy, and I knew who he was, and she told me the story in brief detail: She was raped. And she was like, "That's why I don't feel comfortable around you—it's because I don't know who to trust anymore." I didn't blame her at all. I was pissed at him. I was *really* pissed at him. It made me angry that this guy had ruined a friendship of mine with somebody I cared about. Then when I saw this men-concerned-with-sexual-violence thing, it came together.

As a man doing this kind of work you get stories and stories—it's just exponential. I probably know fifty survivors personally—most of them through campus.

Warren: The first person who told me she had survived a rape—here on campus by another Duke student on Valentine's Day—was during my first year in graduate school. For me it was a real hard lesson learning that just me being sensitive is not enough. This sort of thing was happening to women and it was going to change the way they reacted to all or most men, especially initially. And that prompted me to get involved with this program in Durham with men who batter their wives.

Once it became known on campus that I was concerned about these issues, and once I had a chance to speak at a Take Back the Night march, the number of stories I heard from women just seemed to multiply. One reason MAC has been so important to me is that I feel I've got an emotional support network now—not just feeling utterly overwhelmed by the number of stories that seemed to come flooding in. Probably one in five friends told me—attempted rapes and assaults, but usually rape.

Carlton: When I was growing up I was abused sexually. I just internalized everything and left it there. It was through MAC I could come in contact with people who had a rape encounter and see how they handled it, how they were surviving it, without actually having to admit that I was someone who had been raped also. That was really difficult for me. But to see women have the courage to pick up their lives and keep on going—it's really empowering. I can feel for women a lot more now that I know that it was something that I had no control over and that it wasn't my fault. I can understand that helplessness and that dirty feeling, the pain and sorrow.

Most guys are like, "Well, how do you rape a male?" There are a lot of ways to rape a male. And I would say to any other male survivor, "Don't be ashamed." Even if it happened ten, fifteen, twenty years ago, it still happened, and you're going to have to deal with it. You're going to have to address those feelings. It's not going to be easy, but try and hook up with a group of guys that can really feel for you and care about you. And by caring for women—I guess I took that assumption, that these guys care about women—then they're obviously going to care about my plight and respect me.

Erick: For the women I know that have been sexually assaulted or raped—I'd say twenty to twenty-five percent—it sticks with them; it changes their lives.

Carlton: Your sense of security is gone, and once you lose your sense of security you're never going to get it back.

Erick: There's an awful lot of fear out there—like if there's a woman sitting in a room with me alone, and we're sitting there talking, there's the chance that she is fearful of me.

Carlton: Sometimes I just want to shout, "I'm not going to hurt you!"

Jason: Holding up a sign: "not a rapist"?

Carlton: Yeah.

Andy: My first experience of sexual violence was from the other side, knowing the male who was being accused. During freshman year at Duke, I was faced with a rape case that was going to the Judi [Judicial] Board. This was a huge shock for me—becoming aware of the size of the problem and the frequency with which these acts were going on. It was something I was completely unaware of in high school. Having a very dear personal friend share with me that they were assaulted, coupled with knowing someone accused of the rape—those two things at the same time forced me to try to understand how this could happen. I couldn't just say, "Well, it's obvious these people are incredibly violent," because I wasn't seeing that. How could this happen around me every day and these people don't show me any signs of violent tendencies? How could this be happening with such frequency?

As you begin to get involved, a lot more people, a shocking number, tell you things. It takes you aback, the numbers—between twenty and twenty-five good friends, very close. Mostly women, ninety-some percent. I had one male friend share like that. And there were a number of stories where the male was someone I knew, probably a fourth of them. Actually more than that—probably half.

Talking with other people in MAC and doing programs on sexual violence helped me, because I felt I could do something. In a very basic way that feels good, to fight a situation that before you felt really helpless in. I have a little bit more understanding of how the event could happen—so it's not so much burning hatred towards that individual. I'm not so quick just to discard that person and say, "OK, he raped this woman so now I'm just going to not communicate with him any longer." I don't want to do that. There's definitely resentment and anger, a great deal of anger, and I try to suppress that as much as I can, because when you have these sorts of numbers around you, it's vital that you don't hate and cut that person off just because—. I mean, you become very lonely, obviously.

Q: How do you reach other men?

Jason: Standing up to them never seems to work. It seems to push them farther away, make them reactive. It's a balance of making them feel like I care what they say and being willing to sit down and listen to them for a long time, but then be willing to challenge them. Not saying, "Oh, you're a sexist pig—get the fuck outta here," but when the opportunity is there to say, "What you're saying really bothers me" or "I'd really like to talk to you about this because I'm learning where this is coming from."

Carlton: Don't make men feel like a minority. There are a lot of men out there who really want to understand themselves and their feelings a lot more, and you can really turn somebody off with that raw anger that seems to be associated with feminists. That's intimidating to men. I know it is to me.

Andy: A lot of the successes that I've been a part of talking with fraternity men came from catching them off guard. The minute some discussion on sexual violence comes up they become defensive. When they've gotten in these discussions with women or with non-Greek men, oftentimes it's led to an argument, they didn't feel very good about it, they don't want to talk about it, and so they don't deal with it. If there's something being discussed about a Greek function, they immediately assume that the fraternity men are going to be blamed, and they're going to defend themselves as not being a rapist or whatever. So a lot of the successes have come from surprise, when they realize there's a real conversation that's going to happen and it's not going to become some heated argument—because a lot of men haven't really thought about it much at all, and people really enjoy having an opportunity to reflect about their opinions, to recognize, "Wow, you know, I've thought about this and it really helped."

Erick: I was talking to a good friend and he said, "You know what I think date rape is? I think this woman has sex with this guy and the next morning she decides she shouldn't have done it, so she just screams rape." And I'm like, "Well, you know, I remember not long ago I felt the same way. But if you really think about it, things like that can happen. On a date maybe with somebody that you might know very well or have been seeing for a long time, you could get violent with that person, couldn't you?" And he said, "Uh, I don't know." And I'm like, "Well, have you ever gotten so angry or so frustrated with your girlfriend that you could just—" And he's like, "Sure, I guess so." And there was a relation there, where I could see how he was feeling, and he could see how I was feeling too. I think if he had said that to a woman, she would be very offended—and rightfully so.

Andy: You have to have discussions for the potential rapist, but also focus on how people contribute to an environment or make it easier for a rape to happen. A lot of times they don't recognize how they in a much more subtle way contribute or make these sorts of things easier to happen, by a comment or a particular action in a situation.

Warren: Or by no action.

Andy: Right, exactly, because so quickly they say, "Well, *I'm* not a rapist." They don't think about what environment you're establishing when you're having a party or you're making some joke or you don't say anything in a particular situation. It's better to have dialogue about those issues.

Jason: A lot of men don't hear what feminists are actually saying when it's coming from women. Their words are so devalued, and we value men's words more. My experience has been that it takes some patience, because if somebody said something sexist like "Oh, she deserved to be raped, look at how she's dressed," there's an instinct to want to confront that. But what seems to be more beneficial is to ask questions, maybe let the story weave itself a little more, find a deeper belief system, and figure out what about that issue to confront. I think with some men you can definitely do that.

Warren: My formative experience thinking about male violence was working with men who beat their wives. They were ordered by the courts to attend. The men couldn't leave the program angry because they might go home and beat their partner. That was a real constraint on my need to be vindictive and self-righteous. There was a counselor who put it very well when he said, "Dealing with abusive men is like judo; you gotta grab ahold of their energy and move them someplace they don't expect to end up."

NOTES

1. I tried for two years to get this conversation into print. Among the publications that passed on it are *Cosmopolitan, Details, Elle, Glamour, Mademoiselle, Ms., On the Issues, Rolling Stone,* and the *Village Voice.*

2. Ages and academic concentrations are given as of the date of this conversation.

Chapter Six

Patriarchal Sex

Robert Jensen

Patriarchal sex (example 1): Four male undergraduates at Cornell University post on the Internet the "Top 75 reasons why women (bitches) should not have freedom of speech." Reason #20: "This is my dick. I'm gonna fuck you. No more stupid questions."[1]

Patriarchal sex (example 2): Rhonda was separated from her husband but was on generally friendly terms with him. One night he entered her home. For the next seven hours he raped her. "It was like something just snapped in him. He grabbed me and said, 'We gonna have sex, I need to fuck' " (Bergen 1995, p. 125).

I begin with a working definition of patriarchal sex: Sex is fucking.[2] In patriarchy, there is an imperative to fuck—in rape and in "normal" sex, with strangers and girlfriends and wives and estranged wives and children. What matters in patriarchal sex is the male need to fuck. When that need presents itself, sex occurs.

From that, a working definition of what it means to be a man in this culture: A man is a male human who fucks.[3]

What I'm Trying to Do and What I'm Not Trying to Do

In this essay I want to analyze patriarchal sex and theorize about strategies for moving away from it. In simple terms, I want to think about how we males might stop fucking and stop being men.

I draw on the work of radical feminist theorists and activists, my research on pornography and sexuality, and my experience as a man in U.S. culture in the last half of the twentieth century. I move without apology between personal narrative and reflection and more formal scholarly writing. I reject the conventional academic obsession with splitting off mind and body, reason and emotion, objective and subjective, scholarship and activism. One of the ways I know about the world is by living in it, and the knowledge I have gained has led me to a political position that makes certain actions on my part morally necessary. Decades of feminist and other critical work more than adequately justify this kind of engaged scholarship (e.g., Code 1991; Stivers 1992).

What follows is part of my long-term project of trying to make sense of a system into which I was born, a system that privileges certain people with certain attributes (e.g., white, male, heterosexual, educated—all of which I am or have been at one point in my life) and works to maintain the concentration of power in the hands of a relatively small group of people.

This essay is not a "men's studies" or "gender studies" project. It is a feminist-inspired project (see also Jensen 1995a). I am a man working within feminist theory to try to understand the nature of oppression, specifically in this essay the nature of gender oppression and the role of sexuality in that oppression. My goal is to be a traitor to my gender, as well as to my race and my class. I routinely fail at this goal, though sometimes I get glimpses of what success looks like. I am fortunate to have the support of many feminist women[4] and a few like-minded male colleagues.[5] Integral to that support is their willingness to hold me accountable for my actions and words; the critique is a key part of the support.

Also, this essay is not an attempt to tell women what they should think or how they should behave. I am trying to talk primarily to other men about my struggle and what I have learned from it. I do this work both out of a yearning for justice for those oppressed in patriarchy (women, particularly lesbians, children, and to some extent gay men) and out of self-interest (the desire to live a more fulfilling life in a more just, humane, and compassionate world). I work both out of hope for the future and out of fear.

The Fear

"What's your problem—are you afraid of sex?"

That question has been posed to me often as I have been involved in antipornography work. For a long time my answer was no, of course not. Me, afraid? I'm no prude.

I am not a prude, but I have come to realize that I am very much afraid of sex. I am afraid of sex as sex is defined by the dominant culture, practiced all around me, and projected onto magazine pages, billboards, and movie screens. I am afraid of sex because I am afraid of domination, cruelty, violence, and death. I am afraid of sex because sex has hurt me and hurt lots of people I know, and because I have hurt others with sex in the past. I know that there are people out there who have been hurt by sex in ways that are beyond my words, who have experienced a depth of pain that I will never fully understand. And I know there are people who are dead because of sex.

Yes, I am afraid of sex. How could I not be?[6]

A common response from people when I say things like that is "You're nuts." Sometimes, when I'm feeling shaky, a voice in the back of my head asks, "Am I nuts?"

I have been doing research and writing on pornography and sexuality for about eight years (Jensen 1996, 1995b, 1994a, 1994b). In the past few years I have been trying to figure out how to talk to people who think I am crazy and how to deal with my own fear that they may be right. I have been trying to understand why the attack on the feminist critique of patriarchal sex has been so strong and so successful, and how it connects to the backlash against feminist work on sexual violence.

Here's one tentative explanation: It is too scary to be afraid of sex. To go too far down the road with the radical critique of sexuality means, inevitably, acknowledging a fear of patriarchal sex. And if all the sex around us is patriarchal, then we are going to live daily with that fear. And if patriarchal sex seems to be so overwhelmingly dominant that it sometimes is difficult to believe that any other sex is possible, then maybe we are always going to be afraid. Maybe it's easier to not be afraid, or at least to repress the fear. Maybe that's the only way to survive.

But maybe not. Maybe being afraid of sex is the first step toward something new. Maybe things that seem impossible now will be possible someday. Or maybe we will find that we won't need what we thought we needed.[7] Maybe being afraid is the first step out of the fear and into something else that we cannot yet name.

Expanding the Working Definition of Patriarchal Sex

I was born in 1958 in a small city in the upper Midwest to white parents who, after some years of struggle, settled into the middle class. I went to a Protestant church and public school. I had friends, mostly other boys. We talked about sex and we begged, borrowed, and stole pornography. I watched a lot of television and went to a lot of movies. I had a G.I. Joe doll and toy guns. I played sports. I was a quirky kid in some respects, physically smaller than most and a bit of an egghead from an early age. Maybe my family was a little more emotionally abusive than most, but maybe not. In many regards, I grew up "normal." And I got a normal education in sex.

Here is the curriculum for sex education for a normal American boy: Fuck women.

Here is the sexual grammar lesson I received: "Man fucks women; subject verb object" (MacKinnon 1989, 124).

The specifics varied depending on the instructor.

Some people said, "Fuck as many women as often as you can for as long as you can get away with it." Others said, "Fuck a lot of women until you get tired of it, and then find one to marry and just fuck her." And some said, "Don't fuck any women until you find one to marry, and then fuck her for the rest of your life and never fuck anyone else."

Some said, "Women are special; put them on a pedestal before and after you fuck them." Others said, "Women are shit; do what you have to do to fuck them, and then get away from them."

Most said, "Only fuck women." A few said, "Fuck other men if you want to."

The basic concepts were clear: Sex is fucking. Fucking is penetration. The things you do before you penetrate are just warm-up exercises. If you don't penetrate, you haven't fucked, and if you haven't fucked, you haven't had sex. Frye (1992, 113) defines this kind of heterosexual— and heterosexist—intercourse as "male-dominant-female-subordinate-copulation-whose-completion-and-purpose-is-the-male's-ejaculation." That is sex in patriarchy.

All the teachers (parents, friends, ministers, celebrities, pornographers, movie directors, etc.) tend to agree on the one primary rule about sex in patriarchy: You gotta get it. You have to fuck something at some point in your life. If you don't get it, there's something wrong with you. You aren't normal. You aren't really alive. You certainly aren't a man.

When I was a kid, I'm not sure I really wanted to fuck anyone. But eventually I figured out that if I didn't learn to do it, I was going to be an outcast. So I learned, though later than most of my peers.

My first sex was with pornography. I was about six years old the first time I saw it. For the next two decades, it was part of my life on an irregular basis. I had sex with women in person, and I had sex with women in magazines and movies (masturbating to pornography is a way of having sex, of sexually using the women in it). As far as I can tell from research and conversations with men, I had a fairly typical sex life. I learned to like being in control. That was part of the appeal of sex with pornography: I had control over when I used it, and I was in control of the women in it (Jensen 1996). That was part of the appeal of sex with women: I was the man, and I was in control because men "naturally" take control of sex. Once the details of access with a particular woman were negotiated, I was in control. Patriarchal sex practices vary from person to person, from attempts at more egalitarian interaction to the sadomasochistic. My preferred practices, on the surface, leaned more toward the egalitarian, but when I think about my sexual history I can connect every practice to a need for control, either of the woman or of the woman's pleasure.

When I started to realize that, I realized I was in trouble. When I realized that most everyone around me was in trouble, I started to get scared. When I got real scared, I stopped having patriarchal sex. That meant I stopped having sex with other people, including the people in pornography. At first I didn't do this consciously. I just found it more and more difficult to have sex. At some point I consciously made a decision to quit. As I began to understand more about how deeply I had been trained in the rules of patriarchal sex, it became more clear that I would have to stop participating in that system. I would have to stop fucking. I could no longer pretend that I was "working it out" by trying to put into practice new ideas about sex. Patriarchal sex was too deeply rooted in my body and my psyche. Before I could reconstruct my sexuality, I needed time to deconstruct, free of the pressure to have sex.

The Radical Feminist Critique

By the time I came to understand that I wanted, and needed, to stop having patriarchal sex, I had a framework within which to understand what was happening to me. Radical feminist critiques of pornography and patriarchal sex gave me a vocabulary, a way to make coherent in words what was happening in my body and mind. That made it possible, though by no means easy, to begin the process. Many feminist activists and theorists have contributed to this critique (Cole 1989; Dworkin 1981, 1987, 1988; Jeffreys 1990; MacKinnon 1987, 1989; Russell 1993). Here's my summary.

Men in contemporary American culture (I make no claim to cross-cultural or historical critique; I am writing about the world in which I live) are trained through a variety of cultural institutions to view sex as the acquisition of pleasure by the taking of women. Sex is a sphere in which men (by this I don't mean that every man believes this, but that many men believe this is true for all men) believe themselves to be naturally dominant and women naturally passive. Women are objectified and women's sexuality is commodified. Sex is sexy because men are dominant and women are subordinate; power is eroticized. In certain limited situations, those roles can be reversed (men can play at being sexually subordinate and women dominant), so long as power remains sexualized and power relations outside the bedroom are unchanged. Summed up by Andrea Dworkin (1987, 63): "The normal fuck by a normal man is taken to be an act of invasion and ownership undertaken in a mode of predation; colonializing, forceful (manly) or nearly violent; the sexual act that by its nature makes her his."

One of the key sites in which these sexual values are reflected, reinforced, and normalized is pornography. Domination and subordination are sexualized, sometimes in explicit representations of rape and violence against women, but always in the objectification and commodification of women and their sexuality (Dworkin 1981, 1988; MacKinnon 1987, 1993). This results in several kinds of harm to women and children: (1) the harm caused in the production of pornography; (2) the harm in having pornography forced on them; (3) the harm in being sexually assaulted by men who use pornography; and (4) the harm in living in a culture in which pornography reinforces and sexualizes women's subordinate status.

In a world in which men hold most of the social, economic, and political power, the result of the patriarchal sexual system is widespread violence, sexualized violence, and violence-by-sex against women and children. This includes physical assault, emotional abuse, and rape by family members and acquaintances as well as strangers. Along with the experience of violence, women and children live with the knowledge that they are always targets.

Attention to the meaning of the central male slang term for sexual intercourse—"fuck"—is instructive. To fuck a woman is to have sex with her. To fuck someone in another context ("he really fucked me over on that deal") means to hurt or cheat a person. And when hurled as a simple insult ("fuck you") the intent is denigration and the remark is often prelude to violence or the threat of violence. Sex in patriarchy is fucking. That we live in a world in which people continue to use the same word for sex and violence, and then resist the notion that sex is routinely violent and claim to be outraged when sex becomes overtly violent, is testament to the power of patriarchy. In this society, sex and violence are fused to the point of being indistinguishable. Yet to say this out loud is to risk being labeled crazy: "What's wrong with you—are you afraid of sex? Are you nuts?"

The Wrong Ways Out of This Problem

1

All women and most men I've met are against rape. That is, they are against those acts the law defines as rape. But most aren't against fucking, because fucking is sex and how can you be against sex, which is seen as natural? This view is summed up in the phrase "Rape is a crime of violence, not of sex." But rape is a crime of sex; to desex rape is to turn away from the possibility of understanding rape. This is not to say that men don't seek power over women through rape and that the power isn't expressed violently; it is to acknowledge that men seek power over women through sex of all kinds, including rape.

I think people, men and women, want to believe that rape is violence-not-sex because to acknowledge that rape is sex requires that we ask how it is that so many men can decide that rape is an acceptable way to get sex. Rape is not the result of the aberrant behavior of a limited number of pathological men, but is "normal" within the logic of the system. When

sex is about power and control, and men are socially, and typically physically, more powerful than women and children, then sexual violence is
the inevitable outcome. As Dworkin (1976, 46) argues, "Rape is no excess,
no aberration, no accident, no mistake—it embodies sexuality as the
culture defines it."

This does not mean that every man is a rapist in legal terms. It means
that we live in a society in which men, both legally designated rapists and
nonrapists, are raised with rapist ethics (Stoltenberg 1989). Raping is a
particularly brutal kind of fucking, but the difference between "deviant"
rape and the "normal" fuck is often difficult to see (MacKinnon 1989).
Timothy Beneke (1982, 16), looking at how metaphors frame sex as an
expression of male power and conquest, concludes, "every man who
grows up in America and learns American English learns all too much to
think like a rapist, to structure his experience of women and sex in terms
of status, hostility, control, and dominance."

So the conventional view is that rape can't be about sex and has to be
about violence, because if it's about sex then each one of us has to ask
how deeply into our bodies the norms of patriarchal sex have settled.
Men have to ask about how sexy dominance is to them, and women have
to ask how sexy submission is to them. And if we think too long about
that, we face the question of why we're still having patriarchal sex. And if
we face that question, we may have to consider the possibility of stopping.
And if we aren't having sex, then we have to face the dominant culture's
assumption that we aren't really alive because we aren't having sex.

2

Women aren't victims, some say, and radical feminism has tried to
turn women into victims by focusing on the harms of patriarchal sex.[8]
This is a deceptively appealing rhetorical move. When members of one
class (women) identify a way that members of another class (men) routinely hurt them, those who are hurt are told they are responsible for the
injury because they identified it. If women would stop talking about these
injuries, the logic seems to be, then the injuries would stop. This strategy
seems popular with some women and lots of men lately. I understand
why men take this stance; it relieves them of any obligation to evaluate
their own behavior and be responsible. And I understand why women
don't want to see themselves as always at risk of men's violence and sexual

aggression. But saying you aren't at risk because you don't want to be at risk doesn't take the risk away.

What does the word "victim" mean? Dworkin (1990, 38–39) writes,

> It's a true word. If you were raped, you were victimized. You damned well were. You were a victim. It doesn't mean that you are a victim in the metaphysical sense, in your state of being, as an intrinsic part of your essence and existence. It means somebody hurt you. They injured you. . . . And if it happens to you systematically because you are born a woman, it means that you live in a political system that uses pain and humiliation to control and to hurt you.

Understanding one's victimization is not the same as playing the victim. Acknowledging that women often are victimized is not an admission of weaknesses or a retreat from responsibility. Instead, it makes possible organized and sustained resistance to the power that causes the injuries. By clearly identifying the victimizers (most always men) and the system within which the injury is ignored or trivialized (patriarchy), we make political change possible.

We live in a world in which some people exercise their power in a way that hurts others. It has become popular to pretend that the injuries are the product of the overactive imaginations of whiners. White people routinely tell nonwhite people that racism is not a big problem and that if the nonwhites would stop complaining, all would be fine. Rich people tell poor and working people that there is no such thing as class in the United States and that if we all would just work hard together everything would be fine. Straight people tell lesbian and gay people that if they would just stop making such a public nuisance of themselves everyone would leave them alone and things would be fine. But things aren't fine. We live in racism. Poor and working people are being crushed by a cruel economic system. Heterosexism oppresses lesbians and gays. And men keep fucking women.

Why Try?

If patriarchy is this dominant and patriarchal sex this colonizing, one might ask what hope there is in resistance. Would it not make more sense to go along and get along?

No system, no matter how overwhelming and oppressive, is beyond challenge. Borrowing a metaphor from Naomi Scheman, we can think of patriarchy as being like concrete in the city. It covers almost everything. It is heavy and seemingly unmovable, and it paves the world. But the daily wear and tear produces cracks, and in those cracks, plants grow—weeds, grass, sometimes a flower. Living things have no business growing up out of concrete, but they do. They resist the totality of the concrete.

No system of power can obliterate all resistance. All systems yield space in which things can grow. I have seen resistance to patriarchal sex grow, even flourish, in the cracks. I have friends, the people who helped me sort these things out and move forward, who continue to survive and grow in resistance to patriarchal sex. In my life I have met few people interested in this project of resistance, but it doesn't take many people for me to feel that resistance is worthwhile. But I also seek more than just a few friends who are scattered around the country. I would like to be part of an epistemic community in which these questions can be explored.

Epistemic Communities

What kind of investigation is required for confronting patriarchal sex? I am not after *the* solution to the problem. At times I am not entirely sure about the questions. Lorraine Code (1987, 165) suggests that when epistemology is construed as a quest for understanding, the appropriate question becomes not "What can I know?" but "What sort(s) of discourse does the situation really call for?" It is from conversation and the sharing of richly detailed narratives that understanding, not definitive answers, can begin to emerge.

While we are all individually accountable for our actions, the effort to understand sexuality is not solely an individual task; we have a responsibility to create collectively the tools for this investigation. As Code (1987, 245) suggests, "Thinking individuals have a responsibility to monitor and watch over shifts in, changes in, and efforts to preserve good intellectual practice. . . . In principle, everyone is responsible, to the extent of his or her ability, for the quality of cognitive practice in a community."

Such community can be difficult to form and maintain. Pressures from the dominant ideology, combined with the routine human failings, can make the task seem overwhelming. My experience is that there are different levels of community at which different levels of conversation can happen. I have done most of this work in a fairly small group that includes a core of five to ten trusted friends, colleagues, and students (fellow students when I was in graduate school and—on rare occasions now—students whom I meet as a professor). Beyond that, I sometimes meet others with similar interests and convictions with whom I have important, though perhaps not ongoing, conversations. There is no recipe for how these conversations develop and no criteria for whom I connect with. The conversations cross lines of, among other things, gender, race, age, and sexual orientation, though not without great effort and occasional stress.

But one thing that is constant for me in these conversations is an understanding—sometimes stated but often simply understood—that we won't have sex, now or in the foreseeable future. These kinds of conversations can involve strong emotions and physical responses, and it is easy to want to channel that energy into sex. Also, there are ways in which talking-about-sex can be a type of having-sex. It takes constant monitoring to reject patriarchy's rule and not engage in sex. But I believe it is essential to resist the imperative to have sex because we do not always learn more about our desire by acting on it. I believe that having sex and talking-having sex in my core epistemic community would undermine progress. It would erode trust, not just between the people involved in the sex but in the whole community, and would make it difficult, if not impossible, for the conversation to continue.[9] Such activity suggests that no matter how much one tries to redefine sexuality or talks about change, in the end we're all just interested in fucking each other.

Beyond those small communities in which we are likely to feel most safe in searching to understand sexuality, important conversations can, and must, go on in a larger context. This essay is one attempt to create an epistemic community; implicit (and now explicit) is an invitation for others to engage me in conversation. My search for community at this level happens at conferences, in the classroom, in antipornography and antirape public presentations, and in conversations with a variety of people I meet. Most often, I am sharing things I have learned in my core community with others and asking for feedback. These conversations are unpredictable but always, in some sense, productive for me.[10]

The Work of Women and Men

In her discussion of epistemic responsibility, Code asserts that "knowing well" is of considerable moral significance (Code 1987). On matters of sexuality, knowing well requires attention not just to what our desires are but to where those desires come from. To simply know, "This is what arouses me," without attempting to understand why it does is epistemically irresponsible. Code reminds us that it can be easier "to believe that a favorite theory is true and to suppress nagging doubts than to pursue the implications of those doubts and risk having to modify the theory" (Code 1987, 59).[11] Being epistemically responsible requires that we investigate those nagging doubts.

In this and other work, I tend to focus on the objectification, aggression, and violence that is central to the dominant construction of male sexuality in this culture. I believe this focus is proper, especially because I am a man and I work from my experience as a man. However, these questions about the construction of our sexuality are as crucial for women as they are for men.[12] This does not mean I claim the right to tell women what their sexuality should look like. It means that we all must acknowledge that, to varying degrees, our lives have been shaped by patriarchy and men's values, and that we must examine the effects.

An example: While having sex, a man finds it sexy to put a woman's arms behind her head and hold them down at the wrists, rendering her fairly immobile and intensifying the experience of intercourse for him. The man should consider: How did he come to develop this practice? What is it about rendering a woman immobile that feels sexy? Why does having control over a woman in such a manner intensify his orgasm? All those questions are central to epistemic responsibility; to act morally, he needs to know. But what if the woman in that scenario also finds the practice exciting? What if the sensation of being unable to move her arms while having intercourse intensifies her sexual response? What is it about being immobile that feels sexy?

I believe that women have the same epistemic responsibility as men. However, in a society where women are often blamed for being in some way responsible for the injuries that men inflict on them, such a call for epistemic responsibility can appear to be asking women to blame themselves for the ways they may have internalized patriarchy's values. But this is not about blame or guilt; it is about the search for understanding, for freedom. Just as pornography teaches men to rape, romance novels teach women to be rape victims. Just as fathers often instill rapist values in sons, mothers often teach daughters how to submit to the boys. I believe there are compelling moral and political arguments for men to change. It also seems clear that to survive, women must change.

Hetero and Homo

By the way, I am gay. I lived most of my thirty-eight years as a heterosexual. I was once married, and I have a son. I am out, although what exactly that means for me—beyond a public rejection of heterosexuality and its institutions—is unclear at the moment. But gay-or-straight doesn't much matter. The question of resistance to patriarchal sex is just as important in the gay male world as it is for straight men. As far as I can tell, the majority of gay men fuck in about the same way straight men do. We all received pretty much the same training. In fact, the term "fucking" is thrown around in many gay male conversations with frequency and ease, in a celebratory way. Fucking is taken to be the thing that gay men do; some might even argue that if you aren't fucking, you aren't gay.

If that's the case, then I'm not gay. And I'm not straight. I'm trying to live in the cracks in the concrete.

Imagining Not-Sex

In early versions of this essay I wrote about the task of imagining what a new kind of sex, a nonpatriarchal sex, might look like. I suggested that one of the main problems in this project of resistance is that we lack a language in which to imagine what that sex might be. I felt the need to imagine things beyond our experience, in words that we have yet to find.

I still believe that we lack the vocabulary to talk about this and that creative imagination is at the center of this project. But I no longer think that imagining a new kind of sex is crucial, or even helpful, at this point. I fear that a rush to fill the void left when one starts to disengage from patriarchal sex can ultimately keep us from moving forward; we risk trying to reconstruct before we have adequately deconstructed, before we understand enough about how the norms of patriarchal sex live in our bodies. Obviously, this is not like the flushing of a system to get the toxins out, not a mechanical task that has a clear beginning and end. I expect to struggle for the rest of my life to understand how patriarchy has shaped my identity and sexuality. If I waited for the magic moment of pure clarity to begin a reconstruction project, I would be waiting forever. But I want to guard against beginning the reconstruction process prematurely.

There is an important lesson in my rush to want to fill the void with new imagined conceptions of nonpatriarchal sex. Although I claimed to have been willing to stop having sex for some period of time, my first instinct was to rush toward a reconstruction. That is, in trying to resist the imperative to have sex, I gave in to the imperative to create a new kind of sex so that I could have it. I told myself that because we are humans with bodies and needs for intimacy, the task of imagining something new was crucial. I do have a body, and I need love and intimacy. But the question remains: Would any sex I could imagine at this moment really be nonpatriarchal? Have I disentangled myself from patriarchy enough to even begin that task?

The answer for me is clearly no, I am not in a good position to imagine something new. That is my judgment about myself, and I don't pretend to have the answer for others. I come to this moment with a specific history that shapes what is possible for me. I do not know what is possible for others, and I expect that many men who share the values I describe decide to take other paths toward a similar goal. My point is not to persuade everyone that not-sex is their only option, but to suggest that it is a relevant question for everyone—that it is an option and that there is a compelling argument to be made for that choice. If we want to leave behind patriarchal sex, not only must we confront the likelihood that we might need to stop having sex for some period of time, but we must be willing to accept that we may not have any idea of what will take the place of patriarchal sex for quite some time. In other words, we have to be willing to live a life without sex for the sake of justice, for the sake of ourselves.

So for the time being, I want to imagine not-sex. I reject sex in the hope that someday, maybe in my lifetime and maybe not, I can find a way to be physically intimate outside patriarchy. Maybe we will call it sex, maybe not. At this point, it's not a terribly important question for me.

This move to embrace not-sex may seem a drastic, or even silly, rhetorical move. But I think the gravity of the situation justifies the deployment of new language. As Susan Cole puts it (1989, 132), "We have a long way to go before we uncover the full extent of the damage. We may not see the full repair in our lifetimes and it may not be possible to chart the entire course for change." I no longer trust myself to chart the course for change, to refashion sex into something I can trust. So I seek not-sex, something different than what "sex" means in the dominant culture. I want intimacy, trust, and respect from other people, and I hope that it is possible for those things to be expressed physically. But I don't want sex.[13]

To say that I don't want sex is not to deny my sexuality nor cut myself off from my erotic power, as Audre Lorde uses that term (see also Heyward 1989). Lorde talks about the way women's erotic power is falsely cordoned off in the bedroom, made into "plasticized sensation," and confused with the pornographic (1984, 54). For Lorde, the erotic is a life-force, a creative energy: "those physical, emotional, and psychic expressions of what is deepest and strongest and richest within each of us, being shared: the passions of love, in its deepest meanings" (1984, 56).

Lorde writes about expressing her erotic power in some ways that the culture does not define as sexual and others that the culture might call sexual; she writes of the erotic power flowing both in the act of writing a good poem and in "moving into sunlight against the body of a woman I love." My expression of the erotic at this point in my life need not include such movement against the body of another. What is crucial is not channeling my erotic energy into sex, but finding other ways to feel that power. Lorde writes, "Recognizing the power of the erotic within our lives can give us the energy to pursue genuine change within our world, rather than merely settling for a shift of characters in the same weary drama" (1984, 59).

To be more specific, what does it mean to say that in my intimate (broadly defined) relationships I want to tap my erotic power while practicing not-sex? Does it mean a ban on touch that produces an erection for me? A ban on touch of another person's body in areas that are typically sexualized (genitals, breasts, buttocks)? Is there any way to achieve not-sex intimacy that involves touch?

For me, not-sex is intimacy that resists or transcends oppression. In practice, that has meant different things with different people, depending on my relationship with them and the level of trust. For example, one female friend and I hug frequently, and I feel as if that touch is not-sex and a loving intimacy. A gay male friend and I tend to hug when we greet and say goodbye, and each of us knows that if the other needed emotionally supportive not-sex physical contact we would provide it. But we are not routinely physical out of a commitment to not-sex. In both relationships, there is an erotic element; in neither case is it made sexual.

Masturbation is a more difficult issue for me in thinking through not-sex. I sometimes do it, though I am aware that the fantasies that fuel that masturbation are almost exclusively scripted by patriarchy. There is a difference between self-touch that is motivated by self-love and self-touch that is rooted in those scripts. My struggle with this issue (not to be confused with adolescent guilt over masturbation) remains unresolved, and is one reminder that perhaps I am further from imagining a nonpatriarchal sex than I once thought.

Jim Koplin once said to me that it is at the moment when a man can no longer achieve an erection—when all the old ways of sparking sexual pleasure have failed—that something new is possible. That moment, he said, may be the most creative point in our lives. "Impotence" becomes not a failure or a problem, but the point from which something new becomes possible. In this sense, I strive for impotency; that may be the point at which I am doing something more than shuffling characters in "the same weary drama."

Heat and Light

As I have said, I am not interested in writing a recipe book for nonpatriarchal sex. I do not want to imagine new practices or create new rules for sex at this point in my life. But is there anything one can say about a new path, about where not-sex might lead me?

There is a cliché that when an argument is of little value, it produces "more heat than light." One of the ways this culture talks about sex is in terms of heat: she's hot, he's hot, we had hot sex. Sex is bump-and-grind; the friction produces the heat, and the heat makes the sex good. Fucking produces heat. Fucking is hot.

But what if our embodied connections could be less about heat and more about light? What if instead of desperately seeking hot sex, we searched for a way to produce light when we touch? What if such touch were about finding a way to create light between people so that we could see ourselves and each other better? If the goal is knowing ourselves and each other like that, then what we need is not heat but light to illuminate the path. How do we touch and talk to each other to shine that light? I'm not sure. There are lots of ways to produce light in the world, and some are better than others. Light that draws its power from rechargeable solar cells, for example, is better than light that draws on throwaway batteries. Likewise, there will be lots of ways to imagine nonpatriarchal sex. Some will be better than others, depending on the values on which they are based. The task ahead is not just imagining something new, but being alert to how things that seem new can be rooted in old ideas.

A possible response to this from other men (and women): "Not-sex. Striving for impotency. Are you crazy?"

Sometimes I wonder. But I don't think I am crazy. I feel as if I may be going sane.

REFERENCES

Beneke, Timothy. 1982. *Men on rape.* New York: St. Martin's.

Bergen, Raquel Kennedy. 1995. "Surviving wife rape: How women define and cope with the violence." *Violence Against Women* 1 (2): 117–38.

Code, Lorraine. 1987. *Epistemic responsibility.* Hanover, NH: University Press of New England.

———. 1991. *What can she know?* Ithaca: Cornell University Press.

Cole, Susan. 1989. *Pornography and the sex crisis.* Toronto: Amanita.

Dworkin, Andrea. 1976. *Our blood.* New York: Harper and Row.

———. 1981. *Pornography: Men possessing women.* New York: Perigee.

———. 1987. *Intercourse.* New York: Free Press.

———. 1988. *Letters from a war zone.* London: Secker and Warburg.

———. 1990. "Woman-hating right and left." In Dorchen Leidholdt and Janice G. Raymond, eds., *The sexual liberals and the attack on feminism,* 28–40. New York: Pergamon.

Frye, Marilyn. 1992. *Willful virgin.* Freedom, CA: Crossing Press.

Heyward, Carter. 1989. *Touching our strength: The erotic as power and the love of God.* San Francisco: Harper and Row.

Jeffreys, Sheila. 1990. *Anticlimax: A feminist perspective on the sexual revolution.* New York: New York University Press.

Jensen, Robert. 1994a. "Pornographic novels and the ideology of male supremacy." *Howard Journal of Communications* 5 (1&2): 92–107.

———. 1994b. "Pornography and the limits of experimental research." In Gail

Dines and Jean M. Humez, eds., *Gender, race and class in media: A text-reader*, 298–306. Thousand Oaks, CA: Sage.

Jensen, Robert. 1995a. "Men's lives and feminist theory." *Race, Gender & Class* 2 (2): 111–25.

———. 1995b. "Pornographic lives." *Violence Against Women* 1 (1): 32–54.

———. 1996. "Knowing pornography." *Violence Against Women* 2 (1): 82–102.

Lorde, Audre. 1984. "Uses of the erotic: The erotic as power." In *Sister outsider*, 53–59. Freedom, CA: Crossing Press.

MacKinnon, Catharine A. 1987. *Feminism unmodified: Discourses on life and law.* Cambridge: Harvard University Press.

———. 1989. *Toward a feminist theory of the state.* Cambridge: Harvard University Press.

———. 1993. *Only words.* Cambridge: Harvard University Press.

Russell, Diana E. H., ed. 1993. *Making violence sexy: Feminist views on pornography.* New York: Teachers College Press.

Sommers, Christina Hoff. 1994. *Who stole feminism? How women have betrayed women.* New York: Simon and Schuster.

Stivers, Camilla. 1992. "Reflections on the role of personal narrative in social science." *Signs* 18 (2): 408–25.

Stoltenberg, John. 1989. *Refusing to be a man: Essays on sex and justice.* Portland, OR: Breitenbush Books.

Wolf, Naomi. 1993. *Fire with fire: The new female power and how it will change the twenty-first century.* New York: Random House.

NOTES

1. A copy of the message was posted on several Internet discussion lists and widely circulated, and criticized, in November 1995.

2. I don't use the word "fuck" without hesitation and concern. The word carries with it incredible violence, and I realize that it can feel assaultive to some people, especially women. But in this case I believe that it is the word that most accurately represents what I am trying to describe.

3. My focus will remain on heterosexual men and their sex with women, though much of what I will say here has relevance for gay men. More on that later.

4. Thanks specifically to Elvia Arriola, Rebecca Bennett, Donna McNamara, Nancy Potter, and Naomi Scheman for their roles in helping me understand these issues.

5. Thanks to Jim Koplin, a friend, intellectual partner, and colleague in the antipornography movement. Much of what I write here was first spoken by Jim and by me in conversation. I can no longer trace the origin of some of the ideas;

many are as much Jim's as mine. His affection, support, and wisdom inform this essay.

6. There is another kind of fear that I believe most, if not all, men live with: the fear of not meeting the imagined standard of masculinity, of never being a skilled enough sexual performer to be a "real" man—the stud, the man in total control. That fear is real, as is the alienation from self and partner that results. However, the fear I am describing here is a deeper fear, a realization of how thoroughly sexuality in this culture eroticizes domination and subordination. More on that later.

7. This has proved to be the case in other parts of my life. I live without a car, a television, or meat. At earlier times in my life, I would have thought that impossible. Now I find my life immeasurably enriched by the absence of those things.

8. One popular female writer argues that such "victim feminism" needs to be replaced with "power feminism" (Wolf 1993). Another claims that radical feminists, or "gender feminists," have hijacked the women's movement and betrayed the real interests of women (Sommers 1994).

9. This is especially true when the sex happens across differences in status that reflect potential power imbalances, such as a large age gap, significant wealth or class gaps, and gender. Most devastating, I believe, is sexual contact between people in institutionalized roles of unequal power, such as student/teacher, client/therapist, parishioner/clergy. I believe that sexual activity in such situations is always wrong.

10. I don't want to appear naive about this wider community. As troubling and divisive as these investigations can be in communities committed to feminism and liberatory politics, they can be dangerous in mainstream and reactionary political circles, where people may want to ignore or undermine a feminist analysis. My goal, and the goal of the feminists whose work informs my analysis, is the exploration and celebration of diversity, but the goal of those to the right is often the suppression of diversity. These political realities are important to consider. The kind of open discussion that is crucial to expanding our understanding may be safe in some contexts but not in others, and more safe for some than others. But it is important that the conversation continue.

11. This is not to say that every individual in every situation need engage in discussions about these matters. People whose sexuality is under attack by the established social structure—lesbians, gay men, and, in some sense, many heterosexual women—might feel that social conditions make it unsafe to engage in such open discussion. For example, a lesbian high school teacher in a small town may not be able to be part of a discussion about sexual practices in that community. Still, the idea of epistemic responsibility does suggest we should make whatever efforts are possible to pursue knowledge about sexuality and its social construction.

12. Thanks to Rebecca Bennett for reminding me of the importance of discussing this.

13. In response to a draft of this essay, Jim Koplin suggested that labeling this "not-sex" is reactive rather than inventive and offered alternative terms such as "body-play," "body-connection," or "creative touch." I understand his point, but I think that at this stage in my project I want to hold onto a clear break from sex. At some point in the future, I may shift to such language, but my gut tells me it is too early for me to do that.

Chapter Seven

The Many Paths of Feminism
Can Men Travel Any of Them?

Steven P. Schacht and Doris W. Ewing

Feminists long for men to heal. . . . We dream of a world full of men who could be passionate lovers, grounded in their own bodies, capable of profound loves and deep sorrows, strong allies of women, sensitive nurturers, fearless defenders of all people's liberation, unbound by stifling conventions, yet respectful of their own and others' boundaries, serious without being humorless, stable without being dull, disciplined without being rigid, sweet without being spineless, proud without being insufferably egotistical, fierce without being violent, wild without being, well, assholes.

> —Starhawk, "A Men's Movement I Can Trust"

There are no books that adequately serve as maps providing males of all ages with a feminist education by explaining what patriarchy is, how it works, and why they should be committed to a feminist movement that opposes sexism and sexist oppression.

> —bell hooks, "Men in Feminist Struggle"

When we first read these statements and numerous others offered by an impressive array of prominent feminists in the anthology *Women Respond to the Men's Movement: A Feminist Collection* (Hagan 1992), we did so with both hope and sorrow. Unlike anyone we had previously read on the topic of feminism and men, the women in this anthology not only gave clues but also offered specific suggestions on how a truly feminist man might look. This gave us hope.

Our sorrow came from their descriptions and our own observations of the misguided, often pitiful and destructive members of the growing men's movement in the United States. While many of the men in this movement have presented themselves with a feminist veneer ranging from gender self-actualization to profeminism, to our knowledge none of them have offered any meaningful or realistic maps for becoming a feminist. Moreover, many of the men in this movement have provided just the opposite: reasons a man should not and cannot be feminist-oriented.

This essay is an exploration of the infelicitous attempts men have made thus far to gain a feminist consciousness, and more important, a preliminary delineation of why a man should want such a worldview and how he might go about realizing it. To this end, we first individually and personally explore the promise that feminism holds for all people and the necessity of women and men working together to create larger feminist realities. Next, we briefly critique what are seen as two identifiable groups in the men's movement, "Iron John" type groups and men's studies programs, in the United States. Experiential models for becoming a feminist that women have offered to other women are then examined. Concluding that the men's movement presents serious impediments to men who hope to gain a feminist understanding of any depth and that feminist experiential models also present limitations, we end this essay with some suggestions of pathways men might pursue in realizing and living a feminist worldview.

Ultimately, most of the ideas put forth in this essay cannot be evaluated in any scientific or formal manner. Thus, "its method is to appeal to the reader's own experience; if the result feels in any way enlightening, the argument is validated insofar as it can be" (Dinnerstein 1991, ix). As suggested by this essay's title, what follows is not posited as a definitive statement on whether men can or cannot be feminist or the exact paths they should travel. Rather, we hope this essay will be treated as a serious invitation to men to finally start joining their feminist sisters in one of the most important struggles ever undertaken: the emancipation of all people. Then again, "the only thing worth writing about is what seems to be unknown and, therefore, fearful" (Moraga 1983, 32) and "having the courage to confront the unknown is a precondition for imagination, and the capacity to imagine another world is an essential element in scientific progress" (Delphy 1993, 1).

The Promise of Feminism for All People

Steve

I (Steve) went into sociology and academia to fulfill a real aspiration: to help others and to make a difference for all people. Throughout graduate school I explored numerous theoretical outlooks with hopes of finding the best way to implement my passion. Quickly, however, and one after another, each perspective I examined presented me with blatant inconsistencies. Every theoretical perspective seemed to hold some answers, whether at the micro or macro level, but each seemed too rife with apparent contradictions. As I began to study gender issues and the feminist perspectives that accompanied them, however, the concomitant theoretical inconsistencies and contradictions of other perspectives no longer appeared overwhelming. Further, if one adopted a radical feminist stance, as I have, the forthcoming theoretical solution seemed clear: going to the root of all forms of oppression—gender—other categorical forms of stratification no longer seemed omnipotent.[1]

Currently, the reason I must put my passions into feminism is that not only does it hold the promise of eradicating all forms of exploitation and oppression, but also, and of equal importance, herein lies the future of life on this planet. We have now had thousands of years of a patriarchal reality, and the "progress" of this "civilized" structural arrangement has put us at the brink of self-destruction. In contrast, radical feminism's life-affirming-giving-enhancing values are the only ones veracious enough to reverse the cataclysmic direction in which patriarchal societies are leading us. Quite simply, I believe that feminist values and realities are the only ones that can ensure the survival of this planet. As such, I chose to direct my energies into feminism and life versus patriarchy and death.

Ultimately my attraction to feminism was brought about, and continues to be instilled by, the significant women I have had the honor of knowing throughout my life. In the past I have tacitly sat by and watched a misogynist, male-dominated society attempt (often with great success) to destroy these intelligent and beautiful women. My mother died over fifteen years ago at the hands of a male doctor who misdiagnosed her abdominal pains as simple "female problems" when she had cancer of the colon. I have watched nearly every academic woman who has befriended me struggle on a daily basis with a patriarchal system (the university) that structurally and often individually sets her up for failure. In total, the vast majority of women I have known have been raped in one way or another. The pain that these and other women have experienced has become mine. I can no longer idly stand by and be part of the problem by not doing anything about it. To do so would mean not only that I would be assisting in the destruction of individual women who are close to me, but also that each time I hesitate to act means that another part of me is potentially (and far too often) destroyed. The personal experiences of these women have became my political reality.

As I continue to shed my profeminist glaze—a deceptively sweet and appealing but potentially sticky and destructive exterior—and replace it with a feminist center and being, I find myself being increasingly betrayed and rejected by other men. Conversely, many of my attempts to seek acceptance from feminist women have been met with a cool reception: indifference, mistrust, and even hostility. Having been disappointed so often, many women understandably distance themselves from self-proclaimed male feminists.

Yet while the path I yearn to travel is largely unknown and replete with numerous obstacles, in my lifetime I have been fortunate to have had several strong feminist women personally accompany me on this journey. Not only has their companionship made my travels toward a feminist worldview meaningful, but without their guidance I would truly be lost, forever condemned to a patriarchal existence. I strongly believe that ulti-mately, only women can be midwives in the birth of any sort of feminist consciousness (as reflected in the poem by my mother on the facing page).

I believe there is hope that someday each of us—women and men— laboring together towards a feminist birth, will find ourselves born into a world free of hate, exploitation, and oppression.

Doris

I (Doris) did not come to feminism until my midyears. Growing up in the fifties, I entered college and found that joining a good sorority was more important to my parents than academic achievement (I was a dis-appointment). I became a social worker, a seemingly agreeable career for a woman, and dutifully married a man from a good family with promis-

Birth

I huddle around my pain
  you
could not love me enough
  to help me
with this long labor
your understanding
was removed from you
  at your birth
  as your foreskin
  was removed
    only women
  can be my midwives
accompanying me
  in this endless
    tearing
      agony
        of aloneness
their hands
  touching me
  from the depths
  of their understanding
    supporting
    supplying the strength
    I need
  when my own strength
    is frayed
    and rent
    like a garment
    worn overlong
encircle me
  my sisters
surround me
  and sustain me
in this everlasting birth

as I expand
and contract
  my bones grind together
  my insides
    are torn
      downward
      outward
  huddling over my pain
  learning to move with it
    until
  it is coming
  it is coming
    into the light
  a beginning
a beginning
  this birth of myself
    my body
    shall rejoice
    in its soon to be
    lightness
  a beginning
  a beginning
    of joy
    of self realization
    of affirmation
  clench my hand
    it hurts so
    it hurt so
  I feel its coming
    there is hope
    in my pain

—Jaci (1939–1980)[2]

ing career prospects. While working toward a Ph.D., I noticed that women students were marginalized and that there were no ranked women faculty in the department, but I only tacitly questioned the "natural" order of things. I was more concerned with more "important" issues, such as social justice, civil rights, and world peace.

My divorce came just as the second wave of feminism was gaining national prominence in the United States. Alone with my son, I discovered the practical difficulties of being a female-headed household in a society set up for and administered by men. Questioning all my childhood assumptions, I began to recognize the ways patriarchy and its values were at the root of all my previous concerns. In the early days I felt that women and feminism had the power to change the world with our all-inclusive vision of sisterhood and the enthusiasm of a young and vital movement. We would create a new, life-affirming world order based on acceptance, equality, and liberation for all.

The feminist vision in the United States began to crumble under the pressure to ratify the ERA. It was politically expedient to exclude lesbians from the movement and to focus on gaining privilege for just white middle-class women. Political disappointments generated anger without any clear direction for action. In frustration, women turned on each other, negatively judging those who were perceived as different. The movement fragmented and we lost our vision.

I have always been criticized for not doing feminism right. Liberal feminists consider me too radical, while radical feminists see me as an apologist for patriarchy. I am not theoretical enough for the academic elite, not political enough for NOW, not pure enough for the separatists, and too middle-class for urban organizers. I am criticized for suggesting that men could have a real role to play in feminism. Friends tell me they are not interested in men and unwilling to invest any energy in their issues. They feel that if men are sincere about challenging patriarchy, let them change men and leave women alone.

Clearly a new world order requires both a broad-based recognition of the ways patriarchal values are destructive to women and men and basic changes in our ways of being in the world. There is not one true feminist path, but a multitude of paths that can be adapted to fit the diverse needs of many people. Although it is much less threatening to restrict men's involvement in feminist issues to the men's movement, the truth is that significant change will occur only when women and men work together toward a shared vision. Feminist "fundamentalism" and exclusivity prevent the formation of a critical mass that is necessary for wide-scale social change.

In beginning work on this chapter, convinced men could never be true feminists, I felt overwhelmed by the impossibility of the task. Intellectually I recognized the need to work cooperatively with men, but my previous experiences had taught me to proceed with caution. Such relationships are seldom based on equal power. Either women participate in male-dominated efforts and risk having their efforts co-opted, or occasionally men are accepted into women's space as "honorary women." Our early discussions were often chaotic; I lurched between aggressive confrontation and passivity. It was difficult to trust a feminist man, to be open to the unique perspectives and contributions he could add, not by ignoring gender differences, but precisely because he was a man.

Constructing a feminist bridge between women and men at the personal level requires new ways of relationally doing things so that there can be different experiences and outcomes. Perhaps Steve and I have taken only a few tentative steps into the uncharted wilderness of gender equality, done with the hope that it may create new openings for others, but the work must begin if we are to save ourselves and the planet. Instead of always gathering in gender-exclusive groups, like those discussed below, women and men must combine their energies and create new paths in the pursuit of a shared feminist vision.

The Men's Movement: Dead Ends and Circumscribed Pathways

A basic problem with this approach, and with the mythopoetic men's movement as a whole, is that it moves within the aura of that guiding principle of patriarchy: that male nature characterizes full humanity, that men are central, the core around which all others revolve. . . . Within this worldview, the problems and pain of women are infinitely less interesting, less compelling, less urgent, than those of men.
—Kathleen Carlin, "The Men's Movement of Choice"

Whether it be in the all too familiar exclusive male bonding groups where men can get together to discuss their hopes and personal troubles with the explicit goal of trying to recapture their somehow lost masculinity, or men's studies research that demonstrates that patriarchy is bad for men too, women are marginalized at best, and at a misogynist extreme, sometimes blamed for men's problems. For men who strive to gain insights into how as a society and individually they must change to bring about a feminist transformation that negates gender and other inequalities, the men's movement is what they are almost always offered. This route has been touted not only by men themselves, but also by feminist women. The problem with men pursuing this avenue to gain a feminist understanding is that it presents severe limitations to such an end, and some of the paths in the larger men's movement promote just the opposite: explicit misogyny.

While admittedly, categorizing the men's movement into two distinct groups gives a simplistic picture of a complex array of many different men's groups, we have done this for two specific reasons. First, most of the recent literature on the men's movement loosely uses these same two categorizations (Friedman and Sarah 1982; Kimmel 1987a; Hearn and Morgan 1990; Faludi 1991; Hagan 1992; Ramazanoglu 1992; Kimmel and Messner 1995). Second, in recent years these two groups have exceedingly received more and more academic and media attention. As such, these are not only the most popular contemporary men's groups in the United States, but also the most powerful.

Iron Johns: Dead Ends

> But it is not really difference the oppressor fears so much as similarity. He fears he will discover in himself the same aches, the same longings as those people he has shitted on . . . the immobilization threatened by his own incipient guilt . . . the hatred, anger, and vengeance of those he has hurt. He fears he will have to change his life once he has seen himself in the bodies of people he has called different.
>
> —Cherrie Moraga, "La Güera"

Susan Faludi (1991, 307) rightly identifies Robert Bly (1990) and his scores of imitators as a cottage industry that sprang up to support the larger backlash against women in the 1980s. To support this assertion she describes Bly and his followers' rhetoric and activities as a strict separatist movement where "soft men" can become "wild men" and reject all that is female to shore their weakened masculinities. As she further notes (310), the true subject of Bly and his followers' propaganda "is not about love and sex, but power—how to wrest it from women and how to mobilize it for men."

Every other account of Bly's mythopoetic men's movement we have read by feminists reaches almost identical conclusions (see, once again, Hagan's 1992 anthology). At best, we would hold that Bly and similar groups appear to be nothing more than a reactionary stance against women's perceived gains in status and power that is essentially based in fear. Utilizing a zero-sum outlook, these groups simplistically equate women's advancements with their loss. Through separatism, male bonding, and wild man rituals, Bly and his imitators are nothing more than a misogynist fraternal order of men who are attempting to recapture their perceived lost masculinity and the power that traditionally accompanies men as socially constructed beings.

Then again, there is nothing new about exclusionary male bonding groups that are created whenever masculinity is perceived as being threatened. The Boy Scouts in the United States, rugby football and many other organized sporting events, and an array of other male bonding groups were created and have become more popular during periods when masculinity was perceived to be in decline (Sheard and Dunning 1973; Dunning and Sheard 1979; Donnelly and Young 1985; White and Vagi 1990; Hantover 1992; Schacht 1996). As such, Bly, his followers, and other similar reactionary groups fail to offer any meaningful paths to men who hope to gain a feminist consciousness. In reality, the stance they often take is quite contrary to such an outlook and has the distinct potential to undermine the limited feminist gains that have been realized.

Men's Studies: Circumscribed Pathways

Why, when all experience suggests that men as men enjoy real advantages from the oppression of women, do they work so hard to support the claim that men merely *mediate* capitalist oppression?
—Diana Leonard, "Male Feminists and Divided Women"

Harry Brod (1987, 264), a prominent figure in men's studies, has stated, "the subject matter of men's studies is the study of masculinities and male experiences in their own right as specific and varying social, cultural, and historical formations." He goes on in this article to note that the male sex roles that patriarchy constructs often are very destructive for men. In fact, the majority of research undertaken by those in men's studies reaches just this conclusion: patriarchy is bad for men too (the following anthologies from the men's studies perspective in the United States largely give this impression: Kimmel 1987b; Kimmel and Messner 1995; Messner and Sabo 1990). In other words, what he and numerous others are saying is that yes, patriarchy is bad for women, but of equal importance is the "fact" that such a structural arrangement is also bad for men.

The problem with the present men's studies emphasis, thinly veiled in feminist theory, is that the focus is almost exclusively on men and their problems, and women are marginalized and ignored, as they are in larger patriarchal realities. At best, most of the research undertaken by those in men's studies treats images of femininity as secondary variables, while in even more extreme cases, men's oppressive experiences with patriarchy are analyzed in terms that marginalize women to the point that they are rendered almost invisible (Leonard 1982; Stanley 1982; Canaan and Griffin 1990; Ramazanoglu 1992). Quite simply, one is often left with the feeling that "as long as *any male, anywhere* is suffering, women are selfish to mention that they are suffering, too" (Johnson 1987, 258; emphasis in original).

While in all likelihood, most men in this movement do not consciously intend such an androcentric emphasis, their focus does obscure most of the basic insights of feminist theory and methodology (Roberts 1990; Fonow and Cook 1991; Reinharz 1992; Stanley and Wise 1993). Such an emphasis has also allowed those in men's studies to diffuse the responsibility for oppressive men's behavior and ignore what feminism calls for: a *personal* and *political* transformation of gender relations. That is, as long as the problem of gender inequality is viewed as entirely structural, which often is the impression given by those in men's studies, then the personal behaviors of individual men need not change. Or as Stanley (1982) states,

> Most revolutionary analyses are "structural" ones. They [gay and other men] see oppression as lying outside the behaviors and relationships of everyday life, and so outside of and beyond their responsibility. Such analysis suggests that "the revolution", if it ever comes, will come from outside the activities of ordinary people. . . . When the revolution occurs then everything will be changed. We don't have to change our lives—that has nothing to do with the revolution. (208)

Further, since some men are being oppressed by a patriarchal structure, then their individual and categorical oppression of women is somehow negated and not seen as important, not men's responsibility, and certainly not as terrible as women are telling them it is.

If those in men's studies truly took to heart what most feminist theory proposes—something they purport to center their analyses around (Brod 1987; Kimmel 1987a)—the picture they paint of men and masculinity would be entirely different. For while *some* men do experience oppression in patriarchy, all women experience oppression in some form, and *most*— if not all—men derive benefits from women's oppression. After all, being able to individually and categorically oppress women is why many men put up with their own oppression.

What those in men's studies appear to be most vehemently protesting is that some oppressed and failed men (not to be confused with men who are actively trying to reject being men and the privileges associated with such status) are not receiving the same amount of goodies more successful men do in patriarchy. As such, men's studies is another fraternal brotherhood of sorts—a safe haven for men to advocate men's issues, where the "collective noun *men* as an eternal theme" is passed around among men like an Olympic torch, without recognition of the "interactional, relational, and transitive" role the collective noun *women* plays in its construction (Stoltenberg 1996, 9–10). Perhaps this explains why, to our knowledge, there are no women actively involved in men's studies or, as ridiculous as it may sound, in the larger men's movement in the United States.

Yes, truly feminist studies of men have and should be undertaken (for excellent examples of such studies, see Stoltenberg 1990, 1994; Connell 1995). Even some of the investigations undertaken by those in men's studies have been fairly feminist in orientation (Kimmel and Mosmiller 1992; Hearn and Morgan 1990). However, these rare feminist studies on men by men and the numerous ones undertaken by feminist women are differentiated from most of the research being produced by those in men's studies in the following two ways: (1) the vast majority of research produced by those in men's studies lacks a truly critical focus on men and masculinity in terms of how men's roles and behaviors are relationally oppressive to women, regardless of whether men are oppressed themselves; and relatedly (2) those in men's studies need to recognize that individual men, not just the system, are ultimately responsible for the oppression of women and other men.

If the men in men's studies were actually interested in having a feminist orientation in their research, they would have to depart "from that androcentric, homosocial world where men talk to men about men and come up with some variation of the old solutions that maintain male centrality and dominance," and replace it with an orientation that relates "to women as peers whose basic worth and way of being in the world are recognized as fully as men's." Additionally they would have to "giv[e] up all forms of controlling and abusive behaviors and [learn] new skills with which to negotiate the intricate, demanding transition that lies ahead" (Carlin 1992, 122–23). In other words, for there to be a transformation in gender relations, both the structure and individuals must change. Until those in men's studies are willing "to put their money and power where their mouths are and put money into feminist projects, and to use their power to discriminate positively in favour of women," men's studies will offer little for men who hope to gain a truly feminist understanding and being (Bradshaw 1982, 188).

In sum, while those in men's studies have been successful in establishing academic credibility for their approach and have without question increased our understanding of masculinity as a social construct, the pathway they are presently traveling is far too narrow and circumscribed for men who are ultimately trying to construct and live feminist worldviews.

Experiential Models of Feminism and Their Limitations for Men

In the past twenty-five years numerous authors have proposed various definitions of feminism. While there often are ideological disagreements over exactly what a feminist should stand for, there appears to be some general agreement over how a woman typically becomes a feminist. This consensus seems to revolve around two interrelated themes: (1) similar to Simone de Beauvoir (1953) and other early feminist writers who observed that one is not born a woman, but rather, society creates women, contemporary feminists hold that one is not born a feminist, but rather becomes one; and (2) becoming and being a feminist involves a transformative process that is experientially grounded (Morgan 1978; Johnson 1987; Stanley and Wise 1979; Bartky 1990; Collins 1991; Steinem 1992). Experientially, this means that women begin to become "aware of an alien and hostile force outside of oneself which is responsible for the blatantly unjust treatment of women" (Bartky 1990, 15) and correspondingly realize "that women share a status as members of a subordinate group" (Riger 1994, 275). This transformational process is also seen as entailing a "self-conscious struggle . . . to develop new interpretations of familiar realities

...in order to reject patriarchal perceptions of women and to value women's ideas and actions" (Collins 1991, 27).

Since men cannot experience women's oppression, and it is men exercising their tyrannical authority who are largely responsible for this hegemonic reality, many women and men categorically reject the present possibility of men becoming feminists. Some reject the possibility of men becoming feminist because of personal experiences with so-called feminist men who have turned out to be just the opposite: phallocentric misogynists (Stanley and Wise 1979; Bradshaw 1982; Leonard 1982; Stanley 1982; Showalter 1987). Other women reject the possibility that men can be feminist on the grounds that they do not experience the world as women do (Daly 1973; Jardine and Smith 1987). As Bart et al. (1991, 191) state, "we believe that one must inhabit a female body to have the experiences that make one feminist."[3] Both of these positions are summarized in the following quotes; the first is by a founding member of the current women's movement in the United States, while the second is by a male author:

> I haven't the faintest notion what possible role white heterosexual men could fulfill, since they are the very embodiment of reactionary-vested-interest-power. (Morgan 1970, xxxv)

> Men's relation to feminism is an impossible one. This is not said sadly nor angrily (though sadness and anger are both known and common reactions) but politically. (Heath 1987, 1)

To categorically state that men cannot be feminist, however, is an essentialist argument; such a position also falls into a trap set up by patriarchy itself (Johnson 1987, 282, 304). That is, the reality that patriarchy tries so hard to "ontologically" imprint into each of our brains is that we live in a dichotomous, binary world: knowledge/ignorance, light/darkness, good/evil, love/hate, male/female, and so forth (Hekman 1987; Haraway 1988; Hawkesworth 1989, 539–40; Davies 1990, 510–11; Delphy 1993). Moreover, as Hawkesworth (1989, 544–45) notes, the position that only "women will produce an accurate depiction of reality, either because they are women or because they are oppressed, appears highly implausible," and "adhere[s] to the great illusion that there is one position in the world or one orientation toward the world that can eradicate all confusion, conflict, and contradiction." Since ultimately all perspectives and knowledges are partial and situated (Haraway 1988), a full understanding of oppression requires that we recognize these multiple realities, each valid from the perspective of those having the experiences. Or as Walker asserts with equal insightfulness, "I believe that the truth about any subject only comes when all sides of the story are put together, and all their different meanings make one new one. Each writer writes the missing parts to the other writer's story. And the whole story is what I'm after" (1983, 49).

As a result, like most feminists who reject such a dichotomous worldview, we too reject such a stance and conclude that it is equally not applicable to whether a man can or cannot be a feminist. Thus, while we recognize that men do not experience the oppression that women do, the question then becomes for us, and hopefully others, what pathways might men travel to become truly feminist? That is the issue the rest of this chapter addresses. In doing so, we hope to "not let the danger of the journey and vastness of the territory scare us—let's look forward and open paths in these woods" (Anzaldúa 1983, v).

Pathways for Men to Become Feminist

Women's feminist consciousness is seen as ultimately being grounded in experiences of oppression because they are female, and these experiences are not available to men; therefore, if men are ever to gain a meaningful feminist understanding they will have to travel a new and different path. This is not to say that just because men do not socially experience the world as women do, the paths they might travel to gain a feminist understanding will be less difficult. Our own experiences tell us just the opposite: any meaningful path a man pursues in gaining a feminist consciousness is strewn with roadblocks. What it does mean, however, is that men who aspire to gain a feminist worldview have *no choice but to travel a different path* than women. If men look to feminist women and feminist writings to inform and guide their journey—looking both at women's experiences of oppression and their own and other men's behaviors that cause and support its occurrence—we strongly believe that men will finally begin to meaningfully support their feminist sisters' efforts to emancipate all people.

To this end, we propose that there are four basic principles a man should consider addressing and acting on if he hopes to gain a feminist consciousness: (1) through reading feminist works and *actually listening to women*, he should try to learn about the depth and unjust nature of women's oppression; (2) he should consider asking himself in what ways he personally, and as a man in general (structurally), oppresses women; (3) he should consider ways to reject traditional notions of masculinity that are oppressive to others and replace them with women and feminism as his referent; and in sum (4) he should consider ways to put women's needs as equal to or even greater than his own. These matters that a man should attend to in gaining a feminist consciousness are not seen as necessarily incremental steps, mutually exclusive, or exhaustive; however, in total, they are proposed as some necessary beginnings. Note also should be made that, depending on a given man's ethnicity, race, social class, and sexual orientation, these proposed principles have potentially different meanings and applications. Finally, we would hold that, notwithstanding the direct experiential underpinning for women gaining a feminist consciousness, these principles are quite consistent with a reality that women have seen as feminist (Morgan 1978; Johnson 1987; Stanley and Wise 1979; Bartky 1990; Steinem 1992).

Men who are willing to address all four of these preliminary principles will potentially find themselves cast into a salient new role within the larger feminist movement: a bridge. Feminist women of color have assumed this bridge role in educating their white middle-class sisters of the additional ways they experience oppression, often at the hands of their white sisters (hooks 1981, 1989; Moraga and Anzaldúa 1983; Baca Zinn et al. 1986; Collins 1989). A truly feminist-oriented man can perform four important functions when he assumes a bridge role: (1) he can educate other men and build a strong foundation for feminist social change among them; (2) he can gain access to settings where women are excluded, and utilizing a feminist lens, explore and expose these settings to a larger feminist audience (Schacht 1997, 3); (3) he can serve as a bridge to the established power structures translating feminist agendas to the "good old boys"; and overall, (4) he can provide an important linkage between feminist women and men.

Fear of co-optation and far too many experiences with self-serving men who steal key insights from feminism but give nothing in return have rightly led many feminist women to conclude that men can add little, if anything, to a feminist reality. Clearly, however, the kinds of far-reaching social change envisioned by feminist goals cannot be accomplished without the active support and participation of men. Men who truly have a feminist consciousness can serve as a bridge of understanding between genders separated by tradition for thousands of years. This is the promise truly feminist men hold: an important addition to the larger reality that is presently being constructed. The role of a bridge is both explicitly and implicitly found in each of the following principles of a male feminist consciousness.

Learning the Depth of Women's Oppression

Men can learn about the depth of women's oppression and its unjust nature from two basic sources: (1) a wide array of written feminist works, and (2) feminist women and women in general. Considering the number of feminist-oriented books, anthologies, and periodicals published in the past twenty years, a man will find a nearly inexhaustible array of academic and nonacademic sources to address almost any interest he might have. For men in academia, taking a women's studies course (if one is offered on his campus) or, at the very least, getting a list of readings from those who teach such courses might be an excellent start at becoming sensitive to some of the basic issues feminism explores. For men outside academia, a visit to nearly any bookstore or library will provide a wide array of contemporary feminist works.

Of equal importance for a man who hopes to gain any sort of feminist understanding is learning, perhaps for the first time in his life, how to listen to women. Men are socialized to control and dominate discussions with women (Thorne et al. 1983). Not only is this a personally sexist behavior, but it also severely undermines any possibility of men learning anything from women. If a man truly wants to learn of women's experiences with oppression, quite simply, he should learn ways not to interrupt others when they are speaking and *really try to listen* to what is being said.

We would also suggest that unless asked, he should suspend any advice or judgmental attitudes he might have, and instead try to be understanding and supportive of what is being shared with him. This is not to say that he should not have opinions or share them with others. What it does mean is that he should adopt a critical stance that is supportive and constructive instead of the traditional "one-upmanship": I will get my point across at whatever cost. Ultimately, this new knowledge should lead men to question additional ways they oppress women (and other men).

Questioning the Ways Men Oppress Women

In what ways do I exploit women, put them down, ignore them? And then move from there to find new understanding, new ways to behave.

—Harriet Gill, "Men's Predicament"

While there are untold ways men oppress women, perhaps one of the most basic, rudimentary methods is at the interpersonal level through sexuality. Numerous feminists have examined the way heterosexuality as an ideological practice is used to dominate and control women (Brownmiller 1975; MacKinnon 1982, 1983; Dworkin 1987, 1989; Wilkinson and Kitzinger 1993). Whether it be in the more blatant forms of rape, incest, sexual harassment, prostitution, and the presentations of these found in pornography or in so-called consensual sex, heterosexuality is largely a tool used by men to dominate and control women in all settings (Schacht and Atchison 1993).

Perhaps the bedrock of this ideological practice is the social process of objectification. Or as Andrea Dworkin states, "male supremacy depends on the ability of men to view women as sexual objects" (1989, 113). From a very early age, men in our society are taught to relationally think of themselves as subjects and women (and other perceived lesser beings) as objects and, therefore, not quite human. Expressed through heterosexuality, objectification provides all men with an instrumental practice whereby they can differentiate themselves from "others" so that they can ultimately feel relationally superior to some*thing:* all women.

Recognizing this most fundamental insight begs the obvious question for men who hope to construct and live a feminist reality. Quite simply, men who are trying to break from patriarchy should explore and try to learn new ways of viewing women and men that do not involve sexual objectification. Since one can only rape, sexually harass, or exploit an object, viewing and treating women as real people (subjects) diminishes, if not completely eliminates, men's predisposition to oppress women. Moreover, if men were to start to view all people as subjects, then the whole construct of oppression, in the numerous ways it manifests itself (Young 1988; Bartky 1990), would truly become contested and subject to elimination.

While ending gender oppression may seem like an insurmountable task, there is yet one other context where many women are relatedly oppressed that feminist men can easily question and personally change: the home. Although today most women are employed outside the home, they are still largely responsible for most of the housework and child care. This "second shift" means that the average woman works fifteen hours longer each week than a man (over a year's period this equals an extra month's worth of twenty-four-hour days) and that there is a considerable difference in the leisure time available to men and women (Hochschild

1990). Moreover, since women are also largely responsible for the emotional upbringing of children, by parental example, young women and men through primary socialization learn to expect and accept oppressive gender roles from the onset of their birth.

There are obvious things that all feminist men can do to traverse this oppressive reality found in far too many contemporary homes. To begin with, instead of "helping" with the household chores and child care responsibilities, men should learn how to *equally* share in completing these tasks. To this end, the following are basic questions a man might ask himself: Who primarily does the dishes or scrubs the toilet? Who primarily does the grocery shopping and the laundry? Who is primarily responsible for changing the diapers on an infant or the feeding and bathing of the children? Who primarily attends to the children when they are in need of comfort, support, or a ride to an activity they are involved in? While this is far from an exhaustive list of questions a feminist man might ask himself concerning housework and child care, we would guess that many such men might not like the answers given if they were to truthfully respond to such questions.

Overall, men need to learn how to appreciate and value household labor and child care. Contemporary society pays homage almost exclusively to masculine values and behaviors while at the same time it largely denigrates and belittles the values and behaviors traditionally associated with women. Feminist men, in general, must try to change this orientation.

Replacing Masculinity with Women and Feminism

Men who resist masculine dominance cannot become women, they become failed men and betrayers of masculinity.
— Caroline Ramazanoglu, "What Can You Do with a Man?"

While it is true that men who reject traditional notions of masculinity are betrayers of such an ideology and they cannot become women, such men are anything but failures. If one agrees with Stoltenberg's (1990, 185) assertion that "the belief that one is male, the belief that there is a male sex, the belief that one belongs to it is a politically constructed idea," then rejecting such a position is also a political statement. In other words, while men who betray masculinity are seen as failures in the eyes of patriarchy and its destructive tendency, they would be successful survivors in a life-affirming reality of feminism. Or, as more elegantly stated by Carlin,

Exposing the monster's false power, thus breaking the spell, happens when a man dares to enter the realm of women's reality. A man breaks rank with other men when they make women's reality their referent. All the power of the social order gathers itself to prevent his going there. . . . Where he is going, he risks being regarded with suspicion, of not being readily accepted, because of what he has left. . . . He understands that to save himself means not grasping patriarchy closer, but letting it die—even the part of it that resides within himself. (1992, 124)

Men who truly aspire to have a feminist worldview should not view such a commitment as a part-time activity, to be undertaken when it is convenient or to their advantage. Rather, to become truly committed to a feminist reality means that a man should try to act accordingly in *every* possible setting he finds himself in. Moreover, as Sonia Johnson notes, we believe such a feminist orientation is found in the present, not the future.

When we envision the future without first changing our present feelings, without undoing our indoctrination, we project all our unexamined assumptions into the future, recreating the old reality, making it inevitable. Anything we try to do without grounding ourselves in new and powerful present feelings and perceptions will be compromised from the onset, hopelessly contaminated, simple tinkering at best, perilously complicit at worst. . . . This means that our feelings about ourselves *in the present moment* are the sole source of change, and that they are therefore our only source of power. (1987, 305–6; emphasis in original)

In sum, individually giving up male privilege and replacing it with women and feminism means that men will have to discover new ways of relating to and interacting with women in the present. With women and feminism as his referent, he should always try to "discriminate positively in favour of women" (Bradshaw 1982, 188).

Putting Women's Needs as Equal to or Greater Than One's Own

Discovering himself to be an oppressor may cause considerable anguish, but it does not necessarily lead to solidarity with the oppressed. Rationalizing his guilt through paternalistic treatment of the oppressed, all while holding them fast in the position of dependence, will not do. Solidarity requires that one enter into the situation of those with whom one is in solidarity; it is a radical posture. True solidarity with the oppressed means fighting at their side to transform the objective reality.

—Paolo Friere, *Pedagogy of the Oppressed*

Part of putting women's needs as equal to or greater than one's own entails recognizing that women should have the same rights that, to varying degrees, have always been granted most men in patriarchal societies. The foremost of these is the inalienable "right to physical privacy... essential to personal freedom and self-determination" (Dworkin 1987, 102). Beyond respecting women's right to physical privacy, this also means that men should learn how to respect and honor women's need for a "room of their own." That is, not only should individual women be able to control their own personal space, but men should also recognize women's need for "a room" with other women.

Thus, since a truly cooperative relationship between men and women requires men to give up male power and privilege, men should always wait for an explicit invitation before entering women's space. Once there, men should tread softly and act like they are a guest in someone else's house. This may be quite difficult for many men who are used to being homeowners and arranging the furniture how they please. Feminists will look more at what a man does than what he says: how he treats women at work, at home, and in his personal relationships. Extensive knowledge of feminist theory will not erase a personal style of dominance and control. While in the short run this may mean some small measure of loneliness for feminist men, in the long run it potentially means an invitation on terms that are agreeable to all parties.

Ultimately, men should ask themselves what they can *add*. What insights from a man's feminist perspective can he offer to support and strengthen the activities taking place in a given setting? If there appears to be nothing he can contribute or if it seems that his presence will be disruptive, he should graciously decline the invitation. We believe these rudimentary principles for participation in feminist settings should be considered by all men who hope to assist in the creation of larger feminist realities.

Following these preliminary principles and listening to other feminists for further insights (in the *present* and the *future*), men will find themselves assisting feminist women (and men) in a struggle that not only continues to alter others' reality but theirs with it; men "must be transformers of selfhood—our own and others' " (Stoltenberg 1990, 198).

Moving beyond Patriarchal Boundaries

> Rolling, and pushing out the boundaries, beginning to explore our deeper
> mind where we know so much more than we know we know, so much
> that we never get to consider because we're always staying on the surface
> explaining the same ideas over and over.
> — Sonia Johnson, *Going Out of Our Minds*

Some who read this essay may still insist that a man cannot become a
feminist. This position is based on the same male-female dichotomy that
underlies patriarchy, and it sets up boundaries that men need not go
beyond, excuses men from gaining any sort of feminist understanding,
and spares them from having to change anything in their personal lives.
We believe that the time has come to reject this artificial boundary and
move beyond it. The path we have tentatively outlined in this essay is not
well worn or known to many men, but it is something beckoning, "something real and urgent. Another way, another path, another door. A door
patriarchy says isn't there; *insists* isn't there, which is evidence of its existence. That which doesn't exist doesn't have to be denied" (Johnson 1987,
49; emphasis in original). Although the pathways men have to travel to
exit patriarchy into a new feminist reality have many unknown obstruc-
tions and dead-end forks, we have attempted to delineate some preliminary trailheads, landmarks, and milestones that may be found on this
journey.

While women and men, people of color, people residing in third world
countries, and so forth all have to travel disparate paths in realizing a
feminist reality, our differences are also "that raw and powerful connection from which personal power is forged" (Lorde 1983, 99) and new
realities are constructed. Thus, on our different journeys toward a feminist world, if this reality is to ever exist, we must forge new connections
between autonomous people, regardless of their gender, race, sexual orientation, or other socially constructed categorizations. We believe that
then, and only then, can we truly start to live, instead of slowly dying in
a patriarchal reality.

REFERENCES

Anzaldúa, G. 1983. Foreword to the second edition. In C. Moraga & G. Anzaldúa, eds., *This Bridge Called My Back: Writings by Radical Women of Color*, iv-v. New York: Kitchen Table: Women of Color Press.

Baca Zinn, M., L. W. Cannon, E. Higginbotham, and B. T. Dill. 1986. The Costs of Exclusionary Practices in Women's Studies. *Signs: Journal of Women in Culture* 11:290–303.

Bart, F. B., L. M. Freeman, and P. Kimball. 1991. The Different Worlds of Women and Men: Attitudes toward Pornography and Responses to Not a Love Story— a Film about Pornography. In M. Fonow and J. A. Cook, eds., *Beyond methodology: Feminist Scholarship as Lived Research*, 171–96. Bloomington: Indiana University Press.

Bartky, S. L. 1990. *Femininity and Domination: Studies in the Phenomenology of Oppression*. New York: Routledge.

Beauvoir, S. de 1953. *The Second Sex*. Middlesex, England: Penguin.

Bly, R. 1990. *Iron John: A book about Men*. Reading, MA: Addison-Wesley.

Bradshaw, J. 1982. Now What Are They Up To? Men in the 'Men's Movement'! In S. Friedman and E. Sarah, eds., *On the Problem of Men: Two Feminist Conferences*, 174–89. London: Women's Press.

Brod, H. 1987. Toward Men's Studies: A Case for Men's Studies. In M. S. Kimmel, ed., *Changing Men: New Directions in Research on Men and Masculinity*, 263–77. Newbury Park: Sage.

Brownmiller, S. 1975. *Against Our Will: Men, Women and Rape*. New York: Bantam Books.

Canaan, J. E., and C. Griffin. 1990. The New Men's Studies: Part of the Problem or Part of the Solution? In J. Hearn and D. Morgan, eds., *Men, Masculinities, and Social Theory*, 206–14. London: Unwin Hyman.

Carlin, K. 1992. The Men's Movement of Choice. In K. L. Hagan, ed., *Women Respond to the Men's Movement: A Feminist Collection*, 119–25. San Francisco: Pandora.

Collins, P. H. 1989. The Social Construction of Black Feminist Thought. *Signs: Journal of Women in Culture and Society*. 14:745–72.

———. 1991. *Black Feminist Thought: Knowledge, Consciousness, and the Politics of Empowerment*. New York: Routledge.

Connell, R. W. 1995. *Masculinities*. Berkeley: University of California Press.

Daly, M. 1973. *Beyond God the Father: Toward a Philosophy of Women's Liberation*. Boston: Beacon Press.

Davies, B. 1990. The Problem of Desire. *Social Problems* 37:501–16.

Delphy, C. 1993. Rethinking Sex and Gender. *Women's Studies International Forum*. 16:1–9.

Dinnerstein, D. 1991/1976. *The Mermaid and the Minotaur: Sexual Arrangements and Human Malaise.* New York: Harper Perennial.

Donnelly, P., and K. M. Young. 1985. The Reproduction and Transformation of Cultural Forms in Sport: A Contextual Analysis of Rugby. *International Review for Sociology of Sport.* 20:19–37.

Dunning, E., and K. Sheard. 1979. *Barbarians, Gentlemen and Players: A Sociological Study of the Development of Rugby Football.* Oxford: Martin Robertson.

Dworkin, A. 1987. *Intercourse.* New York: Free Press.

———. 1989. *Pornography: Men Possessing Women.* New York: Dutton.

Eisenstein, H. 1983. *Contemporary Feminist Thought.* Boston: G. K. Hall.

Faludi, S. 1991. *Backlash: The Undeclared War against American Women.* New York: Crown.

Fonow, M. M., and J. A. Cook, eds. 1991. *Beyond Methodology: Feminist Scholarship as Lived Research.* Bloomington: Indiana University Press.

Friedman, S., and E. Sarah, eds. 1982. *On the Problem of Men: Two Feminist Conferences.* London: Women's Press.

Friere, P. 1970. *Pedagogy of the Oppressed.* Trans. M. B. Ramos. New York: Seasbury Press.

Gill, H. 1992. Men's Predicament: Male Supremacy. In K. L. Hagan, ed., *Women Respond to the Men's Movement,* 151–57. San Francisco: Pandora.

Hagan, K. L., ed. 1992. *Women Respond to the Men's Movement: A Feminist Collection.* San Francisco: Pandora.

Hantover, J. P. 1992. The Boy Scouts and the Validation of Masculinity. In M. S. Kimmel and M. Messner, eds., *Men's Lives,* 123–31. New York: Macmillan.

Haraway, D. 1988. Situated Knowledges: The Science Question in Feminism and the Privilege of Partial Perspective. *Feminist Studies* 14 (3):575–99.

Hawkesworth, M. E. 1989. Knowers, Knowing, Known: Feminist Theory and Claims of Truth. *Signs: Journal of Women and Culture* 14:533–57.

Hearn, J., and D. Morgan, eds. 1990. *Men, Masculinities, and Social Theory.* London: Unwin Hyman.

Heath, S. 1987. Male Feminism. In A. Jardine and P. Smith, eds., *Men and Feminism,* 1–32. New York: Methuen.

Hekman, S. 1987. The Feminization of Epistemology: Gender and the Social Sciences. *Women and Politics* 7:65–83.

Hochschild, A. 1990. *The Second Shift.* New York: Avon Books.

hooks, b. 1981. *Ain't I a Woman: Black Women and Feminism.* Boston: South End Press.

———. 1989. *Talking Back: Thinking Feminist/Thinking Black.* Boston: South End Press.

———. 1992. Men in Feminist Struggle: The Necessary Movement. In K. L. Hagan, ed., *Women Respond to the Men's Movement: A Feminist Collection,* 111–17. San Francisco: Pandora.

Jardine, A., and P. Smith, eds. 1987. *Men and Feminism.* New York: Methuen.

Johnson, S. 1987. *Going Out of Our Minds: The Metaphysics of Liberation.* Freedom, CA: Crossing Press.

Kimmel, M. S. 1987a. Teaching a Course on Men: Masculinist Reaction or "Gentlemen's Auxiliary"? In M. S. Kimmel, ed., *Changing Men: New Directions in Research on Men and Masculinity,* 278–94. Newbury Park: Sage.

——, ed. 1987b. *Changing Men: New Directions in Research on Men and Masculinity.* Newbury Park: Sage.

Kimmel, M. S., and M. A. Messner, eds. 1995. *Men's Lives.* 3d ed. New York: Macmillan.

Kimmel, M. S. and T. Mosmiller, eds. 1992. *Against the Tide: Pro-feminist Men in the United States, 1776–1990, a Documentary History.* Boston: Beacon Press.

Leonard, D. 1982. Male Feminists and Divided Women. In S. Friedman and E. Sarah, eds., *On the Problem of Men: Two Feminist Conferences,* 157–75. London: Women's Press.

Lorde, A. 1983. The Master's Tools Will Never Dismantle the Master's House. In C. Moraga and G. Anzaldúa, eds., *This Bridge Called My Back: Writings by Radical Women of Color,* 98–101. New York: Kitchen Table: Women of Color Press.

Mackinnon, C. A. 1982. Feminism, Marxism, Method, and the State: An Agenda for Theory. *Signs: Journal of Women in Culture and Society* 7:515–44.

——. 1983. Feminism, Marxism, Method, and the State: Toward Feminist Jurisprudence. *Signs: Journal of Women in Culture and Society* 8:635–58.

Mapstone, E. 1993. Against Separatism. In S. Wilkinson and C. Kitzinger, eds., *Heterosexuality: A Feminism and Psychology Reader,* 86–89. London: Sage.

Messner, M. A., and D. F. Sabo, eds. 1990. *Sport, Men, and the Gender Order: Critical Feminist Perspectives.* Champaign, IL: Human Kinetics Books.

Moraga, C. 1983. La Güera. In C. Moraga and G. Anzaldúa, eds., *This Bridge Called My Back: Writings by Radical Women of Color,* 27–34. New York: Kitchen Table: Women of Color Press.

Moraga, C., and G. Anzaldúa, eds. 1983. *This Bridge Called My Back: Writings by Radical Women of Color.* New York: Kitchen Table: Women of Color Press.

Morgan, R. 1970. *Sisterhood Is Powerful: An Anthology of Writings from the Women's Liberation Movement.* New York: Vintage Books.

——. 1978. *Going Too Far: The Personal Chronicle of a Feminist.* New York: Vintage Books.

Ramazanoglu, C. 1992. What Can You Do with a Man? Feminism and the Critical Appraisal of Masculinity. *Women's Studies International Forum* 15:339–50.

Reinharz, S. 1992. *Feminist Methods in Social Research.* New York: Oxford University Press.

Riger, S. 1994. Challenges of Success: Stages of Growth in Feminist Organizations. *Feminist Studies* 20:275–300.

Roberts, H. 1990. *Feminist Research.* London: Routledge.

Schacht, S. P. 1996. Misogyny on and off the "Pitch": The Gendered World of Male Rugby Players. *Gender & Society* 10:550–65.

———. 1997. Feminist Fieldwork in the Misogynist Setting of the Rugby Pitch: Temporarily Becoming a Sylph to Survive and Personally Grow. *Journal of Contemporary Ethnography,* 26:332–63.

Schacht, S. P. and P. H. Atchison. 1993. Heterosexual Instrumentalism: Past and Future Directions. In S. Wilkinson and C. Kitzinger, eds., *Heterosexuality: A Feminism and Psychology Reader,* 121–35. Newbury Park: Sage.

Sheard, K., and E. Dunning. 1973. The Rugby Football Club as a Male Preserve. *International Review of Sport Sociology* 3–4:5–21.

Showalter, E. 1987. Critical Cross-Dressing: Male Feminists and the Year of the Women. In A. Jardine and P. Smith, eds., *Men and Feminism,* 116–32. New York: Methuen.

Smith, B., and B. Smith. 1983. Across the Kitchen Table: A Sister-to-Sister Dialogue. In C. Moraga and G. Anzaldúa, eds., *This Bridge Called My Back: Writings by Radical Women of Color,* 113–27. New York: Kitchen Table: Women of Color Press.

Stanley, L. 1982. "Male Needs": The Problems and Problems of Working with Gay Men. In S. Friedman and E. Sarah, eds., *On the Problem of Men: Two Feminist Conferences,* 190–213. London: Women's Press.

Stanley, L. and S. Wise. 1979. Feminist Research, Feminist Consciousness, and Experiences of Sexism. *Women's Studies International Forum* 2:359–74.

———. 1993. *Breaking Out Again: Feminist Ontology and Epistemology.* London: Routledge.

Starhawk. 1992. A Men's Movement I Can Trust. In K. L. Hagan, ed., *Women Respond to the Men's Movement: A Feminist Collection,* 27–37. San Francisco: Pandora.

Steinem, G. 1992. *Revolution from Within: A Book of Self-Esteem.* Boston: Little, Brown.

Stoltenberg, J. 1990. *Refusing to Be a Man: Essays on Sex and Justice.* New York: Penguin.

———. 1994. *The End of Manhood: A Book for Men of Conscience.* New York: Penguin.

———. 1996. "How Power Makes Men: The Grammar of Gender Identity."

Thorne, B., C. Kramarae, and N. Henley, eds. 1983. *Language, Gender, and Society.* New York: Newbury House.

Walker, A. 1983. *In Search of Our Mothers' Gardens.* New York: Harcourt Brace Jovanovich.

White, P. G., and A. B. Vagi. 1990. Rugby in the Nineteenth-Century British Boarding-School System: A Feminist Psychoanalytic Perspective. In M. A. Messner and D. F. Sabo, eds., *Sport, Men, and the Gender Order: Critical Feminist Perspectives,* 67–78. Champaign, IL: Human Kinetics Books.
Wilkinson, S., and C. Kitzinger, eds. 1993. *Heterosexuality: A Feminism and Psychology Reader.* London: Sage.
Young, I. 1988. Five Faces of Oppression. *Philosophical Forum* 19 (4): 270–90.

NOTES

Paper presented at the annual meeting of the American Sociological Association, Washington, DC, August 19–23, 1995. We thank Michael Hill, Tim Knapp, David Morgan, Jeff Hearn, Janet McGivern, and the members of our feminist studies group: Susan Hinze Jones, Lisa Bond-Maupin, Martha Wilkerson, Lesley Champeny, Debra Emmelman, and Shahin Gerami, for their helpful comments on earlier drafts of this paper.

1. In contrast to liberal feminists, who posit equal opportunity and access to societal structures (Eisenstein 1983), I take the same view as other radical feminists that gender oppression is the root of all forms of oppression and that the life-affirming-giving-enhancing values it proposes are the only ones powerful enough to offer an alternative path to the self-destructive path of patriarchy. And although I am also a strong proponent of women establishing autonomous lesbian relationships, lesbian separatism, while a valued choice and truly a lifeline for some women, is unlikely to bring about the far-reaching social changes envisioned by feminist goals. For while this is where strong, autonomous, self-governing feminist women are born, "ultimately, we must struggle together" (Moraga and Anzaldúa 1983, 196). That is, "political separatism which emphasizes differences between people . . . [often] merely serve[s] to maintain the cultural status quo" (Mapstone 1993, 86). Further, as Barbara Smith and Beverly Smith (1983, 126) have posited, what is truly radical is to try "to make coalitions with people who are different than you," and deal "with race and sex and class and sexual identity all at one time . . . that is really radical because it has never been done before."

2. Steve's mother, the woman who planted the seed of his "everlasting feminist birth," was among many other beautiful things a lesbian, a radical feminist, an artist, and a poet.

3. Over the past few years we had, wrongly, come to the conclusion that most women feel that men cannot be feminist. While the above list of people who feel men cannot be feminist is far from complete, in actually reviewing the literature

to write this essay we have found just the opposite: most feminist women appear to feel that men could be truly feminist. Interestingly, many of the accounts that we have read that take a stance against the possibility of men being feminist are written by men (Jardine and Smith 1987).

Chapter Eight

Healing from Manhood
A Radical Meditation on the Movement from Gender Identity to Moral Identity

John Stoltenberg

As a human rights activist whose life and lifework have been enriched beyond measure by radical feminism, I have chosen to inquire, as searchingly as I know how, into the ethical meaning of manhood. Over the years I have observed, in myself and in other penised people, a vast discrepancy between two very different experiences and practices of personal identity. One of them I call moral identity (or "selfhood"), and the other I call gender identity (or "manhood"). I have come to realize that for anyone raised to be a man, at least in Western industrialized societies today, our selfhood—the fullest experience of our own and others' humanity—tends to get contradicted in practice by the behaviors and attitudes required for social maintenance of manhood. The personal identity we experience when we choose behavior in order to "be the man there"—when we choose acts that will make our "manhood" seem real— cannot possibly coexist with authentic, passionate, and integrated selfhood. Because I believe deeply that selfhood not only is a preferable mode of being but also promises a society premised on greater fairness and equality, I am committed to communicating to other penised people this revolutionary shift in how we can experience personal identity.

I understand manhood relationally, transactionally, as something one feels compelled to prove by *doing*. This is a crucial distinction, and it sets my views apart, philosophically and pragmatically, from many other formulations of the subject "feminism and men." I believe that everyone raised to be a man has to some extent been conditioned, by both bribe and trauma, into the same structural gender panic—the same fear of not seeming to be enough of a real man. So the approach I recommend is very different from those who believe that the manhood standard can somehow be revised and redeemed—"reconstructed," "reinvented," "redefined," "remythologized," "revisioned," or rewhatevered. That project is futile, I believe, for at least two reasons: (1) it is based on an inaccurate analysis of the way manhood operates ethically, and (2) it offers no meaningful hope to those at the bottom, many of whom are female, who are most subordinated and disenfranchised in the social construction of manhood.

Manhood is not static; it is not some nebulous array of qualities that one embodies merely by *being*. Nor is manhood some substance or *thing*, a metaphysical or ontological category. Manhood is instead an ethical category: it is experienced relationally and episodically according to a specific set of values in conduct.

There are many differences in the life experiences of penised people, including hierarchies based on class, race, sexuality, and physical stature, and some academics have attempted to describe these differences as varieties of "masculinities." But I believe we can understand and explain those differences more usefully by analyzing the ethics of manhood proving. Those ethics, I believe, are a constant, even as they impact variously on everyone. Viewing manhood as an ethical category makes plain—with tangible evidence from real life—the metastructure of social subordination. This transactional model of manhood takes accurate account of a given human male's experience of relative social powerlessness, *and* locates his gender identity in whatever acts of power he chooses over and against others, *and* explains the interconnection. The transactional model of manhood is thus a unified theory. Pointing toward interpersonal and social justice, the practical possibility of our healing from manhood is also a revolutionary vision.

Both selfhood and manhood are relational and ethical constructs, but experientially they are different identities because the ethics by which they are realized are profoundly different. The ethics of manhood proving— the values in the conduct by which manhood is made to seem socially and subjectively "real"—are in complete contrast to the ethics of affirming one's own and another's selfhood—the values in the conduct by which justice occurs interhumanly and socially. In order to discover the transcendent potential of selfhood, and in order to heal from manhood, we must understand exactly what the ethics of manhood proving are.

As a society we sort out kids who are born with penises and we raise them to have a lifelong panic about experiencing subjectively the feeling of being a real-enough man. But manhood as a personal identity belief— as a subjectivity—cannot occur except fleetingly through a relational act.

We construct the meaning of manhood socially and politically through our acts; it does not derive from our anatomy. The difference people perceive between "the sexes" derives mainly from social and political dominance, expressed interpersonally in an ethic that must put someone down so that someone else can be "the man there."

The problem of how to be "a real-enough man" has no solution compatible with justice. The more important problem, actually, is how to become one's own best self. And this cannot happen if one is striving to prove manhood. Whenever any human tries to act like a real-enough man, his action must have negating consequences for someone else or else the act doesn't work.

All of us have been treated or regarded as "less real" by *someone* who has been struggling to prove manhood. Now and then, of course, some of us have also treated or regarded others as less real in our struggle to be the man there.

To heal from manhood, we must learn to love justice.

Our humanity—our authentic selfhood—can be honored and understood only through loving justice. And I define loving justice this way: an act of intense desire for, and attraction toward, fairness, also: that quality of fairness which exhibits love as well.

The tricky thing is that one cannot love justice and love manhood at the same time. In my book *The End of Manhood,* I advocate amplifying ("turning up the volume on") one's sense of oneself as a moral choice maker, as someone who tries to find the most just thing to do circumstantially. A consequence of making that commitment, I believe, is that over time one pays less and less attention to whether what one is doing is the "man" thing to do. Because choosing selfhood means choosing an ethic of loving justice over an ethic of loving manhood, its expression is not so much a rejection (of the social gender into which one has been cast) as an affirmation (of a preferable mode of ethical relating, out of a preferable sense of self). For anyone raised to be a man, this is a profound and radical relocating of identity. I sum it up mnemonically in the epigraph to *The End of Manhood:* "The core of one's being must love justice more than manhood."

My heretical hope is that as more male human beings understand the fundamental dichotomy between manhood and selfhood, and learn in our everyday relationships to apply the practical lessons of that insight, there will be among us all more and more loving justice, and more and more of us will say "I" and "you" as if we each are equally real.

All humans who grow up to be a man are raised to pass tests of loyalty to manhood. These tests can be routine or episodically treacherous. Anyone who has been raised to be a man will recall this happening when you are confronted by another man who intimidates or scares you.

In the moment of the confrontation—when another man's threat rears up, when his opportunity to hurt or humiliate you becomes clear to you both—no amount of mental or physical preparedness seems to prevent your falling for the test. Naturally you wish to save your neck. But more important, you wish to pass the test of your loyalty to manhood, which another man may have impugned. At the flash point of confrontation, it is unlikely that your mind has time to reflect on the fact that this test of your loyalty to manhood also tests your *disloyalty* to selfhood.

There is a classic dramatic plot line that occurs every time two humans raised to be a man—flush with fight-or-flight fury—decide to lock horns in contest in order to pass the manhood test. This is how the drama goes when there is a duel at downstage center and you are a featured player in it. When you and another man are in combat defending the manhood act, there are three (and only three) possible resolutions:

1. *You lose.* He manages to humiliate you or hurt you in such a way that he comes off more manly.
2. *He loses.* You manage to hurt or humiliate him so that he will learn not to mess with you.
3. *You both agree to pick on or put down someone else.* You end up in a truce, a tacit treaty that must have a third party—someone you both agree has a relatively inferior manhood act or someone who is simply female. With (and only with) that third party for contrast, you both become comfortable enough to concede that your mutual manhood acts pass muster.

The sellout of selfhood begins here, in this truce, in the gendering ethics of this endlessly recurring drama, in this pact between would-be men trying to experience their social gender by proving their manhood to each other. Once this agreement is struck—once someone offstage has been betrayed or disparaged in order that the curtain will ring down on two former combatants taking a bow arm in arm—something has drastically altered in the moral character of each human who played out the manhood act in order to convince another player. Once the duel becomes this particular deal, once this gender bond between "men" is forged at the expense of someone else who is "less manly"—someone queerer, younger, poorer, less abled; someone of an ethnicity despised; or someone simply female—each human's loyalty to selfhood has been abandoned for the sake of loyalty to manhood.

Note that whenever manhood is on the line, its zealous aspirants do not suddenly check in for a chromosome test or bang on a drum or curl up with an epic poem. Either they fight it out or else they gang up to derogate some third party. In this sense manhood is always an ethical, not a metaphysical, category.

In all transactions whereby male humans confer "manhood" on one another, specific others must be excluded and treated as inferior. For the ethics of this "manhood act" to work effectively, there must be a point of reference who is treated unjustly (be it disparagingly or violently—it's a continuum), and the mere fact of male genitalia does not exempt one from being this point of reference over and against which certain other male humans mark their "manhood" status.

Once you start observing the dynamic that happens whenever manhood is contested, you begin to see it happening over and over again everywhere. A given human raised to be a man might sometimes enact the transaction as contestant; that same human raised to be a man might be the butt of other men's manhood-proving pact. This structural theory of manhood helps explain a lot that is not explicable if one looks only at what happens between men and women. Manhood proving happens originally between would-be men, producing widespread inequalities and hierarchies of status, and the dynamics and the consequences are all interrelated.

One obvious and blatant expression of the manhood act happens whenever men do violence against women: they are proving manhood in other men's eyes. The same structural dynamic is happening whenever men do violence (including economic, racist, and homophobic violence) against other men: they are proving manhood relationally and transactionally according to the master plot I just described. That which animates their social dominance over other male humans is the same compulsion to pass as sufficiently real exemplars of manhood. These systematic social ethics of manhood proving offer extremely low odds for escaping manhood's downside, as can be observed in the lifetime of any human male over and against whom other human males have allied on account of race, wealth, sexuality, and/or physique.

This is male bonding at its worst, of course. But if any two anatomical males are obsessed with manhood, when is their proof of it any more just, and when is their male bonding any better? The surviving fall guys may not require stitches, but the dominant ethics of manhood-proving behavior are a constant. This reiterated pattern of male bonding, writ large, also functions internationally, nation-state to nation-state. It not only conceptualizes how manhood proving fuels men's oppression of women; it also accurately theorizes how manhood proving drives groups of men's oppression of other men.

Violence proves and privileges manhood in a way that myths and sexual anatomy cannot. Derisive violence against third-party scapegoats is especially prized, because it keeps men safe from the violence of other men (at least some of the time). But disparagement that proves manhood has subtler forms as well, and the master plot's ethics are always operative: You lose. Or he loses. Or you jointly pick on or put down some other loser.

Millions of boys grow up with a life-threatening case of undiagnosed gender anxiety. If their "manhood" is ever in doubt, they must somehow rise to the challenge and *prove* it. Often the kid learns from traumatic experience: the way to prove manhood incontrovertibly is to commit some act of injustice or derogation against someone else. He knows how, because it happened to him. Every day this high-stakes gender drama is the stuff of countless schoolyard tiffs, sidewalk scuffles, and father-son feuds. Yet even when this drama is sublimated into games and team sports, coaches persist in a coarse pedagogy of humiliation. Poor performance is derided with antifemale taunts.[1] In locker rooms and practice sessions a fresh generation of young male athletes gets misogynistically shamed, rather than genuinely inspired, to excel. Little wonder so many penised humans grow up anxiously aspiring to manhood, a personal identity category that cannot withstand equality.

So long as our culture maintains its hallucination that there is such a thing as "manhood," male infants will continue to be coaxed into a lifetime of gender anxiety, trying to prove they qualify for this fiction, and injuring or humiliating someone else will remain a "defining moment" in the life of every would-be real man.

This recurring test of "manhood" has implications for the capacity of any penised human being to feel empathy. In order to stay on guard against another man's judgment on his manhood, he will have to cancel out, close down, his human capacity for empathy, since if he inadvertently feels any, feels *with* someone else, he will be disadvantaged in the next test of his loyalty to manhood: he may not be sufficiently able to distance himself from the selfhood of a third party so that he and another penised person can pass muster in each other's eyes as "real-enough men." It takes years to teach a male human infant the ethics of manhood proving— humiliations by bullies and bigger and older men, slings and arrows of derision by peers. We should not expect male humans to learn the ethics of selfhood affirming overnight, but the process will be completely different.

In my book *The End of Manhood* I explain that we teach social gender to penised kids with one culture-pervasive lesson. It can be summarized like this: "Not to be a man is to be less than nobody." I explain how fathers and other adult men, especially, pass that lesson on to sons. I chart many of the rewards and punishments that make the lesson stick. I explain what sons tend to do in order to still their fears of what other men will think of their manhood, in order to feel real by treating someone else as less real. I explain how that splits the self.

I also explain that we pass on to some lucky children what I call the lesson of selfhood, which goes like this: "To be human is to be somebody."

If you were raised to be a man, you got some proportion of the lesson of manhood along the way, perhaps burned into your brain, perhaps bruised into your body, perhaps simply because you were bribed: "Not to be a man is to be less than nobody." You probably also got some proportion of the lesson of selfhood: "To be human is to be somebody." And you've been standing astride the chasm between those two lessons ever since, teeter-tottering, flip-flopping, because the lessons are contradictory. Manhood and selfhood are dichotomous.

Either you are trying to act like a real-enough man, in a moment of choice making (and the only way you can do that is by treating or regarding someone as less real than you, so that some other manhood contestant will not think you are faking), or else you are living the lesson of selfhood, in a moment of choice making, and you are temporarily oblivious to the judgment of other men on your manhood, and that is when you discover you are never more real than when someone else is real to you.

Manhood/selfhood. Flip-flop. You cannot experience them both at the same time. And empathy automatically tilts you toward selfhood, which can only be experienced reciprocally, horizontally, human self to human self. So if you feel you had better feel real as a real-enough man, then you are simply going to have to tune out empathy. You cannot feel empathy and act like "the man." Cannot be done.

Professional healers listen to people present the pain they have felt when someone tuned out empathy with them and treated them like less than nobody. Happens all the time. And professional healers' job is to somehow help the pain go away—the pain of being treated as less than nobody—through empathy, through *feeling with*. Then and only then can healing begin.

Empathy helps someone remember the lesson of selfhood: "To be human is to be somebody." Empathy helps heal, because empathy reminds someone they are real and they matter.

Our culture is in crisis because we do not teach the ethical difference between selfhood and manhood. We do not model how to love justice more than manhood. We still believe manhood is somehow, somewhere, metaphysical—some *thing* you can be. And it is not. Manhood does not exist. It is a cultural delusion. We simply keep teaching gender anxiety. We make each other *crazy* with gender anxiety. We keep teaching conformity to social gender expectations as if that is any kind of solution. It is not. It is the problem.

Humans are no more born with manhood than they are born with anxiety about whether they have it.

As human infants born penised, some of us started out prepared to experience manhood at times and selfhood at other times.

To whatever extent we were taught the lesson of manhood, we were left with a recurrent experience of gender-anxiety waves: a tension in the chest or throat, a palpitation in the heart, a spring tension in musculature, some episodic heebie-jeebies. In effect, these anatomical hot buttons are a remnant of our autonomic reflex system with the social gender schema branded on. For anyone to "get" the meaning of manhood so as never to forget it, the lesson had to boot to a body and brain in a physical, palpable way. That is what those disconcerting gender-anxiety waves do now and then—they make you feel like attacking or ducking for cover when your abstract manhood seems in danger.

One of the reasons so many humans feel manhood like a fire in the belly is that when waves of gender anxiety strike, they seem emotionally and physically overwhelming. They play out involuntarily through your blood circulating, your breath inhaling, your nerve signaling, your muscle contracting. Just because manhood is make-believe—it has no material basis whatsoever—does not mean your body and brain cannot be tricked into responding as if manhood is as vital to your survival as is keeping your body out of the way of speeding trucks. (Not surprisingly, gender anxiety in penised people also accounts for a common sort of erection—insistent yet disconnected from any empathic reality between the penised person and anyone else.)[2] So powerfully is the lesson of manhood imprinted onto our autonomic nervous system that you can sometimes feel as if you would be utterly numb, plowed down, limp, or dead without your manhood.

The good news: Just as there is a physical, resonating reminder in us of the lesson of manhood, there is also a physical, resonating reminder in us of the lesson of selfhood.

The body's memory of human selfhood is not always easy to detect, and it does not announce its presence with the persistent hullabaloo of gender-anxiety waves. The lesson of selfhood is nevertheless resident in us. It is in us and it is between us.

People sometimes call these feel-with feelings "empathy." To me that word seems a bit puny, so I coined a new term: *moral sonority*.

Moral sonority means "feelings that are resonant with interhuman affiliation." *Moral sonority* means "feelings that are therefore communicable from one human being to another."

Moral sonority means those feelings that seem like emotional mirroring or mimesis, except they are not imitation; they are as real as your own.

Moral sonority means those feelings that seem as though a viaduct has opened between you and another, a flooding passageway for fluent emotion exchange, or as though you and another have suddenly grown a common skin, a membrane for emotional osmosis, except that the feelings seem not so much to be *transferred* as to well up from within you, *in yourself, with* another self, *in joined witness* to your joint selfhood.

Moral sonority means those feelings that do not compute as feelings appropriate to social gender, and so they sometimes unnerve us; they were not the feelings we were expecting to have; they were not the feelings we always thought we needed in order to feel certain our manhood was real.

Moral sonority means those feelings that transparently tell us we are in the presence of another living human being, and we are the very being to whom that very life is present.

Moral sonority means those feelings that so rock us and astound us with our common humanity that we are speechless, agog.

Some of us feel these feelings more deeply than others do, more or less often, in some situations but never in others. There is an enormous range of people's experience of these feelings, just as there is an enormous range of people's experiential learning of selfhood.

Sometimes we penised folks feel our moral sonority right alongside our gender-anxiety waves. Even though we cannot experience the reality of our selfhood and the fiction of manhood in the same act, in the same ethical stance, in the same choice, we can sometimes experience moral sonority and gender-anxiety waves simultaneously.

It is our challenge as human beings to learn to tune in to moral sonority more and tune out gender anxiety. We shall all be more whole, and we shall all become better healers, to the extent that any individual one of us gives up trying to prove manhood.

Throughout history the jockeying for credibility between two or more manhood contestants has meant conquest, betrayal, and violence for billions of human beings, whether third parties to a temporary truce or ongoing losers in a permanent war. This insanity can cease only when one by one we each learn the commitment and the skills to empower one another's selfhood and to disempower the manhood act by laying to rest our subservience to it.

The way to experience this interpersonal potential of loving selfhood is practical, everyday attention to the matter of justice in interpersonl relating. Loving justice as human healing—what a concept.

Healing transpires when one's selfhood is witnessed and not betrayed. Healing transpires when one's selfhood feels safe and sustained, seen, and not alone.

Moral sonority is how anyone learns selfhood. Moral sonority is how anyone passes it on.

The measure of health and healing cannot be conformity to social gender, because no one gets to be "the man there" without someone underneath. Too many of us have been underneath. Underneath is a place where no one belongs. Choosing loyalty to manhood over selfhood leads inevitably to injustice. And to the extent that anyone you meet comes away from that encounter with the message that conforming to the lesson of manhood is a desired end, you have committed a kind of crime against human selfhood, theirs and yours.

But loving justice more than manhood relocates personal identity in selfhood—relationally, reciprocally, realistically. Loving justice more than manhood replenishes the selfhood of each one you encounter—and replenishes your own selfhood in each moment of relation.

The challenge is not to substitute some ostensibly lower-risk version of gender panic but instead to displace it altogether. The ethical courage that no longer feels compunction to accede to the manhood standard is not unknown to us. Episodically such choices can be, and have been, made in our lives. Such selfhood-affirming moral courage would become more familiar, and more constant in our personal relations and political outreach work, the less we insisted on giving it a gendered and genderizing name, which merely keeps us loyal, at some level, to other men's judgment on our conformity to social gender.

That's not necessarily rejecting gender identity. It's often more like just letting it go—and letting folks see that that's OK.

How do penised humans model and communicate the possibility of selfhood to other folks raised to be a man? That is partly what is at issue in the subject "feminism and men," because our fear of what "other men" might think about us "as men" so often keeps us from speaking (and living) feminism's liberating truth.

This is what I have learned about speaking from my selfhood to someone apparently committed to manhood: I believe it helps to think of one's own tiny expression of moral courage as a particular act of communication that has within it an empathic and justice-affirming ethical stance already—a medium that bears within it a selfhood-affirming message. All one can do, after all, is act in hope that someone else might witness, recognize, intuitively understand, and be emboldened—even if they are in lockstep with a power bloc of male bonding.

It is easy to forget that inside another "manhood mask" there resides a human being struggling to be free. I know well the feeling of peer-pressured panic: What will happen to me, what costly stigma will befall me, if I am found out, if my ungendered selfhood stands nakedly exposed to ridicule and reprisal in a manhood-proving contest? But over time I have learned to try to keep mindful that the ineluctable conflict between selfhood and manhood is not just within me; it's going on in just about everyone else raised to be a man as well. If I play out yet another manhood-proving number in my choice of how I address someone else raised to be a man, I am unlikely to elicit in the other any recollection of selfhood; and I am unlikely, in the event, to elicit even my own. But when I speak as if there is a gender-free selfhood with whom to communicate, that necessarily changes what I say, changes the "I" who is saying it, and (I act in hope) may help change the one who hears. Selfhood-to-selfhood communication is always based on the leap-of-faith hypothesis that I can bear witness to another's selfhood, just as another can behold mine.

Of course, the other person raised to be a man may not hear, may not get the message at all. It may not be the right time in that person's life. I may be the wrong message bearer. That person's gender panic may, at the moment, be unbreachable. Someone else, pandering to that panic, may have recently made a more persuasive case for reiterating manhood, and so the act of my words is tuned out.

And yet, it seems to me, the public and private act of choosing selfhood, of loving justice more than manhood, is not only a worthy pursuit, it is the future. We are none of us more real than when someone else is completely real to us.

I suggest that in our outreach communication with other penised people we frankly reassess how we depict and describe what really are the alleged benefits and downside costs of manhood as against selfhood. The lived benefits of selfhood, of regarding other selves as being as fully human as oneself (without insistence on asserting oneself as being "the man there") are, I believe, pragmatically experienceable. My catchphrase "You are never more real than when someone else is completely real to you" echoes, I believe, an experience that vast numbers of people have had in their lives, even if only fleetingly.

On the hierarchical vector of race, many people have had this transcendent experience: they have been intimate companions, loyal allies, across the social-political racial divide, and it has been as if, for a moment suspended somewhere outside political strife and power plays, a human-to-human ethical interaction has occurred that is as close to an "I-Thou" encounter as people can possibly know. The fullness of such a moment arises not from an "ought" so much as from a found and recoverable mode of being in the moment through the equality-based ethics of one's acts. And the fullness of such a moment happens temporally, sometimes transiently, because it arises solely from the particular ethics of a particular interaction at a particular time. Such a moment could not be possible, could not even be imagined, if the person who is, socially speaking, "white" brought to the encounter a headful of fears and panics (perhaps anticipating shaming from other "white" people for being a traitor) and therefore insisted on acting in ways that authenticated membership in the racial identity "white." Quite the contrary, such a transcendent and proximate moment depends utterly on declining to specify oneself as "white."

I urge that as we address people raised to be "a man," we find ways to recall—and reinforce by naming, by publicly recognizing—the pragmatic possibility of meeting one another (including across the vector of social gender) in a way that does not insist on being the man there; for to insist is to preclude the possibility of the moment of human-to-human revelation, just as to insist on being "white" would be, across the vector of race, to preclude the possibility of a mutual relationship grounded in the possibility of loving justice.

Our challenge is to make visible the tangible and pragmatic benefits that actually do occur selfhood-to-selfhood, in our lives of loving justice, in our moment-to-moment relating. We have to find the language. We have to find the way to express those tactile and interactional moments when choosing to recognize someone else's selfhood was the fullest choosing of our own at the same time.

We are too often at a loss for words in this regard. Too much of our language is stuck in the win/lose, cost/benefit-ratio vocabulary that is still reinforcing of manhood proving and gender anxiety.

The longing for a sense of sustainable safety for one's selfhood is only rarely acknowledged in communication with folks raised to be a man. How does one communicate with such people without becoming the butt of their (socially inculcated) propensity to ally against someone perceived as having less manhood than they, in order to (re)assure themselves that manhood can still be (and be *theirs*)? How, in other words, does one choose the ethics of selfhood affirmation without prompting a bonding frenzy against oneself?

I want to hold up to view—at least for those of us who have made it our lifework to communicate a vision of justice meaningfully with folks raised to be a man—a disquieting question: Are we indeed helping to create that needed sense of selfhood safety by furthering the illusion that there is a manhood mask somewhere out there (one of a variety of "masculinities" perhaps?) that is not so discomfiting as all the rest, not so

necessarily dependent on at least some episodic act of injustice? To do so—
to promise safety for "selfhood" within terms still specified by
"manhood"—are we not telling a lie to ourselves, to our own *selfhood*
selves?

But if we let it be known, even understatedly, that our deepest preference would be to speak selfhood-to-selfhood (without the mask, without
having to prove or insist on our manhood credentials), might that be just
the first step that someone hearing us has been dying inside to know it is
possible to take?

Support for such courage is still in short supply. And it is a crucial part
of the political healing work that we have yet to do.

The cutting-edge question for the next millennium is this: Why must
human experience be "gendered" at all? Why must *any human* continue
feeling the urgency to keep manhood feeling "real"? Why need we tolerate
any longer the injustice that is intrinsically required in order to shore up
the myth of manhood?

Answering this question privately and publicly will become the most
radically liberatory project in human history. How you choose to have a
personal identity, how you choose to situate yourself in relation to hierarchical identity categories, ultimately has political consequences. One
cannot possibly and positively be "the man there" without somebody
underneath. Nor can one be "white" or "Aryan" without personally helping to keep the category "real" by helping to keep selected others outside
it or put down. Any personal identity that is premised on identification
with a dominant social category is also premised on disidentification and
inequality.

Manhood is a personal and social hoax that exists only through interpersonal and social injustice. Manhood is the *paradigm* of injustice. *Refusing to believe* in manhood is the personal and ethical stance of resistance to all injustice done in its name. And refusing to accept the
manhood imperative—the lie that there *must* be a discrete and boundar-
ied gender identity to "belong" to—is a personal and political principle
of revolutionary liberation beyond any amplitude we can now imagine.

You help liberate anyone whenever you say "I who am a human self
like you" to "You who are a human self like me." Not incidentally, you
also help liberate yourself.

Refusing to believe in manhood is the hot big bang of human freedom.

NOTES

A shorter version of this essay was delivered as a keynote address to "Changing Minds towards the Millennium," an international conference for mental health practitioners and academics, September 26–27, 1996, at the Royal Geographical Society, London.

1. Some examples: "Take your skirt off and get aggressive," "You're playing like a bunch of sluts," "You're playing like a bunch of girls," "What are you, on the rag," "What's wrong, does your pussy hurt?" "You're acting like a bunch of wimps," "You don't deserve to be called men." From Andrea Parrot, Nina Cummings, and Timothy Marchell, *Rape 101: Sexual Assault Prevention for College Athletes* (Holmes, Florida: Learning Publications, 1994).

2. See *The End of Manhood: A Book for Men of Conscience* (Bridgewater, NJ: Replica Books, 1998), chap. 12 ("What's Supposed to Turn a Real Man On?"), chap. 19 ("How Can I Have Better Sex?"), and chap. 20 ("Looking Really Turns Me On—So What's the Matter with That?").

Chapter Nine

A Good Man Is Hard to Bash
Confessions of an Ex-Man-Hater

Kay Leigh Hagan

I remember well my first conscious exchange with a Good Man. Tom was the best friend of a man I had been dating for several months, and a warm acquaintance—though hardly a friend—of mine. I had asked him to meet me for coffee one day after a troubling incident with my lover when I feared he might hit me. He had not, but as I closed and locked the door behind him that night, I was shaken by the possibility. And I was also deeply in love. I called Tom for a "reality check," to find out if he knew of any history of physical violence, and to seek his advice.

After listening carefully to my fitful story, he asked, "How much abuse do you think you ought to tolerate in this relationship?" I only had to consider this for a moment. "Well, some. I mean, if I'm serious about him, and if I want the relationship to work, to last, there will be ups and downs. I don't think I should run away when it gets hard. I should be willing to tolerate a little abuse if I really love him." Tom paused, looked me gently but directly in the eyes, and said, "Kay, in a loving relationship, abuse is unacceptable. You should not have to tolerate any abuse to be loved." This surprising notion had not entered my mind.

Something in my worldview, in my self-esteem, in my understanding of love and power changed forever in that moment. What had I expected from Tom? Certainly that he would defend his friend, reassure me that he would never be violent, tell me everything would be okay, perhaps volunteer to talk to my lover. Instead, his reaction encouraged me to love myself, to take responsibility for my own well-being, and to reject violence even in its subtler forms. I did not expect him to hold up a compassionate mirror to the historical legacy of sexism I was playing out unwittingly in my own partnership. I did not expect Tom to be my ally—this was another option I had not considered.

What enabled him to respond in this way? As it happens, Tom later became one of the founders of an organization dedicated to stopping male violence against women.[1] His insight was based, I know now, on years of study and self-reflection using a feminist analysis of power to understand the context and range of men's abusive behavior toward women, starting with his own. This first experience with a man who has taken both a personal and public stand against male supremacy was not my last, but its intimate nature left an indelible impression on me. I sensed the revolutionary potential of radical alliances between men and women, and I decided to believe in them. I am proud to say that I have several such male allies in my life today. The lover referenced above is not among them.

What should women expect from our male allies—our partners, relatives, lovers, friends, neighbors, coworkers, colleagues—those men we love and respect, who claim to love and respect us? Some of the answers to this question may lie in its opposite.

The Merits of Man-Hating

I spent my first years as a feminist discovering the world anew: suddenly I realized society as I had accepted it was not necessarily the only way society could be. Applying this new political template to my observations, it appeared for the most part that society was in fact constructed by those in power for their benefit at the expense of others—most emphatically (I noted at the time), by men at the expense of women. Further, I was disturbed to discover that by my lack of consciousness, I cooperated with this situation, even colluding with my own oppression in many ways. Already an aficionado of the examined life, I became quite fascinated with the dilemma of internalized oppression. In truth, I was mesmerized by it.

For some years, identifying all the ways women are oppressed consumed me in a righteous fury. Having not understood for my first thirty years that male supremacy is a ruse, I made up for lost time by reading, writing, and reconsidering my assumptions and perceptions about men and women. I began to move through the world in a different way, nurturing myself, questioning authority, replacing men with women in the center of my life, and generally affirming women in any way I could, most importantly at this point in my own choices.

Understandably, in that early rush of liberation I found myself relating to men differently, often confronting them about assumptions of privilege and superiority. After years of accepting sexism as "just life," suddenly I noticed its injustice everywhere, and viewed all men as its perpetrators and benefactors. I felt disgusted with the basic attitudes of men in general: how disturbed they were when I spoke up, how defensive and offended they acted when faced with their history of unjust advantage, how conveniently ignorant they professed to be of their artificially heightened status. Having shifted from the extreme of obedient denial to its opposite of hypervigilance, I found men, as a whole, insufferable. I recall it was during this period that I was first accused of being a man-hater. Although I intuited the fallacy of this charge at the time, I could not verbalize a defense because, on some visceral level, the label felt accurate. However, I was to learn over the years that even a woman's slightest deviation from utter devotion to male supremacy is likely to be deemed "man-hating," or at the very least "male-bashing." The visceral resonance I felt was actually the thrill of breaking that taboo.

The Turn

Of course, as my initial focus of scrutiny I would be compelled by that area where I felt most comfortable: as a target of oppression. But feminism, honestly pursued, does not allow its advocates to settle in to such a position for long. More than any other discipline, philosophy, spiritual path, belief system, or worldview I've encountered, feminism requires that we keep asking questions, that we make connections, especially those that disturb our assumptions. When a wise activist colleague suggested—more than once—that I might consider widening my area of inquiry and self-observation to include other forms of oppression, such as racism, classism, and ableism, I eventually took her advice. And promptly stumbled over the dead elephant in the living room.

In these social constructions, my position was not nearly so enchanting to me. With white skin in a white supremacist system, middle-class status in a classist system, full mobility, vision, and hearing in a system that despises disability, I was flipped to the other side of the injustice equation.

The dead elephant in the living room of my self-esteem was privilege: that inheritance of profound institutionalized advantage I possessed—unbidden, unearned, and previously invisible to me—bestowed by a system that arbitrarily prized and rewarded certain of my characteristics. Particularly confusing was the fact that I seemed to believe I deserved these advantages, on the basis of—what? My whiteness? My mobility? My college degree? This was, after all, the same system I railed against for its absurd gender hierarchy. Did I believe that receiving advantages from such a system was valid and moral, that only its dispensation of penalty and restriction was objectionable? Clearly my socialization, which I was carefully examining for evidence of internalized messages of inferiority, also included an intricate set of expectations based on presumptions of superiority. It occurred to me that if I stand against oppression, then I must stand against privilege as well. Mustering a reluctant determination, I now became obsessed with understanding my internalized privilege with the same depth as I was learning to understand my internalized oppression. Onward through the fog.

While I am at the early stages of what clearly will be a lifelong pursuit, at the outset I can tell it is not going to be easy. Privilege is quite smarmy, marked by a kind of arrogant ignorance. (Prince Charles comes to mind here.)[2] Where oppression casts us into the sharp-edged realms of deprivation and desperation without a buffer, privilege creates a cushion of distance and protection from the "great unwashed," fostering a distorted sense of reality framed by willful ignorance. Becoming more aware of privilege does not exactly fill me with that warm glow I experienced earlier in relation to my rekindled female pride. Indeed, for people of conscience, acknowledging privilege is not nearly as fun as claiming oppression. Rage and righteousness are much more appealing to me than regret and reparations. The connections feel harder to make, and my resistance is difficult to overcome, indeed, even to perceive as such. Nevertheless, certain benefits of this inquiry are already becoming obvious. As I work to raise my consciousness and to discern how to be an ally to people of color, poor people, and people with disabilities despite my privilege in these areas, I have had an epiphany concerning men. Where once I was mystified by what seems to be their complete denial of a social system that systematically advantages them for being male, I realize now they are simply wrapped in the soft prison of their privilege—as I am. Suddenly, I can empathize.

The Big Picture

> The conundrum humanity faces is this: We are on a sinking ship, but the only materials we have to build a ship that will float come from the ship itself. The problem is that: we must tear down the old ship before it sinks, rebuilding it at the same time without destroying the needed parts.
>
> —Joel Kramer and Diana Alstad, *The Guru Papers*

My most optimistic read of contemporary society is that we are in a long and awkward transition phase from Patriarchal Hell to Feminist Utopia. In short, this Hell valorizes authoritarianism—expressed by the practices of supremacy and submission—and in it we have each inherited a mixture of unearned privilege and undeserved oppression. Feminism, often myopically caricatured as a "battle of the sexes," is in fact a social change movement challenging the very concept of domination as an ethical organizing principle. By questioning male supremacy and the gender caste structure that implements it, feminism reveals the seminal elements of the system of dominance as a whole, exposing the connections and shared values among sexism, racism, heterosexism, classism, and other oppressive social structures. The worldwide historical resistance to challenging sexism might indicate its position in domination's house of cards.

While I am consistently rewarded for being white, educated, able-bodied, and middle-aged, I am penalized for being female and lesbian. Most of us experience such a mixture of superiority and subordination, and move mindlessly through the culture, responding automatically to the overt and covert cues prompting behaviors and beliefs appropriate to our relative social status in the immediate situation. While we frequently perceive neither our oppression nor our privilege, we maintain and collude with both by our daily choices—a state of being Mary Daly has called Robotitude. The mission of people of conscience, as I view it, is to become conscious of this value system and how it affects us, to reclaim our right to self-determination, then to shift the paradigm however we can, at whatever level possible, to the said Feminist Utopia, a place where all have enough, kindreds make communities, mutual respect and compassionate conflict reign, the earth is sacred, universal safety is the rule, and domination, oppression, and privilege are nonsense terms. Riane Eisler speaks of the shift from a culture of dominance to a culture of partnership. While it may seem a long way from here to there, the first essential steps—being internal ones—are always at hand.

I believe the role of feminist advocates here is that of a "transition team" for this paradigm shift. Like the transition teams that facilitate the peaceful shift of power from one presidential administration to another, feminist advocates are uniquely qualified to stimulate society's shift from dominance to partnership. Feminism provides an analysis of power that demystifies the compelling culture of domination, as well as a societal vision that defines an appropriate strategy for change. As we strive to comprehend the ways all of us have been indoctrinated into Patriarchal Hell (a social order, by the way, that has had over five thousand years to establish itself), we must work together to actualize in practical and daily ways the shift from one value system to another, to create bridges of transition to a culture of partnership, to be living heralds of that utopian world. We cannot know how long this task will take, but the task itself is upon us: our ship is sinking, and we need all the help we can get. I bring all this up to emphasize the critical importance of allies. In spite of our individual inheritance of privilege and oppression, we must find ways to build alliances with those who share our values and vision. Subscribing to this larger view of feminism has prompted another important change in my personal stance: from "man-hater" to recruiter.

Radical Alliances

The identification of potential allies in this quagmire is definitely a challenge. While oppression binds us in a straitjacket of deprivation and self-loathing, privilege numbs us in a medicated haze of denial and self-aggrandizement. Whatever our particular mix of privilege and oppression, we move into awareness and self-determination accompanied to some degree by outrage, shame, despair, guilt, resentment, cynicism, defensiveness, and suspicion. Trust, a necessary aspect for alliance, seems unlikely. Even foolish. How to do this?

After taking some tentative steps to challenge the skewed internal perspectives created by both oppression and privilege, I am coming to understand that I can learn something about how to be an ally by drawing from my lived experiences in each to inform the other. To wit: when men or heterosexuals seem insensitive and arrogant to me, I can mentally change places—visit my race privilege, for instance—to get an intimate clue about their exasperating attitudes. Well-intentioned offenders may need only a gentle reminder to adjust their sensibilities, while the in-grained supremacist requires a more assertive intervention or a wider berth. And when I feel confounded, defensive, or hurt by the anger of people of color or people with disabilities toward me or the system in general, I can visit my experience of oppression as a woman and lesbian to gain some insight into their urgency and impatience with my inability— or unwillingness—to "get it." I can remember how vitally important it is to be believed, even if I am not understood. By using this internal shift of perspective, I can sometimes circumvent the kneejerk reactions of resig-nation and retreat that prevent me from taking action, speaking up, reaching out, or otherwise creating the opportunity for change, for con-nection, for alliance.

In grappling with the dilemma of privilege, I have often wished those who are victimized by it would just, please, tell me what to do to make it right, to fix it, to get it. While I understand the inappropriateness of asking the targets of oppression to educate the perpetrators, I have found also that the protected condition of privilege itself can inhibit me from becoming aware of the very characteristics I must change in order to become trustworthy and authentic—that is, to become a potential ally myself. The privilege of privilege is not having to acknowledge my privi-lege.[3] Oddly, a stock Christian image seems helpful here: Christ—or in this case, perhaps, Nemesis—is knocking at the door, but there is no latch on the outside. The door can be opened only from within. I believe the soft prison of privilege has such a door. While I have honed with zeal the ability to detect the many ways I collude with my own oppression, I have a great deal of difficulty—or probably more accurately, resistance to—identifying the more subtle, daily practices of my privilege, both in-ternalized and bestowed. Only to the extent that I can do this am I able to challenge those practices and make the choice to use my privilege with integrity. This is the message of Nemesis.

Looking for Mr. Good

The road men are taking toward the goal of liberation has but one obstacle that will prevent them from reaching the mark of transforming growth we call liberation; that obstacle is male supremacy.
— Harriet Gill, "Men's Predicament: Male Supremacy"

So how can women recognize our potential allies among men? The likely candidates—the Good Men[4]—do exhibit distinguishing characteristics. Here are some that come to mind:

Men who are allies of women acknowledge and reject the notion of male supremacy and the unjust gender caste system that supports it. They understand that while they are not personally responsible for creating this system, they have inherited its benefits and internalized its values. Because they take a stand against this belief—in public and in private—they are often regarded by most other men as defectors from patriarchy. Good Men cop to male privilege; they wrestle with it, work on it, worry about it, and always strive to use it with integrity.

For both men and women, Good Men can be somewhat disturbing to be around because they usually do not act in ways associated with typical men: they listen more than they talk; they self-reflect on their behavior and motives; they actively educate themselves about women's reality by seeking out women's culture and listening to women while not imposing themselves on sacred ground. They avoid using women for vicarious emotional expression; they can offer observations about a woman's internalized oppression without judgment or sarcasm; they ask permission before touching. When they err—and they do err—they look to women for guidance, and receive criticism with gratitude. They practice enduring uncertainty while waiting for a new way of being to reveal previously unconsidered alternatives to controlling and abusive behavior.[5] They intervene in other men's misogynist behavior, even when women are not present, and they work hard to recognize and challenge their own. Perhaps most amazingly, Good Men perceive the value of a feminist practice for themselves, and they advocate it not because it's politically correct, or because they want women to like them, or even because they want women to have equality, but because they understand that male privilege prevents them not only from becoming whole, authentic human beings but also from knowing the truth about the world. They continue to open the door.

Because they offer proof that men can change, the Good Men in my life have ruined me forever as a man-hater—I am unable to believe that men, as a lot, cannot be redeemed. Granted, I have lapsed into this view before, and no doubt will do it again when the next unthinkable incident of male violence against women crosses my path. There are times when man-hating seems the appropriate response. But ultimately, I believe that man-hating is the easy way out: not only does it oversimplify a deep and complex problem (and thus prevent us from finding any real solutions), but in a strange way it lets men off the hook. The demonized man can easily be dismissed as hopeless. But when I dare to expect more of men, to insist on their full humanity, intelligence, and responsibility, the image of an ally emerges and working together becomes a possibility.

Radical allies across privilege and oppression give a most precious gift when we tell the truth about ourselves and what we perceive about each other. Which is to say, once again, what may appear to some as man-hating may very well be something else far less personal, something broader with more historical context, something about changing the world.

NOTES

1. For more information, contact Men Stopping Violence in Atlanta, Georgia (404-688-1376), an organization dedicated to ending violence against women. From their mission statement: "As we work to help men change their abusive behavior, we recognize that individual change is dependent upon changing social systems which support the private and institutional oppression of women. We believe that groups of men can work together to change patriarchal values and belief systems that oppress women and children and dehumanize men themselves. In this struggle, we look to the battered women's movement to keep the reality of the problem and the vision of the solution before us. Our work must support their work."

2. I refer here to the child-rearing practices of English royalty, challenged by the notorious Princess Diana, who insisted on exposing her sons to all classes of people in all walks of life so they would have broader understanding and direct experience of society—unlike their father, whose traditional upbringing for the most part "protected" him from "commoners" and created a cultivated ignorance.

3. Terrence Crowley, in conversation.

4. Admittedly, my use of this term is somewhat facetious, and I risk not only readers' misunderstanding of my position but also fostering illusions, and so here I will attempt to clarify. To suggest, even in jest, that men can be categorized as "good" or "bad" ignores the reality that institutionalized male supremacy accrues benefit to all men regardless of their intent, effort, and level of consciousness or conscience, and that the violent and abusive behavior of some men affects the relationships of all men and women (causing women to enlist understandable caution or deference against the potential of violence when relating to men in general). At the same time, our acceptance of male arrogance as the norm tempts us to bestow the value of "good" or "exceptional" onto men who display respect,

kindness, and humanity, thus rewarding them for attitudes and behaviors one might expect of any decent human being. In addition, some men may embrace and relax into their relative "goodness" as an avoidance response to the prospect of acknowledging their unjust privilege, and as a distancing tactic to distinguish themselves from the "bad" men ("I've never hit a woman, and I don't like men who do"). To explore this point further, one might review these observations, substituting, for example, "white supremacy" and "good white person," reflecting on the complex dynamic of internalized and institutionalized privilege. Despite these convincing and provocative arguments, which obviously deserve thoughtful consideration, I have used the term "Good Man" here as a simplistic device to identify men of conscience working against male supremacy, in the hope that readers will be encouraged to investigate the deeper implications and perhaps question my categorization themselves. My appreciation to Terrence Crowley, Richard Bathrick, and Michael Kimmel for their insights on this issue.

5. Kathleen Carlin develops this point in her essay "The Men's Movement of Choice," in *Women Respond to the Men's Movement: A Feminist Collection*, edited by Kay Leigh Hagan (San Francisco: HarperCollins, 1992).

Part III

Reconstructing Gender Relations

Feminism, Men, and the Study of Masculinity
Which Way Now?

Matthew Shepherd

In this chapter I explore some of the issues I feel are of importance in discussions about "feminism and men." In the first section I consider what feminism is, what I believe feminism should aim to be, and the position that men can take in relation to this. In the second section I will try to apply this standpoint to the concept of "masculinity" and consider the implications of this for the understanding of gender.

Relating Feminism and Men

In recent years there has been much heated debate among academics about the relationship between feminism and men. Associating the two has prompted anger, dismay, sometimes disgust, and always much discussion. "What right do men have to muscle in on feminism, a woman's preserve?" "Isn't feminism and men a contradiction in terms?" "Isn't feminism about women and for women?" These are all very serious and worthwhile questions, and all have been widely written about. As such, any alliance between "feminist" men and feminist women has been fraught with caution and confusion. For most men these questions are completely irrelevant and of no interest. For some men, however, it has rightly prompted a lot of self-reflective thinking. In *White Guys,* Fred Pfeil (1995) comments on the "apologism" men have expressed about proclaiming to be feminist, particularly noting the dialogue surrounding Jardine and Smith (1987). He stridently asserts that he will boldly proclaim his feminism, and then quietly starts apologizing again during the course of the book. Men are uneasy about their role in feminism.

So what should be the relationship between feminism and men, and men and feminism? I would suggest that this is dependent on what you choose as a definition of feminism and what you believe its goals should be. If the arguments of people like Judith Butler (1990, 1993) or Judith Grant (1993) are taken seriously, the men/feminism association becomes much less problematic. Indeed, the potential exists for the connection between feminism and men to become no more controversial than the connection between feminism and women. An important point that needs to be stressed is that the terms "feminist" and "woman" are not synonymous. In fact, such an equation is dangerous, for it blurs what should be the fundamental objectives of feminism. Judith Grant has very clearly argued this point. The experiences of a woman are not necessarily indicative of the standpoint of a feminist. It is only with what she terms an interpretative "feminist lens" (109) that women's experiences come to be part of feminism. Women's experiences range from "untouched by feminism" to "hostile towards feminism" or "complicit in the maintenance of male exercises of power." Feminism may claim to speak for all women, but all women do not speak for feminism. Feminism is a political way of thinking and, like all political thought, its attractions cut across sex. What is required is for people to have a feminist *consciousness*.

Hence, in bell hooks's examination of feminism, *Feminist Theory: From Margin to Center* (1984) there is strong criticism of the way feminists (who she believes have primarily been white, middle-class, tertiary-educated Western women) have assumed to speak for every woman, using their experiences to generalize for all women, and in the process privileging their own voice. This prompts her to suggest that many of the founding principles and aims of the feminist movement have been misdirected. hooks goes on to outline her own definition of feminism:

> Feminism is the struggle to end sexist oppression. Its aim is not to benefit solely any specific group of women, any particular race or class of women. It does not privilege women over men. It has the power to transform in a meaningful way all our lives. Most importantly, feminism is neither a lifestyle nor a ready-made identity or role one can step into. (1984, 26)

She proposes that rather than saying, "I am a feminist," we should be stating, "I advocate feminism." This applies as much to men as to women who support the idea she outlines above. This emphasizes what I feel is the most important thing about advocating feminist beliefs: desiring a fundamental, radical change of dominant value systems that have produced sexist oppression. In this way, I believe that men (although not necessarily materially) ultimately have as much to benefit from feminism as do women: a society where everyone has the opportunity to live fair and equal lives.

Of vital significance then is the continuation of the constructive critique of feminism. Just as we are critical of society, we need to be critical of ourselves. To critically self-reflect can be a positive experience if it can raise awareness of other people's feelings. Many people, not least the women it is supposed to be representing, have felt misrepresented or even excluded from feminism and by feminists: feminism has had little or no relevance to their life experiences. As hooks states, men have been cast as the enemy. What is needed is not a "battle of the sexes," but a battle for fundamental change. This will obviously be led by women, but it does not have to exclude men who genuinely want to see change.

This leads to one of the underlying questions of this anthology: what sort of supportive roles might men play in the creation of larger feminist realities? Of course, men should be supportive of feminism, but from the arguments I have sketched above, it may not have to be that they hold just *supportive roles*. The old adage "actions speak louder than words" is something of a truism. More than just speaking advocacy of feminism, men must prove it. The personal is political, and therefore the way we all live our lives is vitally important in the expression of feminism. We must bring feminist ideals into our everyday actions. My own Ph.D. research on "masculinity" has emphasized the importance of *practice*. Far more important than beliefs, attitudes, or intentions are our actions and the results of our actions, which are inextricably linked to the exercise of power. Even the most fervent of feminists can be complicit in maintaining male power when feminist ideals are not acted on. Although not always obvious, our actions as individuals have consequences that reach the level of community and society. Men especially have a duty to check their actions, to eradicate the ways they contribute to sexist oppression. I feel that a society that truly embraces social justice can be achieved only by women and men working together. As Rosemary Radford Reuther states,

> The struggle against patriarchy cannot be won simply by a women's movement. Patriarchy is itself the original men's movement and the struggle to overthrow it must be a movement of men as well as women. But men can only be authentically a part of that struggle if they are able to acknowledge

the injustice of their own historical privileges as males and to recognise the ongoing ideologies and economic, political and social structures that keep such privilege in place. (1992, 17)

The challenge of feminism is to break away from strict male-female and masculinity-femininity dichotomies and move toward a progressive politics of change that puts into practice a feminist theory that recognizes differences but unites people under a common cause—to end sexist oppression.

Applying the Theory in Practice: Setting an Agenda for Masculinity Research

Hopefully, this has made clear my understanding of feminism and the important role men could take in relation to it. I would now like to go on to examine the topic in more detail and to suggest ways men can make a difference, with reference to my own particular field of interest, masculinity. I have become increasingly dissatisfied with the burgeoning "masculinity" literature. As Carrigan, Connell, and Lee (1985) traced, the study of masculinity would never have come on to the agenda without the critical influence of feminism. Sadly, much contemporary writing on "masculinity" tries to repay very little of this debt of knowledge to feminism, and some is even openly hostile. The initiative in researching masculinity needs to be retaken by advocates of feminism, and a central way of achieving this is to reassess what we mean by "masculinity."

In my Ph.D. study I have tried to apply feminist theory and methodology to an investigation of "masculinity." As the research has developed, however, both my preconceptions about "masculinity" and what I have learned from feminist debates have become confused. From the interviews I conducted I discovered that "commonsense" notions of "masculinity" and "femininity" no longer made sense to me. This threw into doubt the place of feminism, as I understood it, and my relation to it: thinking of men and women as polar opposites seemed not only far too simplistic but also obstructive to an understanding of gender. More important, as far as my work was concerned, I became increasingly doubtful of the existence of "masculinity" and "femininity" as objects of knowledge beyond the historically constructed concepts manipulated in discourses of sex/gender. It seemed to me that the existing literature had insufficiently located and defined either term. With particular reference to the "masculinity" literature, I found that any and all the words, actions, and attitudes expressed by any man or men was described as relating to "masculinity." Although the literature often urged that biological essentialism be rejected, actions by men, such as playing football, were considered to be indicative of "masculinity," while the same actions undertaken by women were still reckoned to be indicative of "femininity." A dualistic, dichotomous way of thinking is still being perpetuated through such work. This has the effect of continuing normative prescriptions of gender by suggesting that there exist identities—"femininity" and "masculinity"—to which all women and all men belong. Pluralizing the terms to masculinities/ femininities proves no less deterministic, because both are equally biological in their fixity. For me, very little light is being shed on gender *relations* and too little attention is being paid to the key issue—power.

Existing conceptualizations have failed to adequately answer the question, What is masculinity? I discuss my reasoning more fully elsewhere (Shepherd forthcoming), but this failure has prompted me to feel that it is best to forget these catch-all understandings of "masculinity": they become meaningless. Ideally, I would dispense with the term altogether. However, I would suggest that it could be retained as an analytic term to describe certain actions. This has a number of implications in terms of understanding ourselves as men and women and the place of feminism in sexual politics.

I have concluded in my research that rather than understanding "masculinity" as an identity of men, we should perhaps understand it as a *practice* that can be employed by either sex (wittingly or unwittingly): an exercise of power that creates, reinforces, and maintains sexual inequalities and sexist oppression; a way of exercising power based on the discursive construction of a ("masculine") superior and a ("feminine") inferior that encourages and perpetuates sexual differences in power so that men as an apparent "class" can exercise power over women as an apparent "class." In sum, it is an exercise of power based on sexual inequalities that benefits men, but one that can advantage individual women in relation to other women. It is not an identity, it is neither psychologically nor biologically determined, but it is the foundation for the daily practices that uphold male power at the primary expense of women. There are many advantages to such a narrowly honed definition of masculinity (not least that it is a lot less ambiguous), provided that it could gain common currency. It is also one that, I believe, has relevance to feminism, feminist scholarship, and research into "masculinity," which is so often avowedly profeminist but very often unrecognizable as feminist in content.

I quoted earlier hooks's definition of feminism as "the struggle to end sexist oppression" (1984, 26). My definition of masculinity can be regarded as a way of searching for the root cause of "sexist oppression." It is an attempt to isolate and highlight the ways male power operates. It is an analysis of the actual, *practical, everyday* ways male power is perpetuated. This covers a wide range of practices. Masculinity can be practiced in conversations, through the use of language, through individual acts of coercion or violence, in discriminatory practices and policies of companies, state regulations, welfare provision restrictions, sexploitation, and so forth. It is a definition of "masculinity" that hopefully has something to offer feminism: it is an analysis that is focused neither solely on men nor solely on women, but on gender relations, on power relations that advantage men. In a small way it also addresses a challenge from critics. I have found that the equation of feminism with women's experiences has been used in a very negative way by some of the men I have interviewed.

An example of this is what I call the "Thatcher syndrome." As everyone knows, Margaret Thatcher was Britain's first woman prime minister. This fact is manipulated. It has been frequently suggested to me that Thatcher's success as a woman proves that women have now reached equality with men—hers is taken as representative of all women's experiences. But in the definition that I have put forward, this example can be analyzed as an illustration of masculinity. Much of Thatcher's legislation created and perpetuated sexual inequalities that supported male domination and male power. On a more local scale, I found this logic to be extended to all women that men relate to in their everyday lives: an example of any woman who does not appear sexually oppressed is used to suggest that *no* woman is sexually oppressed. The objective should not be to draw generalizations about the sexes but to locate the specific conditions that maintain gender inequalities.

The reconceptualization I have proposed here has implications for the study and understanding of masculinity. A sustained, wider acceptance of "masculinity" as something that is not an identity would have the effect of destabilizing the simple equation of masculinity with men and femininity with women. The result of this would be, for instance, to highlight the mythopoetic men's movement's fable of the search for a "true masculinity"—men's identity—for what it is: a way of maintaining male power. It would mean that the study of masculinity would not be confined to the study of men. This would have the effect of removing the "celebrating men" feel of so many masculinity studies and would challenge the legitimacy of a male-only focus: there are many antifeminist works on masculinity that have thrived on the justification that "feminism is all about women's experiences, this is something about men." It would also mean that a study of masculinity could use the words and actions of men and women to illustrate the negative impacts these can have on women and the production of sexist oppression. This study would apply Grant's interpretative feminist lens (1993) to women's and men's experiences.

Plenty has been written in the "masculinity" literature of the need to change "masculinity." Some authors hold that there is nothing wrong with the identity "masculinity," but that it only needs to be refocused and channeled in new directions. The suggestion is that this will bring about a society that is much more sexually egalitarian and that this is the way to radically alter gender relations. Indeed, the subtitle to Lynne Segal's book *Slow Motion* is *Changing Masculinity, Changing Men*. I would like to challenge such a view. I believe such thoughts blur the realities of gender relations and are based on a misnomer. If we accept the logic that "masculinity" is an identity, we can say that changing "masculinity" to more "positive" forms will change men and benefit women. For instance, there has been much focus in feminist literature on men and housework, centering on men's noninvolvement in the household economy. In its own way, this has been very successful, and men are doing much more work in the home than in the past. But I would suggest that such changes are illusory. There has been very little real change in attitudes and values, and the discourses of women that uphold male power are untouched. I would contend that it is these discourses that must be changed before fairer gender relations can be attained: there is more to changing gender relations than changing "masculinity" to a more "positive" form. What is required is a fundamental change in dominant value systems that privilege and empower men and devalue women; what is required is the development of feminist consciousness. This is not possible within the paradigm of masculinity as men's identity.

Therefore, the study of masculinity needs to become the study of power relations. I would agree with an article in the "radical men's magazine" *Achilles Heel* (number 15) that called for "the men's movement" to be "world changing" and not "navel-gazing." Rather than looking for ways to "heal the wound of men's hurt" under the guise of "changing masculinity," we should utilize a distinct feminist focus on masculinity that aims at important social change. It offers the way to get back to the important issues for men and "masculinity"; discussing the influence of feminism on early writings on men and masculinity, David Morgan writes, "These themes clearly shaped many of the writings about men and masculinities, emerging most obviously in discussions of sexual and domestic violence, pornography, sexual harassment and divisions of labour within the home and in the labour market" (1992, 6). This focus has been largely lost in recent research on masculinity, partially the result of thinking about "masculinity" in terms of identity and therapy, and not in terms of gender at the social scale. Topics such as "healing the wound" and "we're told that we're powerful but we feel powerless" just smack of the powerful justifying their desire for more power. The focus must be on undermining the powerful and unmasking the ways their power is exercised.

But can this "agenda" be put into operation? Can feminist theory be used to research this relational understanding of masculinity? Yes, if masculinity research focuses on power and centers analysis on the different scales at which the practices of masculinity occur. In my own research on masculinity in two workplaces, this meant that the gathered qualitative materials, which included in-depth interviews with both men and women, were related to organizational policies, such as equal opportunity programs, and how these policies were carried out (they were found often to be ineffective because certain men in positions of authority could flagrantly disregard them); interactions between employees to establish how masculinity is practiced at a micro-level; and individuals and their relations with colleagues, organizational demands and their work. Hence, the objective was to locate specific exercises of power that created or maintained sexual inequalities. It was discovered that this involved the discursive construction of women as "naturally" inferior to men, as capable of only certain types of work, and as fitting particular "roles"—as mothers, homemakers, and servicers of men. The consequence was that men and those women who actively upheld the dominant value system were able to achieve material advantages. Such findings, which may be of practical significance, cannot be discovered in research focused purely on individuals and their identities.

Bob Connell (1995) has stressed the need for research to focus on the intersections between gender and other structures, such as labor politics and education. He argues that this will allow progression beyond one-dimensional strategic thinking toward an "alliance politics" (238) of joint action between women and men. This approach is reflected in his femi-nist-influenced research, which has variously concentrated on gender in workplaces, in schools, and most recently on four distinct groups of men. His work has begun to broaden the understanding of masculinity, to stimulate a move away from masculinity as a taken-for-granted concept. He is one of the few writers on masculinity who have adopted feminist theory and genuinely had something to offer back to feminism. It is a lead that everyone interested in masculinity should seriously consider fol-lowing.

For those men who are actively trying to live feminist worldviews (and I count myself among them), the emphasis really must be on putting the theory into practice. The role of men is important:

> Men who advocate feminism as a movement to end sexist oppression must become more vocal and public in their opposition to sexism and sexist oppression. Until men share equal responsibility for struggling to end sex-ism, feminist movement will reflect the very sexist contradictions we wish to eradicate. . . . In particular, men have a tremendous contribution to make to feminist struggle in the area of exposing, confronting, opposing, and transforming the sexism of their male peers. (hooks 1984, 80–81)

For men, this means putting forward feminist viewpoints, advocating feminism publicly, and challenging the sexism they encounter. *Women Respond to the Men's Movement* (1992) outlined what many feminists want men's role in gender change to be. Some key points stressed are that any movement of men must work in solidarity with women; that men must want to make the world a better place for everyone, not just moan about how hard it is to be a man in a man's world; that "liberation from the malaise of masculinity" means letting go of male privilege; and that break-ing down the dualism of feminine/masculine is vital in dissipating the gender system. Thus, men need to be antisexist, antipatriarchal, feminist, and gay-affirmative (Hearn and Morgan 1990). There is a role for men in feminism, and it is a central one, but men must critically engage with a reconceptualized notion of "masculinity," one that is concerned with the actions of the individual at the level of the social.

REFERENCES

Butler, J. 1990. *Gender Trouble.* New York: Routledge.

———. 1993. *Bodies That Matter: On Discursive Limits of Sex.* London: Routledge.

Carrigan, T., R. W. Connell, and J. Lee. 1985. "Toward a New Sociology of Masculinity." *Theory and Society* 14:551–604.

Connell, R. W. 1995. *Masculinities.* Cambridge: Polity Press.

Grant, J. 1993. *Fundamental Feminism.* New York: Routledge.

Hagan, K. L., ed. 1992. *Women Respond to the Men's Movement.* San Francisco: Pandora.

Hearn, J., and D. Morgan. 1990. *Men, Masculinity and Social Theory.* London: Unwin-Hyman.

hooks, b. 1984. *Feminist Theory: From Margin to Center.* Boston: South End Press.

Jardine, A., and P. Smith, eds. 1987. *Men in Feminism.* New York: Routledge.

Morgan, D. 1992. *Discovering Men.* London: Routledge.

Pfeil, F. 1995. *White Guys.* London: Verso.

Reuther, R. R. 1992. "Patriarchy and the Men's Movement: Part of the problem or part of the solution?" In K. L. Hagan, ed., *Women Respond to the Men's Movement.* San Francisco: Pandora.

Segal, L. 1990. *Slow Motion: Changing Masculinity, Changing Men.* London: Virago Press.

Shepherd, M. Forthcoming. "Re-thinking Masculinity." *masculinities.*

Chapter Eleven

Feminism and Masculinity

*Reconceptualizing the Dichotomy of
Reason and Emotion*

Christine A. James

In the context of feminist and postmodern thought, traditional conceptions of masculinity and what it means to be a "Real Man" have been
critiqued. In her book *The Man of Reason*, Genevieve Lloyd critiques the
distinctive masculinity of the "man of reason" and the effect it has had
on the history of philosophy. One major feature of the masculine-
feminine, the dichotomy of reason and feeling, is the main focus of this
chapter. In exploring the history of symbolic conceptions of masculinity
in ancient Greece, the Renaissance, and the present, one finds that the
oppression of women is integrally linked to the traditional tie between
masculinity and reason. There have been many efforts in recent feminist
philosophy to rewrite or redefine "Woman" in such a way as to alleviate
the oppression of women.[1] I argue that rewriting Woman for this purpose
is problematic, primarily because any rewriting of this type must occur in
the current historical context of hierarchical dualisms, like Man-Woman,
masculine-feminine, male-female. These binary oppositions arguably find
their roots in Pythagorean philosophy and can be traced through the
Renaissance to our current historical context.[2] It is these dualisms that
have traditionally valued the masculine side of the Man-Woman dichotomy more than the feminine.[3] Further, it will be argued that the hierarchical dualism of Man and Woman is so pervasive that if we rewrite or
redefine the inferior, deprivileged side of that dualism, we cannot correct
its devalued status. Instead, we redefine that which is undervalued but
retain its devalued status. This particular aspect of attempts to critique

hierarchical dualisms like reason and feeling has been reflected in the writings of many feminists, male and female. This chapter will show that when women attempt to redefine the dichotomy by revaluing the traditionally feminine (like feelings and emotions) over the traditionally masculine (like reason), their work is often mistakenly criticized for being purely political; conversely, when men attempt to redefine the same dichotomy in an attempt to allow men to "get back in touch with their feelings," to be nurturers, their work is described in terms of providing a better epistemology. The current literature on masculinity explores alternatives to rewriting or redefining Woman that try to avoid the problem of status remaining with redefinition. This alternative is rewriting or redefining Man. By redefining Man, one may be able to reconceptualize the privileged side of the hierarchical dualism in such a way that it is no longer privileged. Deprivileging, as well as redefining, Man is possible because while the devalued side of a hierarchical dualism tends to keep the same status when redefined, it may be possible to redefine the privileged side of the dualism in such a way that it loses its privileged status. Unfortunately, many of these attempts to rewrite or redefine masculinity have faults of their own. Finally, this chapter will discuss more promising possibilities for new definitions of Man, as well as a vision of better interaction between the work of women and men in general.

Feminist Reconceptualizations of Reason and Emotion

It is the historical foundation of the relative status of femininity to masculinity, and by analogy Woman to Man, that has made the notion of rewriting or redefining Woman so attractive. It has seemed plausible that if we rework the symbolic associations Woman has been assigned through the centuries, we could somehow relieve the oppression of Woman as well.

While such a redefinition of Woman seems to be a noble project, it unfortunately suffers from many problems. Any shift or change in meaning at the level of the symbolic meaning of Man and Woman must take place within a historical context. As many examples in feminist literature show, our current historical context still places Man and Woman in a hierarchical dichotomy in which Woman, female, and the feminine are severely undervalued. Any rewriting of Woman done while it occupies this subordinate position will maintain its devalued status and leave itself open to misinterpretations that will serve to perpetuate the hierarchical status quo. As Lloyd points out, "our ideas and ideals of maleness and femaleness have been formed within structures of dominance—of superiority and inferiority, 'norms' and 'difference', 'positive' and 'negative', the 'essential' and the 'complementary'" (1984, ix). And the male-female dichotomy itself has operated not as a straightforwardly descriptive principle of classification, but as an expression of values. It necessarily follows that any redefining of Woman or Man, what counts as male or female, will take part in these same valuations and contextual issues. And when motivated by the hope of achieving a political goal (such as the removal of oppression for women and men who are currently forced to live with and within these constraining notions of masculinity and femininity), those who seek to redefine Man must pay attention to this same problem.

Lloyd describes the focus of her book as the pervasiveness of the historical conception of reason as masculine. She notes that

> Past philosophical reflection on what is distinctive about human life, and on what should be the priorities of a well-lived life, has issued in character ideals centered on the idea of Reason, and the supposed universality and neutrality of these ideals can be seriously questioned. . . . The maleness of the Man of Reason is no longer superficial bias. It lies deep in our philosophical tradition. (1984, ix)

Besides noting the pervasiveness of masculinity in our conceptions of the good life, Lloyd views the very nature and definition of this maleness as ripe for critique. Lloyd outlines the symbolic associations by which maleness has traditionally been defined, noting that maleness was "associated (by the Pythagoreans) with a clear, determinate mode of thought, femaleness with the vague and indeterminate" (1984, 3). The association of maleness with clarity of thought persisted and was incorporated into the form-matter distinction that was so central to Greek thought. "Maleness was aligned with active, determinate form, femaleness with passive, indeterminate matter" (Lloyd 1984, 3).[4] In the later Platonic dialogues, the distinction between form and matter is inextricably related to the distinction between body and soul. For Plato, the rational, active, thinking soul rightfully rules over not only the body, but also the two nonrational parts of the soul: the appetitive and the courageous.[5] Platonic philosophy posits a constant struggle between the rational and the nonrational soul, which must by definition be subordinate. Lloyd notes that later Judaic and Christian thinkers elaborated on this Platonic theme in ways that connected it explicitly with the theme of man's rightful domination of women, aligning woman with the nonrational soul that must be subordinate to man, the rational soul (Lloyd 1982, 7).[6]

Evelyn Fox Keller further describes how these ancient notions of reason and masculinity were not only maintained but strengthened with the rise of science in the Renaissance and the seventeenth century. "Our inquiry confirms that neither the equation between mind, reason, and masculinity, nor the dichotomies between mind and nature, *reason and feeling,* masculine and feminine, are historically invariant. Even though the roots of both the equations and the dichotomies may be ancient, the seventeenth century witnessed a marked polarization of all the terms involved— with consequences as crucial for science as for our own understanding of gender" (Keller 1985, 44). An example is Sir Francis Bacon, arguably a founder of modern science. Bacon describes the proper goal of science to be a "chaste and lawful marriage between Mind and Nature that will bind [Nature] to [man's] servitude and make her [his] slave" (Farrington 1951, 187). Bacon's marriage would be one in which "the emphasis was on constraint, on the disjunction between mind and nature, and ultimately on domination of woman by man" (Keller 1985, 44).

Attempts to revalue the feminine often fall into the trap of their underlying societal and intellectual structures.[7] Theorists of masculinity argue that a redefining of masculinity or "the masculine" should be able to shake the underlying normative structures. The central aspect of these hierarchical dichotomies, which this chapter will focus on, is that of reason and feeling. As Lloyd has shown, it is the association of masculinity with reason, femininity with feeling, that has had such a profound and lasting effect on our cultural consciousness in numerous historical contexts.[8] While Lloyd clearly illustrated the historical alignment of masculinity with reason and femininity with feeling, Alison Jagger presents an attempt to revalue the feminine or "feeling" side of that alignment. Jagger gives a new description of emotion that claims that emotion is an important part of all knowledge, and can be used by feminists as an important part of women's experience.

Jagger notes how the rational has typically been contrasted with the emotional, but points to the fact that emotion was never excluded completely from the picture: "the emotions were thought of as providing indispensable motive power that needed to be channeled appropriately. Without horses, after all, the skill of the charioteer would be worthless" (1989, 145). In the modern period, the relationship of reason and feeling changed: "reason was reconceptualized as the ability to make valid inferences from premises established elsewhere . . . the validity of logical inferences was thought independent of human attitudes and preferences; this was the sense in which reason was taken to be objective and universal" (146). Furthermore, Jagger claims that this modern redefinition of rationality required a corresponding reconceptualization of emotion, achieved by portraying emotions as nonrational and often irrational urges that regularly swept the body, rather as a storm sweeps over the land (146). According to Jagger, this view took many forms, most notably evolving into British empiricism and its successor, rationalism. Jagger attempts to challenge these views by suggesting that "emotions may be helpful and even necessary rather than inimical to the construction of knowledge" and proposes a new epistemological model that reflects the importance of both reason and feeling (146).

Jagger outlines this new model by arguing that emotions are best understood as social constructs. We tend to experience our emotions as involuntary, individual responses to situations, and infer that those emotions are presocial, instinctive responses determined by our biological constitution (Jagger 1989, 150). Jagger argues that this view is mistaken, and that emotions are actually social constructs. This is evidenced by the fact that children are taught deliberately what their culture defines as appropriate emotional responses to certain situations (150). Another aspect of the social construction of emotions is their intentional structure: "if emotions necessarily involve judgments, then obviously they require concepts, which may be seen as socially constructed ways of organizing and making sense of the world" (151). In addition, Jagger asserts that emotions are active engagements, that they do not simply overtake us as the modern model would assert. The social-constructivist approach of Jagger's model for a new epistemology may be the first place to look for a possible explanation for why women's attempts to rewrite or redefine hierarchical dualisms like reason and feeling tend to be seen as purely political, rather than having epistemological importance. Perhaps understanding emotions as socially constructed simply goes against the "commonsense" understanding people have of their emotions. Moreover, as other feminists may assert, exposing emotions as social constructs may be another way to devalue them.

Jagger further asserts that in the context of Western culture, people have often been encouraged to control or even suppress their emotions. Consequently, it is not unusual for people to be unaware of their emotional state or to deny it to themselves and others (155). This lack of awareness, especially combined with a neopositivist understanding of emotion that construes emotion as just a feeling of which one is aware, lends plausibility to the myth of dispassionate investigation (155). It is this myth of dispassionate investigation, the use of reason unaffected by emotion to gain truth, which Jagger hopes to argue against by exposing that values and emotions do always enter into all aspects of theorizing, including problem choice as well as the scientific method itself (156). Further, Jagger argues that women are the main group in our society that tends to be allowed and expected to feel emotion, while men—and primarily white men—are expected to always be in control of their emotions. "White men's control of their emotional expression may go to the extremes of repressing their emotions, failing to develop emotionally, or even losing the capacity to experience many emotions" (158). Thus *both* men and women are at a disadvantage with regard to norms of emotional expression or nonexpression, but Jagger argues that women are in the most depriviliged position.[9] With regard to how the silencing of women can be remedied, Jagger advocates the use of what she calls "outlaw emotions." Outlaw emotions are conventionally unacceptable emotions, emotions that people experience and that deviate from the norm. These emotions, when experienced by a group, can form the basis of a subculture that systematically opposes the prevailing perceptions, norms, and values (Jagger 1989, 160). Jagger claims that "feminists need to be aware of how we can draw on some of our outlaw emotions in constructing feminist theory and also of how the increasing sophistication of feminist theory can contribute to the reeducation, refinement, and reconstruction of our emotional constitution" (160).

While this vision for resistance sounds very promising, I think it is important to be wary of two different ways the use of outlaw emotions may actually work against women. First, the idea of women banding together and expressing outlaw emotions does not seem to challenge the stereotypical view of women as overly emotional—we may simply replace our devalued, depriviliged emotionality with new sets of emotions. More important, women who utilize these outlaw emotions run the risk of being misunderstood as hysterical or insane because of our current societal context. Second, it would be wise to explore cases in which the dominant group, white males, experience outlaw emotions. It would seem, based on Jagger's account, that if white men do experience outlaw emotions, those emotions would somehow no longer be outlaw emotions at some point; the subversive culture would be taken up into the dominant culture. And if outlaw emotions for men might include nurturance for children, then our later discussion of May and Strikwerda will provide an interesting example of men utilizing such emotions to their families' and their own advantage. The suggestion of outlaw emotions is promising, but it is clearly open to critique.

Reconceptualizing Masculinity in Terms of Reason and Emotion

Jagger's attempt to revalue emotion stands as an important example of how a feminist theorist might rework hierarchical dualisms like reason-feeling in working toward the goal of alleviating the oppression of women. But potential difficulties with Jagger's work also point to the fact that any attempt to redefine Man or to rework the hierarchical dichotomies like masculine-feminine and reason-feeling needs to pay careful attention to previous attempts to redefine those dichotomies so that it may avoid the problems and criticisms that affected those attempts. Promising attempts to redefine or reconceptualize masculinity have grown in number and diversity in recent years. Many of these reconceptualizations of masculinity show an awareness of and deference to feminist goals, such as removing women's oppression; but they also explore the more general goal of doing away with oppressive normative gender roles under which both men and women live. The reconceptualizations of masculinity described in Larry May and Robert Strikwerda's collection *Rethinking Masculinity* may provide some promising revisions and redefinitions of Man. The text begins with an outline of two of the more extreme reconceptualizations of masculinity, one presented by John Stoltenberg, the other by Robert Bly.

Stoltenberg argues that because men have forced women to occupy subordinate gender roles, the very categories of masculine and feminine must be replaced with something radically different (May and Strikwerda 1992, xiii). It is to be noted that "what is positive in Stoltenberg's book is the 'idea' that men can choose something different from the traditional roles they seem to be thrown into" (xiii). Stoltenberg's position is more subtle than May and Strikwerda's description: in essence, Stoltenberg argues that "manhood," defined as the personal, behavioral identity that is committed to gender, committed to "being the man there," cannot coexist with "authentic, passionate, and integrated selfhood" (Stoltenberg 1993, xiv). I agree with Stoltenberg on this insight, but our prescriptions for what to do vary slightly. While Stoltenberg argues very carefully and effectively that reconceptualizations of masculinity are hopeless, I still seek a promising revision of masculinity. I would also argue that, because of the pervasiveness of the hierarchical dualisms discussed earlier, even if individuals can become different in their relational interactions as Stoltenberg hopes, other characteristics besides gender may then become the standards by which some individuals achieve a higher "symbolic status" than others.[10]

Another reconceptualization of masculinity is presented by Robert Bly. Bly claims that women, primarily since feminism, have created a situation in which men, especially young men, feel weak, emasculated, and unsure of themselves, and that older men must lead the way back to a tradition in which "the divine also was associated with mad dancers, fierce fanged men" (May and Strikwerda 1994, xv). Bly holds up the myth of the Wild Man as an exemplar of the direction men must take and never challenges the hierarchical dualisms that are so integrally linked to the tension he perceives between men and women. Arguably, the notion of the Wild Man merely reinforces clichés about "real masculinity" instead of trying to foster a new relationship between men and women, as well as the masculine and the feminine.

Four other revisionings of masculinity are present in *Rethinking Masculinity*. These are Brian Pronger's description of the "gay jock," Leonard Harris's essay on Martin Luther King, Jr., and May and Strikwerda's two essays on the father-as-nurturer and men's intimacy.

Brian Pronger gives an analysis of masculinity in "Gay Jocks: A Phenomenology of Gay Men in Athletics." Pronger defines masculinity as a strategy for the power relations between men and women, and as a strategy that serves the interests of patriarchal heterosexuality (1992, 44). By understanding masculinity in this way, gay men provide a very powerful example of how to reconceptualize masculinity. Pronger describes the ease with which gay men can be friends with women, and the mutually comfortable nature of such relationships: "all the gay men I interviewed told me their relationships with women are very good; the men feel themselves to be on equal terms with women, and women seem to trust these men more than they do other men" (44). Pronger further notes that this "ease of social intercourse makes possible personal relations with women that are not patriarchal. The patriarchal signification of the masculine/feminine spectrum of behaviors, therefore, has little meaning to gay men in their personal lives" (45). Although Pronger acknowledges that these descriptions take place only in the realm of personal interactions, and that gay men therefore probably do experience patriarchal privilege in wider social contexts, these experiences do provide an important insight into masculinity as a political strategy.

After exposing the strategy of masculinity, Pronger calls for a reinterpretation of the meanings of masculine and feminine behavior. "Gay men can come to see that the power relations for which the semiotics of masculinity and femininity constitute a strategy have little to do with their lives. The meaning of masculinity, consequently, begins to change. Although masculinity is often the subject of sexual desire for gay men, its role in their lives is 'ironic' " (45). By "ironic," Pronger refers to a specifically gay irony.[11] Of course, this is an insight that is known primarily to gay men, and so serves only as a good starting point for raising awareness about what masculinity is or possibly could be. It is also important to note that not all gay men may take part in this insight, since frequently gay men have attitudes toward women and feminism that are as misogynist as the worst heterosexual men's attitudes (Connell 1995, 159).

One possible aspect of a redefinition of masculinity comes form Leonard Harris's essay "Honor: Emasculation and Empowerment." This essay focuses on the honoring of heroes such as Martin Luther King, Jr., and Malcolm X. Each man exemplified, in different ways, a vision of communal love for the black community. This "love, in both cases, represented a form of empowerment in a direct sense, i.e. it was a good through which one engenders, among other things, the ability of others to impose their will" (Harris 1992, 202). It is to be noted that this kind of empowering can be achieved in many ways: parents help empower their children by caring, nurturing, and guiding, and partners empower each other by support, dialogue, and aid. Martin Luther King, Jr., especially presents a promising new model for masculinity, that of a caring, nurturing, empowering man with a vision of communal love.

As promising as this vision of communal love might seem, it is not entirely without problems. Pronger's and Harris's work calls attention to the fact that masculinity is a socially constructed entity, and as such, masculinity cannot simply be incorporated into some of the more traditionally feminine virtues. These virtues are the kinds of feelings (such as love and compassion) that Martin Luther King, Jr., was honored for, and that can be difficult to separate from the more negative behaviors of aggression, threats, and demands. As Harris notes, the conflation of the traditionally feminine and masculine virtues with less desirable behaviors when we attempt to form them into one coherent whole is highly problematic.

May and Strikwerda attempt an analysis of this kind in both of their pieces, "Fatherhood and Nurturance" and "Male Friendship and Intimacy." In "Fatherhood and Nurturance," May and Strikwerda attempt to analyze the possibility for and the benefits of men gaining the traditionally feminine attribute of nurturance in the context of caring for their children. Central to this nurturance is paying attention to feelings, especially their children's feelings, but also their own. "Fathers will have to *face their own feelings* of regret or shame for having inappropriately punished as well as the need to rebuild trust and a positive sense of self-worth in the child . . . in addition, their work in the family will be something about which they can feel a sense of accomplishment" (May and Strikwerda 1992, 88). Here May and Strikwerda offer an exciting possibility for a new vision of masculinity. Arguably, they address the problematic dualism of feeling-reason by giving men a role in which they must face up to their own feelings as well as those of their children. May and Strikwerda also have a means by which men's work in the home can be revalued: men can feel a new sense of accomplishment about their fathering role. May and Strikwerda carefully outline their project, contrasting their model of a nurturing father with older, traditional models. After arguing for men to take on a more nurturing role with their children, they acknowledge that a time of transition will be necessary. This time of transition will occur with the first generation of men to act as nurturers, who still have the traditionally socialized masculine attributes of toughness, aggressiveness, and an alleged prowess in the public sphere:

> In this time of transition, nurturing fathers could use their socialized public skills to provide positive socialization especially for their girl children. Due to their socialization, men are better able to teach kids how to fend for themselves, especially how to assert themselves into a sometimes hostile world or sandbox. Given the differential socializations already experienced by adults today, fathers will be somewhat better at such roles than mothers. And by this we do not mean merely teaching girls to throw the ball "properly" (that is, not like a girl). Rather, we have in mind taking children on regular outings to the playground or museum or just to the corner store and talking to one's children about strategies for coping with disparate

problems, especially with male strangers, that can be encountered along the way. (89)

This seems at first glance like a very sweet idea—fathers showing their children the ropes of how to get along in the world. Unfortunately, it falls short at many key points. The passage makes many dubious assumptions about men's prowess in certain areas of life. It is wrong to assume that men's prowess is indisputably a good thing (in essentialist claims about men and women's capabilities: "fathers will be somewhat better at such roles than mothers"), and that the male-socialized way of handling situations is the best way of doing things ("men are better able to teach kids how to defend themselves"). It seems to me that in May and Strikwerda's hypothetical situation, many of the negative socialized masculine roles can be passed on to either sex. Furthermore, the possibility of negative socialization being passed on brings up the question of when, if ever, this transitional stage will end. What keeps certain negative roles from being passed on?[12] Thus May and Strikwerda have a very promising notion in the model of the nurturing father, but they put the model to bad use.

Broader Implications for Reason and Emotion Reconceived

In the final sections of the chapter I will describe what I believe these contrasting examples from Jagger and May and Strikwerda can illustrate about current attempts to reconceptualize reason and emotion. I assert that the proper way to understand this issue is twofold. When men do the work of revaluing a deprivileged side of a dichotomy like "feelings," they are perceived as achieving an *epistemological* goal: attempting to get at a more accurate vision of what men are really like, uncovering the hidden emotions, or some other piece of better truth that also fulfills a practical value in rectifying a perceived lack, an Aristotelian lack of intimacy or of full emotional growth. When women do the same work it is perceived as aimed primarily at political goals (removing women's oppression), and having the potential to reinforce stereotypically feminine behaviors via essentialism. This gendered double meaning of reconceptualizing dichotomies like reason and feeling, masculinity and femininity is implicit in May and Strikwerda's project:

> Much feminist writing has focused on a reassessment of female experience in order to counter oppression against women. The social practice of men

failing to develop and express their feelings does have the consequence that men in general are more able to oppress than would be true otherwise. Phenomenologically speaking, however, men simply do not see themselves as oppressors in this way. It does not seem to us that most men intentionally oppress women by failing to disclose their feelings; rather, many men are not even aware that they could be acting otherwise. Nonetheless, they do increasingly see themselves as *lacking* in intimate relationships. Thus we try to provide a positive sense of what male friendship could be like in a less oppressive society. It is our hope that if men do become more caring with each other, they will also become so with the women and children in their lives, thus making it less likely that oppression will continue at its present level. (Strikwerda and May 1992, 96–97)

May and Strikwerda show that their project is teleologically oriented not just to remove oppression—indeed, the removal of women's oppression is a happy side effect of men achieving greater intimacy in relationships among themselves! Instead, May and Strikwerda are primarily interested in providing a positive sense of what intimate male friendship can be like, primarily to help remedy men's lack of intimacy. My intention is not to criticize the whole of May and Strikwerda's project based on this aspect of it, but it illustrates well the reasons feminist literature and the literature of masculinity are still treated in very different ways. Arguably, this difference in treatment goes back to those same hierarchical dualisms.

How to Reconstruct Masculinity

The reading of women feminists' work as primarily political and of men's work as correcting perceived lacks as well as serving a better epistemological project harks back to Aristotle's distinction between a happy life as defined by political work and then the better happy life defined by a life of theory and study.[13] The charge of essentialism leveled against female feminist theorists seems to be a valid concern for other feminist theorists, because of the pervasiveness of these dualisms. Quite tellingly, our exemplary male theorists' vision of male friendship seems forced to buy into some of the old dualisms linked to the symbolic associations of the feminine and the masculine as well. On May and Strikwerda's model, male friendships can begin with doing activities together (ancient Greek activity/passivity dichotomy revisited), and then slowly as men learn to reflect more on their emotions and be more in touch with their feelings, they can begin to express traditionally feminine emotions like caring (Strikwerda and May 1992, 106–7).

Another collection of current writings on masculinity offers a more plausible and optimistic suggestion for dialogues between genders, a suggestion that can also serve as a means toward escaping the problem of hierarchical dualisms. *Engendering Men: The Question of Male Feminist Criticism* (Boone and Cadden 1990), as its title suggests, reflects further work by men with attention to gender, feminist insights on gender, and the seemingly "genderless" quality of masculinity within patriarchy. This collection has a clear focus on literary theory, and includes important insights into the work of women writers like Anne Bradstreet, Emily Dickinson, Sylvia Townsend Warner, and Wendy Wasserstein, as well as queer theorists and the concept of "gay reading." The most compelling suggestion found in this collection is the call for simultaneous reading of male and female traditions and canons, a notion credited to Myra Jehlen, Sandra Gilbert, and Susan Gubar. Such simultaneous readings allow (for example) the reading of work by Gwendolyn Brooks in comparison to Paul Laurence Dunbar and Claude McKay. All too often in women's studies courses, only the work of women is read; all too often when one thinks of literature on masculinity one thinks of male authors. Instead, the insights of both men and women, both members of the hierarchical dualisms that shape our societal context, should be read together. This notion of simultaneous readings is a promising way to avoid the problem of constructing women's and feminists' work as "Other."[14] The avoidance of "Otherness" is a promising first step toward alleviating the problem of the hierarchical dichotomy of masculinity and femininity. By reading the work of men and women together, and by analogy the work of members of different races and classes together, one can see the possibility for opening up new dialogues and a new, less hierarchical relationship between members of those groups.

Suggestions for how men can assume feminist viewpoints, and for how masculinity itself can be reconstructed in a feminist context, can be drawn from the literary theorists' concept of simultaneous readings. Rather than viewing the theoretical work of a woman as "Other," or as primarily political, we should view that work as having the same value as that of a man. This means that feminist insights should and must be regarded as epistemologically valuable, as broadening and enriching our knowledge about the world. A necessary condition for this view is a "devaluing" of the work of men: men's theoretical work and men's insights can no longer be given an unquestioned status as the final yardstick by which good knowledge and truth are judged; the work of women, including feminist women, also holds means by which we can "get at the truth."

Arguably this "devaluing" of men's work is actually not a devaluing at all; it is more plausible to say that such devaluing is really simply seeing men's work for what it is and for what it actually implies. Moral theorists, from Aristotle to Kant, describe moral agency in ways that actually have much in common with a feminist worldview; it is an unhappy historical contingency and fact that they limited their descriptions of moral agents to the men of their time. For Aristotle, only male citizens of the Greek polis, not women or male slaves, were fully moral beings for whom the life of contemplation was prescribed. For Kant, only the male landowners of his day were considered to be fully morally responsible. Yet each of these moral theorists outlines theories that, if taken to their conclusion without the historical influence of oppression of slaves and women, should include everyone as moral beings. For example, when Kant enjoins us, via a rephrasing of the Golden Rule in the *Groundwork of the Metaphysics of Morals* to "treat others never only as a means, but as ends in themselves," and to respect other human beings as rational moral agents, he really ought to mean that this rule holds for men as well as women. In essence, feminist theorists, and especially feminist theorists who maintain a focus and concern for issues of race, do Kantian moral theory better and more consistently that Kant himself.[15]

I take this point to be similar to that behind the quotation with which John Stoltenberg opens his book *The End of Manhood:* "The core of one's being must love justice more than manhood."[16] Here Stoltenberg illustrates the guiding premise of his book, that justice and fairness to everyone's selfhood should override the concerns of traditional manhood. Similarly, I would argue that once we realize the historical contingencies affecting male theoretical work (in a sense, devaluing it), and revalue feminist insights, not only as political but as epistemological, then the path a feminist man should follow becomes somewhat clearer. This realization has commonalities with Starhawk's statement that "if men want to be liberated, they must be willing to let go of the institutionalized advantage they have in every arena of society. Sometimes the advantage is clear to behold—higher pay for the same work, for example" (1992, 29). While the examples above are primarily theoretical, a similar prescription holds for the everyday lives of men and women. Instead of viewing a woman who works in a predominantly male field as merely a political anomaly, a "token," or an example of affirmative action, views that share in a construction of Otherness, we should view her as qualified, capable, hired for her ability to do a job, not to fill a quota. This entails a "devaluing" of the male-dominated field, in the sense that the job can no longer be seen as inherently more valuable simply because more men do it. One example would be physicians and surgeons as opposed to midwives and nurses: traditionally, the work of the doctor is seen as more valuable because it takes more schooling, steady hands, and experience; but the work of nurses and midwives is traditionally dismissed as non-complicated, rote temperature-taking, dispensing of medicine, assistance at birth, or mere emotional nurturance and care. Slowly this view is changing, and is being exposed as a caricature of what nurses and midwives actually do. A major force in this "devaluing" to "revaluing" process is the emergence of Ph.D. programs in nursing science, such as the one at the University of South Carolina. In the process of studying for the Ph.D., nurses do research on various aspects of their work, and expose the complicated nature of nursing. For example, insights from hermeneutic analysis of texts as well as feminist philosophy of science have been used to voice the complexities of caring for patients and helping patients deal with stress. Such literature goes beyond the merely political goal of attaining status for nurses, it also argues effectively that the knowledge of a nurse has as much value as that of an M.D. or surgeon.[17] Similar changes in how women's and men's works are valued should be utilized by men interested in adopting a feminist point of view: work traditionally done by men has no monopoly on insights and truth-getting, and the work of women can, and does, have insight and promising ways to get at truth.

The pervasive influence of hierarchical dualisms like feeling-reason permeates both everyday experience and theoretical work. While attempts to redefine the feminine or to revalue traditionally feminine ways of knowing and doing have been sharply criticized or devalued as mere politics, the same kind of work when done by men is couched in terms of a better, more well-rounded epistemology. While I find both men's and women's explorations of hierarchical dualisms to be important work, I also believe that it is important to realize how pervasive and ingrained certain hierarchical dualisms are in our collective consciousness. One way we can learn to appreciate, be aware of, and possibly supersede these hierarchical dualisms is by avoiding constructions of Otherness and opening new dialogues between all members of society. Through new dialogues a "devaluing" of the masculine side of the ancient hierarchical dichotomies and a revaluing of the traditionally feminine or female will occur. In this way, a realization of the epistemological value of feminist insight will result for men and women.

REFERENCES

Boone, Joseph A., and Michael Cadden, eds. 1990. *Engendering Men: The question of male feminist criticism.* New York: Routledge.

Connell, R. W. 1995. *Masculinities.* Berkeley: University of California Press.

Farrington, Benjamin. " 'Temporis Partus Masculus', An Untranslated Writing of Francis Bacon." *Centaurus* 1 (1951).

Harris, Leonard. 1992. "Honor: Emasculation and empowerment." In Larry May and Robert Strikwerda, eds., *Rethinking Masculinity: Philosophical explorations in light of feminism.* Lanhorn, MD: Rowman Littlefield, 191–208.

hooks, bell. "Men in Feminist Struggle: The necessary movement." In Kay Hagan, ed., *Women Respond to the Men's Movement: A feminist collection.* San Francisco: Pandora.

Jagger, Alison M. 1989. "Love and Knowledge: Emotion in feminist epistemology." In Allison Jagger and Susan Bordo, *Gender/Body/Knowledge: Feminist reconstructions of being and knowing.* New Brunswick: Rutgers University Press.

Keller, Evelyn Fox. 1985. *Reflections on Gender and Science.* New Haven: Yale University Press.

Lloyd, Genevieve. 1984. *The Man of Reason.* Minneapolis: University of Minnesota Press.

May, Larry, and Robert Strikwerda. 1992. "Fatherhood and Nurturance." In Larry May and Robert Strikwerda, eds., *Rethinking Masculinity: Philosophical explorations in light of feminism.* Lanhorn, MD: Rowman Littlefield, 75–94. Originally appeared in *Journal of Social Psychology* 22/2 (fall 1991).

Merchant, Carolyn. 1980. *The Death of Nature: Women, ecology and the scientific revolution.* San Francisco: Harper and Row.

Omery, Anna, et al. 1995. *In Search of Nursing Science.* Thousand Oaks, CA: Sage.

Pronger, Brian. 1992. "Gay Jocks: A phenomenology of gay men in athletics." In Larry May and Robert Strikwerda, eds., *Rethinking Masculinity: Philosophical explorations in light of feminism.* Lanhorn, MD: Rowman Littlefield, 41–58. Originally appeared in Michael Messner and Donald Sabo, eds., *Sport, Men and the Gender Order.* Champaign, IL: Human Kinetics, 1990.

Starhawk. 1992. "A Men's Movement I Can Trust." In Kay Hagan, ed., *Women Respond to the Men's Movement: A feminist collection.* San Francisco: Pandora.

Stoltenberg, John. 1990. *Refusing to Be a Man: Essays on sex and justice*. New York: Meridian Books.

————. 1993. *The End of Manhood: A book for men of conscience*. New York: Dutton.

Strikwerda, Robert, and Larry May. 1992. "Male Friendship and Intimacy." In Larry May and Robert Strikwerda, eds., *Rethinking Masculinity: Philosophical explorations in light of feminism*. Lanhorn, MD: Rowman Littlefield, 95–110. Originally appeared in *Hypatia* 7/2 (summer 1992).

NOTES

1. "Rewriting or redefining Woman" has held different meanings for different theorists. This chapter will primarily employ Judith Butler's sense of the phrase, in which "Woman" does not really signify any one woman, but rather a performance of womanhood that is in line with certain symbolic meanings of femininity, certain gendered codings of masculine/feminine behavior, dress, and so forth. Thus a redefining or rewriting necessarily entails some change in these symbolic structures and codings.

2. One example can be found in the *Oxford English Dictionary*'s definition of "masculine" and "feminine." Echoing the ancient Greek association of masculinity with activity and femininity with passivity, the *OED* defines these terms so that power is the distinguishing feature of masculinity, while lack of power is the distinguishing feature of femininity. "Masculine" is defined as having the appropriate excellences of the male sex: "manly, virile, vigorous, powerful," while "feminine" is defined in a deprecatory sense as "womanish, effeminate." The *OED* definition of "effeminate" provides an even clearer example of how femininity and masculinity are still entwined: the *OED* defines "effeminate" as "to make unmanly, enervate. To grow weak, languish" (Pronger 1992, 44).

3. Here I refer to the Pythagorean table of opposites, which was formulated in the sixth century b.c., and specifically aligned the female with the bad or inferior side of ten hierarchical dichotomies, such as limited/unlimited, odd/even, one/many, right/left, male/female, rest/motion.

4. This alignment is explicitly described in Plato's *Symposium*, as in Diotima's speech, which metaphorically links the highest form of love with activities that are procreative and intellectually creative, and that occur only between men. A similar theme is present in much of Aristotle, as in the Aristotelian distinction between form and matter (Metaphysics VI I Z, 15–17), and the relationship of that distinction to reproduction. On the Aristotelian view, the father was seen as providing the formative principle, the real causal force of generation, while the mother provided only matter that received form or determination, and nourished what had been produced by the father (Lloyd 1984, 3).

5. Plato describes the human soul in the *Republic* (book IV) as well as the *Phaedrus* (246a6). As presented in the *Republic,* the doctrine is traditionally traced to the Pythagoreans via Cicero's *Tusculanae Disputationes,* 4, 5, and 10.

6. One example of these "later Judaic and Christian thinkers" would be St. Thomas Aquinas and his vision of an organic state: "Aquinas presented an integrated system of nature and society based . . . on hierarchical gradations. Each part had its own place, rights, duties, and value, which together contributed to the perfection of the whole universal community. Both nature and society were composed of parts so that the purpose or end of the lower was to serve the higher, while that of the higher was to guide the lower toward the common moral good. Each part sought the perfection of its particular nature, growing and developing from within" (Merchant 1980, 72). Moreover, Aquinas posited a hierarchal order that ascribed descending ranks to angels, men, then women.

7. "Unless the structural features of our concepts of gender are understood, any emphasis on a supposedly distinctive style of thought or morality is liable to be caught up in a deeper, older structure of male norms and female complementation. The affirmation of the value and importance of 'the feminine' cannot itself be expected to shake the underlying normative structures, for, ironically, it will occur in a space already prepared for it by the intellectual tradition it seeks to reject" (Lloyd 1984, 105).

8. Intricately related to the dichotomy of reason and feeling is the conceptualization of feeling as passive, reason as active.

9. This is another point at which Jagger may be critiqued. While Jagger correctly points to the devalued status of women on the traditional reason-feeling dualism, she incorrectly places the emphasis of her critique on the myth of dispassionate inquiry. It seems more plausible, given the arguable tracing of the reason-feeling dichotomy to the Pythagoreans, and the relatively recent advent of scientific inquiry as described here, that it would be more accurate to blame any silencing of women on the pervasively masculinist or promasculinist nature of those dichotomies rather than on the more recent myth.

10. By "symbolic status" I refer again to the relative values ascribed to the various sides of hierarchical dichotomies. After achieving androgyny, I would argue, we would simply find something other than gender to ascribe value, such as race (black-white) or class (rich-poor) and thereby keep people in their place. What we need to search for is a way to avoid dualistic valuing altogether.

11. "Gay irony is a unique way of knowing that has its origins in the social construction of heterosexist society" (Pronger 1992, 48). Thus gay irony reflects an awareness of masculinity as a fluid, flexible social construction: "for many gay men, masculinity and femininity cease to be experienced as what one *is,* and they become, quite consciously, ways in which one *acts*"(Pronger 1992, 45).

12. It should also be noted that while May and Strikwerda's concern about sexual assault or abductions of children is good, one must remember that coach-

ing children about male strangers is somewhat misled because the vast majority of those crimes are committed by someone who the child already knows and trusts (perhaps the male role model May and Strikwerda describe).

13. This reading of May and Strikwerda against Jagger is especially ironic, since Jagger's explicitly stated goal is a better, specifically theoretical epistemological model that includes feeling and reason, while the notion that May and Strikwerda get at better truth about men's emotions seems to naturally follow from their discussion of men perceiving a lack in their own lives.

14. By the construction of Otherness, I mean the way work done by women in a given field may be pointed out as Other than or outside the norm; thus a hierarchical and dualistic relationship between male and female is maintained (for example, describing someone as "one of the best female jazz musicians," rather than as simply "one of the best jazz musicians").

15. For an example, see the work of bell hooks (specifically on feminism, race and masculinity: 1992, 116).

16. See also *Refusing to Be a Man: Essays on Sex and Justice* (Stoltenberg 1990, various essays).

17. For examples of this literature, see Anna Omery et al., *In Search of Nursing Science* (1995, various essays).

Chapter Twelve

The Multiple Genders of the Court
Issues of Identity and Performance in a Drag Setting

Steven P. Schacht

> Drag is also disorienting. To become truly familiar with
> its queens and their flair for dramatizing life's absurdi-
> ties is to have one's perspective changed dramatically.
> —Julian Fleisher, *The Drag Queens of New York*

The clamor from countless simultaneous conversations wafts through the smoke-filled club. Flashing and gyrating ceiling lights seemingly keep rhythm to the thunderous, pulsating technotronic-sounding music. Scantily clad waiters hurriedly make their rounds through the constraining crowd of nearly two hundred people, cheerfully, sometimes flirtatiously ensuring that everyone's glass is full. Warm glances, verbal greetings, and hugs and kisses are freely exchanged by the mingling participants of this jovial gathering. The personable, electronically energized atmosphere invites all present to actively partake in the evening's activities.

At 9:15 P.M., after individually welcoming and visiting for over an hour with nearly everyone in the bar, Tina Louise Sapphire Dior, Empress XXIV and co-emcee for tonight's show, gestures for me to follow her, and we make our way over to the podium next to the stage. With her reddish back-combed hair done up in a tight swirl towering at least six inches above her head, she gracefully carries herself in an elegant, tight-fitting black sequined jumpsuit with matching black four-inch high heels. Her appearance is underscored with conspicuous but impeccably applied makeup and very long, bright red fake fingernails. I am wearing a black tuxedo, pleated white shirt, bow tie, and black patent leather shoes that a friend in the setting has generously loaned me. The jacket is meticulously embroidered with sparkly red beads that glisten under the lights.

After placing her cocktail and hand purse under the podium, the DJ turns off the background music and hands Tina a microphone from his booth. In a spirited voice, the show formally begins.

> *Tina:* Welcome to the Emperor and Empress scholarship show. Give your-self a hand for showing up, you guys. [*Applause.*] Ah, now, we can do better than that. This bar is fucking crowded. Give you guys yourself a hand. Come'n. [*Much louder applause.*] Goodness. Right now it gives me absolutely a privilege and honor to introduce my co-emcees for this evening. Ladies and gentlemen, please welcome first, Her Serene High-ness, Miss Debutante XIX, Paige DeMonet Sapphire Rockafeller. [*Pause. Tina looks around.*] Oh well, she's playing pretty Barbie somewhere, so she'll show up when she shows up. [*Enter Paige, hands held high holding her cocktail and purse, carefully running in small steps from the audience. She is wearing high heels, a white jumpsuit, and really big blond hair. She looks like a statuesque cross between a giant Barbie doll and Marilyn Monroe. Applause and some laughter.*] Ladies and gentlemen, your spe-cial emcee for this evening. An incredible man you know. Ah, it takes a lot to get into the gay community, especially being heterosexual.
>
> [*Interrupting.*] Paige: Ya' right.
>
> *Tina:* Shut up you. [*Crowd laughter.*] Ah, ladies and gentlemen, my other co-emcee—and I'm absolutely honored to stand by this man's side— Mr. Steve Schacht. [*Applause.*]

The following two and a half hours witness a constant parade of over twenty-five lip-syncing performers participating in the show, which will raise $622 for the Imperial Sovereign Court of Spokane (ISCS) Scholar-ship Fund. As is typical of charitable events put on in our culture, the majority of those present are elegantly dressed and end up spending more money on the evening's entertainment (drinks) than donating to the cause. Unlike mainstream society, this show is being sponsored and staged by an organization of gay and lesbian individuals who have adopted a variety of gender performances and identities.

This essay analyzes my ethnographic experiences of being a valued, esteemed straight male participant in an almost exclusively gay and les-bian drag setting. Although the scenes I predominantly draw on are grounded in my experiences of co-emceeing the event briefly introduced above (videotaped by one of the participants, who graciously gave me a copy for my research) the essay also is based on my two years of involvement in the ISCS and over four years in various other female impersonator settings in seven cities.[1] Specifically, it explores a setting where at least six discernable gender identities relationally exist, and analyzes the implications this has for challenging preexisting gender inequalities.

While most of us in the social sciences have come to intellectually recognize the socially constructed basis of gender (and to a lesser extent sexuality and race), we nonetheless tend to treat female and male as essential categories in our analyses and interactions with others. Stated slightly differently, we operate with the assumptions that all men will have male personality characteristics and correspondingly act like men (and vice versa for women). Such an outlook fails to take into account the performance nature of gender and how fluid gender identity and behavior are, varying significantly from setting to setting and over one's lifetime. The next two sections of this essay explore the fictitious basis of gender dimorphism and how the members of the court, through their attitudes and actions, demonstrate the truly variable, sometimes ephemeral nature of gender.

My attraction to and involvement in the world of drag queens, as a feminist ethnographer and activist, is not the result of some explicit feminist statement made by the members of this context. Quite truthfully, none are to be found. Rather, my fascination with female impersonation is that despite the dominant society's obsessive attempts to maintain rigidly hierarchal gender roles, participants of this and similar settings have still arisen from the larger cultural milieu to demonstrate that gender relations are nothing more than a caricature and ultimately a farce. That is, I have learned from their convincing gender performances that there is not necessarily one innate way of doing male or female, but rather a infinite number of possible ways to do gender (Schacht 1997). By example, the drag queens have taught me that I can learn new ways of relating to others (Schacht 1996b). As a feminist with a lifetime of experiences as a man, this means exploring and developing radically new ways of relating with others and the world around me that are not predicated on privilege, power, and oppression. I end this chapter by arguing that when we recognize the diversity of gender identities and the corresponding performances that exist, an emancipatory image emerges that both questions the apparent necessity of a dichotomous worldview and points to ways of being that question preexisting inequalities.

Beyond the Apparent Reality of a Dichotomous Worldview

It has become conventional to imagine a linked system of two sexes, two genders and two sexual orientations. But it is as appropriate to see sex and sexual orientation as aspects of the gender system rather than separate from it. Once that reorientation is made, the six-part system of sex, gender and sexual orientation can be reshuffled into a four-part gender system. It produces a more parsimonious and coherent system, and one in which it is never presumed that there is a biological reality that exists outside of the culture produced by our minds.

—Randolph Trumbach, "London Sapphists"

Much of Western thought and most, if not all, preexisting hierarchical realities are based on the socially constructed notion that we reside in a dichotomous, binary world: male/female, men/women, straight/gay, white/black, rich/poor, reason/emotion, winners/losers, good/evil, and so forth (Hekman 1987; Haraway 1988; Hawkesworth 1989; Delphy 1993; James 1997). Depending on the setting in which they might occur, these relational approaches to existence prescribe two—and only two—possible outcomes that inevitably and quite conveniently sort all people/things into discrete superior or subordinate statuses. Yet during our lifetimes we all are confronted with situations that do not readily conform to the expectations of a dualistic reality. This certainly has been the case with my involvement in various drag communities. Here, instead of just two conceivable genders being present, as one might "normally" expect, within the statuses of sex, gender, and sexual orientation, I have found myself surrounded by a multitude of possible gendered outcomes.

On the evening of this ISCS fund raiser, when the six-part system of sex, gender, and sexual orientation is reshuffled, six instead of just four discernable gender identities (e.g., straight men, gay men, straight women, and gay women as reflected in the above quote) are relationally being performed. In degrees of their relative importance in this setting, these six are gay drag queens, gay drag kings, lesbian drag kings, lesbian drag queens, straight men, and straight women. In exploring each of these gendered states of being, like many social theorists (Butler 1990, 1991; Connell 1995; Lorber 1994; Stoltenberg 1996; West and Zimmerman 1987), I take an approach that recognizes that what it means to be "male" or "female" can be understood only in terms of "what it should not—most

206 STEVEN P. SCHACHT

typically seen in the dominant culture as can not—be" and how correspondingly one relationally interacts with those who are supposed to be
one's antithesis (Schacht 1996a, b; 1997, 10). The same is true of other
social identities/statuses, such as straight/gay and rich/poor, all of which
ultimately are relational in constructed, performed, and consequential
meaning. When we consider sex and sexual orientation as additional matrices in the gender system, we see a spectrum of relational states of being.
That is, out of the intersection/tension between supposedly discrete binary
states of being—female/male (sex), woman/man (gender), and straight/
gay (sexuality)—emanates a multitude of lived gender identities and performances.

In exploring what it means to be a man, woman, or otherwise in our
society, I have also adopted the position that drag demonstrates gender
identity to be a form of performance for which there are no original
scripts. Or as more elegantly stated by Butler,

> Drag constitutes the mundane way in which genders are appropriated,
> worn, and done; it implies that all gendering is a kind of impersonation
> and approximation. If this is true, it seems, there is no original or primary
> gender that drag imitates, but *gender is a kind of imitation for which there
> is no original*; in fact, it is a kind of imitation that produces the very notion
> of the original as an *affect* and consequence of the imitation itself. (1991, 21;
> emphasis in original)

And while, as I have discussed elsewhere, there often are oppressive hierarchical realities to gender imitation in drag settings (Schacht 1997), regardless of who is playing what role, viewing gender identity as a fluid form
of performance—instead of a fixed state of being—still creates anxieties
for dominant/straight outsiders and points to subversive possibilities in the
larger culture (Butler 1990, 1991; Garber 1992; Schacht 1996b).

What I am saying in this essay is based on my creative attempts at
performing a gender identity in terms of what I perceive myself to be—
a feminist ethnographer, writer, and activist. Somewhat inversely, the
participants of this setting have imitatively adopted gender identities that
largely adhere to the values of the dominant culture with no intention of
subverting or challenging them. In fact, from my observations and experiences I would say that they are situationally quite successful in realizing cultural standards of gender identity in both their actions and appearance (especially many of the drag queens). However, having so
convincingly performed these gendered ways of being, but "essentially"

being born the wrong sex, they inadvertently throw into question the notion of innate gender identity and behavior.

The Court and Its Multifarious Cast of Gendered Players

I always say "we're born naked and the rest is drag." Any performer who puts on an outfit to project an image is in drag. Everything you put on is to fit a preconceived notion of how you wanna be seen. It's all drag. Mine is just more glamorous.

—RuPaul, quoted in Roger Baker, *Drag*

The following gender identities are not offered as mutually exclusive or exhaustive states of being. After all, they each very much overlap in that gender identities are relationally performed, and on any given evening in this setting, there are several people present who fall into more than one, between, or outside each of these conceptual categories. For instance, bisexuals, transvestites, and preop transsexuals who sometimes frequent this context would not at all readily fit into/conform to the performances being worn/undertaken that are outlined below. There sometimes also are male cross-dressers who patronize this bar who only partially transform their appearance; for example, a very male-looking face is worn with very feminine-looking clothing (or vice versa). All these individuals, although somewhat marginalized in the setting, would nonetheless be intermediaries of what are already proposed intermediate gendered ways of relationally being. Thus, while I recognize the limits of my expanded perspective, the following outlines the genders I found most saliently and generally present in this setting as reflected in this particular evening's activities.

Gay Drag Queens

Perhaps because of the seemingly all-encompassing transformation they undertake, the drag queens—all of whom are gay men—are the most venerated members of the court and in many ways its icons. In fact, those who most successfully imitate/conform to conservative cultural standards of feminine beauty and being a woman are very much the group's leaders. An "absolutely" and "flawless" (two terms frequently used in this context to describe those seen as the most beautiful) woman always removes all visible body hair, does a face with noticeably but elegantly applied makeup, and wears large sculptured hair and hyperfeminine attire: tight-fitting jumpsuits (for less formal occasions) or designer gowns, sparkling, elegant jewelry, and high heels. The drag queens' actions involve quite traditional ways of being a woman. Often resembling contestants of some beauty pageant, drag queens take small, dainty steps with their legs kept together, sit upright on the edge of their seats with legs closely crossed, carefully sip their drinks through straws, and in general, act in a coquettish manner when interacting with men.

Tina and Paige, my co-emcees for this event, personify these externally adopted and internally prescribed feminine ideals. Both present quite convincing/flawless images of exceptionally attractive women, and are quite popular for their stage performances and their facilitation of the court activities. Accordingly, they both hold important elected positions in the group. As previously noted, and indicative of her recent arrival on the drag scene, Paige holds the title of Miss Debutante XIX, a designation reserved for queens that are seen as up and coming stars. Tina, who has been doing drag for over ten years, holds the most important and powerful position (elected or appointed) in the court: Empress XXIV.

While infrequently a male persona, such as myself, or a lesbian will serve as an emcee, a handful of prominent drag queens are responsible for organizing and hosting nearly all the shows staged by the court. Beyond organizing the given event, emceeing involves providing filler entertainment between performances, giving affirming individual recognition when announcing each of the performers, acknowledging the importance of the audience, and in general, setting the tone for the evening's activities. In decidedly masculine tone and delivery, but hyperfeminine in appearance and personal mannerism, the drag queens who emcee not only command the largest audiences but oversee most of the group's activities. They are the sovereign leaders of the court. But, while drag queens convincingly *appear to be* real women (especially the ones who emcee), they assume and exercise masculine authority in the setting, and thus end up escaping and distancing themselves from the reality of *experientially being* a woman in the outside world.

Like all gender identities, female impersonation is contextually grounded and directed at an audience. Given that none of the queens in the court don female attire outside this context, and several appear and act quite masculine when out of drag, they perhaps best illustrate the temporal and situational nature of gender identity. Their success in adopting women's gender identity is judged in terms of how convincingly they can perform what are seen as traditional and stereotypical feminine gestures and ways of being.

Beyond how convincingly she presents herself as a beautiful, glamorous woman, a given queen's notoriety is also based on her stage presence in terms of how much spirit and creativity she puts into her lip-sync performance. While this is accomplished a variety of ways behind the voices of a multitude of famous female singers, the most esteemed performers are always the ones who play to the emotions of the audience. Both Paige and Tina are well-received performers and typically are tipped quite well. The following is a brief description of Tina's routine the night of this fund raiser.

Tina

Paige: Ladies and gentlemen, please welcome her Most Imperial Majesty, Tina Loise Sapphire Dior. [*Enter Tina, now wearing a silver and gold spaghetti-strap sequined gown and matching high heels. In the background is played one of her signature songs.*]

Tina: "I want one moment in time . . . please give me one moment in time . . . and I will give eternally." [*Tina lip-syncs the words in an almost exaggerated but still convincing hyperfeminine manner. Her quivering lips are further accentuated by her fully extended, agitating fingers and jiggling body movements. Whenever the verse "I will give eternally" is heard she gently draws her hands over her chest. Over twenty people come forward to tip her. While she frequently curtseys to individual audience members, her head is always held high in an upright manner and she looks each of her admirers in the eyes. Individual dollar bills are placed gently but firmly in her outstretched hands. Her performance is quite polished and professional in delivery; in appearance and demeanor she appears to be a cross between a Las Vegas showgirl and a female nightclub singer.*]

While Tina ultimately and quite successfully plays to (commands) the entire audience in attendance, both while emceeing and during her routines, some of her most sincere performance gestures are specifically directed at the gay drag kings present.

Gay Drag Kings

As I have outlined in more detail elsewhere (Schacht 1997), the gay "men" of the court are paradoxically the relational signifiers for the importance and power of the gay drag queens.[2] That is, in direct contrast to the dominant culture, where women often masquerade as the appropriate contrast and confirmation of men and masculine authority through their adopted/forced stance of supportive deference (Lacan 1983; Butler 1990, 44–47), gay drag kings inversely assume this relational position in this context. Like all the participants present, they accomplish this through their appearance and relational actions.

In varying degrees of obviousness, gay drag kings always wear very masculine-looking attire.[3] Typically sporting a thick moustache and short, neatly cropped hair (both personal "grooming" details that I did not include in my masculine presentations of self), they wear tight-fitting blue jeans (or sometimes leather pants) and t-shirts or western shirts at less formal occasions. Suit coats or tuxedos covered with beads and/or rhinestones are donned at more important functions. Other masculine-appearing accoutrements frequently include items such as cowboy hats and boots, bolo ties, large medallions attached to a necklace worn by all drag king title holders (both lesbian and gay), tennis shoes, thick leather belts, and solid, heavy-looking rings.

While gay drag kings generally have a conventionally dominant appearance and style about them (they walk with broad, strutting steps and sit with their legs spread apart), in relation to the gay drag queens they play secondary, often behind-the-scenes roles that could be considered traditionally feminine in practice. For instance, the men of the court often are expected to serve as personal attendants and dressers to various drag queens by carrying their outfits and assisting them when changing. Several of these men also do beadwork and other sewing duties for several of the gay drag queens. They also are responsible for an array of other behind-the-scenes activities, such as building sets for court-sponsored events and videotaping them, for which formal recognition rarely is given. During shows, they are expected to escort drag queens when they tip other performers and often will dedicate their routines by serenading a popular gay drag queen.

Like members of other subordinate groups in our society, gay drag kings also are responsible for reinforcing the gendered norms of the setting. Not only do they maintain their own image and position in the court, but by adhering to the gendered values of the gay drag queens, they directly support the importance of the established, "flawless" queens. Thus, unsponsored newcomers or gender benders[4] who challenge the prevailing images of female beauty are summarily boycotted; they do not receive tips and are referred to (sometimes in their presence or directly to their faces) in hostile terms: "Miss Thing. Why don't you go home and figure out which gender you are?" or "What an ugly bitch. Wonder who taught her how to dress/do her makeup?" Such actions and statements clearly define what is acceptable in this context and who is seen as the rightful leaders of the group: flawless gay drag queens who present upper-class images of glamorous feminine beauty.

While drag kings have adopted a hypermasculine identity for shows and act accordingly during them, several act in quite effeminate ways otherwise. That is, if someone outside this setting were to meet certain drag kings, they would probably conclude that they had just met gay men. Often speaking in a higher-pitched voice, with stereotypically limp wrists partially extended, and hips sashaying, they successfully and perhaps purposefully fulfill outsiders' expectations of what a gay man is supposed to be. In fact, from my numerous experiences in external contexts, I would say that drag kings act far more effeminate than drag queens outside of the setting. Here again, the performance nature of gender identity is found to be situationally grounded and quite fluid.

Two individuals present this evening who exemplify a gay drag king in both their appearance and actions are Eddy Ford Kennady-Smith, Imperial Prince XIX, and Richard Ford, an appointed His Imperial Majesty Enchantor. Both attend nearly all in-town events sponsored by the group and frequently attend out-of-town shows as representatives of the ISCS Richard, most typically casually dressed in jeans and t-shirt, always appears quite masculine with his full moustache. Almost always refusing to perform, he has quietly spent the evening behind a camcorder taping the evening's activities. Although Eddy is not nearly the behind-the-scenes participant that Richard is, the following description of Eddy's lip-sync performance tonight further illustrates the gendered roles drag kings undertake in this setting.

Eddy

Tina: Ladies and gentlemen, please welcome this next gentlemen. He will do absolutely anything I ask. I don't even ask him to show up, and he'll be there. Ladies and gentlemen, His Imperial Highness, Crown Prince XIX, Eddy Ford Kennady-Smith. Give it up for him you guys. [*Enter Eddy to the stage replete with a thick moustache and wearing blue jeans, multicolor western shirt, and cowboy boots. He lip-syncs the words to a*

song about Billy the Kid and shooting bad guys with Colt 45's sung by a
male country western recording artist.]
Eddy: "I miss Billy the Kid . . . now that he's dead . . . I wonder where he
is." [*Frequently clenching his fists, Eddy delivers his performance in a*
swaggering, assertive manner. He receives the nearly twenty audience mem-
bers with a firm grip when taking their tips, and frequently bows his head
in deference, especially to the drag queens.]

Although assuming a somewhat different relational location in the court,
in both appearance and action, gay drag kings are quite similar to many
of their lesbian sisters/brothers in this setting.

Lesbian Drag Kings

Lesbians constitute about one-third of the active members of the court.
In their actions and presentation of self, the vast majority of these participants (close to 80 percent) would be considered butch lesbians; or from
the framework in which I am writing, lesbian drag kings. Similar to the
gay drag kings, lesbian drag kings have adopted very masculine-appearing
styles of dress and personal mannerisms. Short, feathered-back hair is by
far the most frequent hairstyle sported. Since makeup apparently is seen
as more appropriate for the queens (both gay and lesbian), lesbian drag
kings use no makeup of any sort. The most typically worn attire for
informal occasions includes blue jeans, cowboy boots, leather jackets, and
tight-fitting western shirts (some appear to have taped their breasts to
flatten their chests). For more important functions tuxedos (often covered
in beads or rhinestones) and other formal male attire are donned. From
just their appearance, one could easily mistake several of them for "real"
men if one was not told otherwise. Most if not all of these lesbians also
"wear" a masculine identity appearance in other public contexts. This is
different from the gay drag queens, who appear as women only for shows.

Lesbian drag kings also carry themselves and act in a stereotypically
masculine fashion. For instance, broad, almost swaggering, steps are taken
when walking, legs are never crossed but instead comfortably spread apart
when seated, and by far the most popular beverage is a beer drunk out of
a long-neck bottle. Most speak in a deeper, more authoritative voice.
Often with lesbian drag queen girlfriends in tow or on their arms, they
very much act like "the man" with their partners. Most songs selected for
their lip-syncing routines are from male (often country) and lesbian sing-

ers (such as Melissa Etheridge) and are performed with masculine gesture. In general, both performing or simply interacting in the context, they exude an unfaltering confidence—almost cockiness—that is most frequently associated with men in the dominant culture. Thus, largely rejecting hyperfemininity, both inside and outside the setting, they have set up a tetrarchy of sorts where they command a smaller, subordinate audience in comparison to the gay drag queens.

Six of the past twenty emperors have been lesbian drag kings, and several have also held lesser "male" titles (such as crown prince and Mr. Wrangler) in the court. As such, in both appearance and status, lesbian drag kings, like the "men" of the court, also fulfill the function of relational signifiers of the gay drag queens. And while they are not as fully immersed in this role in the sense that they do not serve as dressers or sew outfits, lesbian drag kings often will escort gay drag queens to tip other performers and also are responsible for an array of behind the scenes activities (such as building stages, selling raffle tickets, or being door attendants) for which very little formal recognition is given. Likewise, while gay drag queens make up special names for their female personas (e.g., Tina and Paige), both lesbian and gay drag kings almost always keep their real first names.

Unlike the gay drag kings, however, whose actions are almost entirely directed at the gay drag queens, lesbian drag kings play to an audience that is of only minimal concern to the gay men—other lesbians. Thus, while I have never seen a gay drag king or queen devote their performance to (serenade) a lesbian, lesbian drag kings most frequently dedicate their songs to lesbian drag queens and sometimes to gay drag queens and kings. The following description of Donna's performance this evening, a past and present emperor (she is referred to as the Baby Butch Emperor), highlights a song dedication and the gendered manner in which it is accomplished. Also note (and perhaps this further reflects their secondary status in this setting), that since lesbian drag kings perform with their real first names, gender ambiguity often results when they are announced ("please welcome *His* Imperial Majesty, the Panda Bear *Emperor herself* . . . *Donna*"). One can further speculate that gay drag queens emceeing conceivably see themselves as "more real" in the roles they play—assuredly more powerful—than their lesbian ("girl" and "baby butch") counterparts trying to play a male identity.

Donna

Tina: Ladies and gentlemen, I kind of like bribed, I pleaded, and finally went to the girlfriend for this next number. I said if this girl doesn't sing, you ain't giving it up. . . . So obviously you gave it up. . . . Didn't you? [*Lori, Donna's girlfriend sitting in the audience, and appearing quite embarrassed, sheepishly nods yes.*] Good for you. Ladies and gentlemen, this is a dedication from one lover to another, to Lori from Donna, because she thinks you're cute as a button. And you are! Ladies and gentlemen, please welcome His Imperial Majesty, the Panda Bear Emperor herself . . . please welcome the Baby Butch Emperor, Donna. [*Enter Donna to the stage wearing tight-fitting Levi jeans, held up by a thick black belt replete with a large buckle, red western shirt with black t-shirt underneath, and cowboy boots. The song, by a male country artist, blares in the background.*]

Donna: "Love is unconditional . . . you will always be the miracle that makes my life complete." [*Immediately after lip-syncing a line or two, Donna picks up a dozen red and white roses, brings them to Lori in the audience, and gives her a kiss. After returning to the stage, she receives tips from nearly twenty people. When taking the money, instead of dropping her head in deference like some gay drag kings and lesbian drag queens often do, she looks the individual in the eyes, and takes the money out of her/his hand firmly, almost like a handshake. Toward the end of her routine, she tosses the money she has collected onto a speaker, turns, and assertively gestures to Lori with one finger to come up to the stage. She draws her hand down across her lower face, like men feeling their whiskers, bends down onto one knee, and then pulls Lori up to her to give her a passionate kiss. This ends the performance.*]

Not only does Donna always appear and act very masculine in this context, but as the above description suggests, a significant part of her performance is based in having relational contrasts present (her feminine partner) to further demonstrate what she is not.

Lesbian Drag Queens

Feminine-appearing lesbians in this context are somewhat of a rarity. Most lesbian drag queens, like Lori above, are partners of lesbian drag kings, and only a handful have ever held court titles (one empress and one princess). Their corresponding influence on the court's activities is extremely limited. I would speculate that this is partially the result of the fact that only the gay drag queens are seen as the rightful heirs to images of traditional feminine beauty in this context. This is especially apparent in the fact that the few lesbian drag queens who are accepted and perform are all noticeably heavier than the gay drag queens, and as such are not perceived as much of a threat to those seen as fairest in the land/court. Nevertheless, lesbian drag queens also subscribe to conservative ideals of feminine beauty in that they tend to have longer hair and paint their nails; wear makeup, dresses and gowns, and high heels; speak in higher-pitched voices; and sit, walk, and in general carry themselves in a "lady-like" manner.

They use songs by female recording artists, and their lip-sync performances often tend to be quite similar to those staged by gay drag queens. The following is a description of Carrie's (the reigning Crown Princess) routine the evening of the fund raiser. She is the only one of a small handful of lesbian drag queens who attend shows who performs with any regularity.[5]

Carrie

Tina: This next performer has done an absolutely incredible, incredible job in my book. Ah, she only asked me one thing when I asked her to be Crown Princess, and that's we become friends. And we have gone way beyond that. I consider this person to be my confidant and I absolutely love her. She has something she wants me to read. [*Tina picks up a card from the podium and begins to read it.*] I want to thank everyone for coming to last weekend's show. I am going to do a song I got cookie dough on. [*Carrie is known for distributing her homemade chocolate cookies to various court members. Tina has started to have a puzzled look on her face, but then smiles, puts down the card, and continues.*] Oh, last weekend she wanted to do this number but got cookie dough on it. And she got it off. Thank god Carrie. [*Tina picks up card and resumes reading.*] Rick [*a male who is the reigning Crown Prince*], I'm glad you are here. This song's for you. Love you. Ladies and gentlemen, please welcome Her Most Imperial Crown Princess ... Ladies and gentlemen, Carrie Bixler Kennady-Smith. [*Enter Carrie to the stage wearing a black satin sequined gown, black boa, black high heels, and a sparkling necklace and matching dangling earrings. Her back-combed hair is done up into a loose bun on top of her head; ringlets hang down along the sides of her face. She has bright red nails and lipstick, and noticeable eyeshadow and base makeup. In the background a song by a female performer is being played.*]

Carrie: "I believe in love . . . I believe in dreamers . . . I believe in mom and dad . . . I believe in miracles . . . And I believe in you." [*Frequently sashaying back and forth and tipping her head from side to side, she lip-syncs the words to this song in a feminine manner very similar to how a gay drag queen might perform it. When taking tips from audience members she curtseys and bows her head, with eyes downturned, in apparent deference. She ends her performance by looking into the video recorder, smiling, and rolling her eyes in a seemingly cutesy fashion.*]

Carrie's presence, although somewhat atypical in this context, still very much represents another gendered identity relationally playing to a largely masculine audience of lesbian and gay drag kings and sometimes gay drag queens.

Straight Men

The presence of self-identified straight people in this setting is typically infrequent. However, on the evening of this fund raiser, and because of my participation in the court and especially since I was guest emceeing, there were fifteen straight people in attendance; six were men. All were students of mine (or their friends) from a university where I taught at the time.[6] Most straight individuals who have attended shows with me, especially straight men, usually are quite apprehensive about going for their first time and are visibly nervous once they arrive. It has often taken a fair amount of persuasion on my part to convince them that attending a drag show might be a fun learning experience, and typically my spouse and I have had to reserve tables just for our sponsored visitors and then serve as their comforting chaperons for the evening. I introduce my guests to my friends in the setting and sometimes make reassuring comments that since they are sitting with me, everyone knows they are straight and nothing bad is going to happen to them. On several occasions, before I was even given the opportunity to introduce them, straight men have anxiously blurted out things like "I am straight and with Steve" or "This is my girlfriend and I'm one of Steve's students." (Sometimes statements like this have been met with comments such as "That's too bad, not everyone's perfect" or "What a shame/waste, you're so cute.") Frequently I have also had to escort them on their first trip to the restroom.

While part of their apparent reservation about going to a show is the result of the homophobic nature of our society, it is perhaps equally the consequence of now being in a context where they are a minority group member when most (to varying degrees) are used to interacting in situations where they are dominants. This is even more true for the straight men; for some of them this is the first time they have ever felt like a minority group member. In addition, they typically come from conventional settings where two genders are accepted as "reality" and are now entering a setting where at least six genders are present. This potentially reveals the performance nature of all gender, which throws into question the basis of their own masculine actions. Even if one is a good male actor in other settings, if one is unsure of the gendered expectations of attending a drag show one can easily leave it with the unsettling feeling of being a pretender—at the show and potentially elsewhere thereafter.

To compensate, they typically respond in ways that make known their dominant status in other contexts. Thus, I have seen several straight men physically attach themselves to straight women present—an accompanying girlfriend, another student who they know from school, or on a couple of occasions, my spouse—and try to appear as heterosexual as possible. This is even more apparent should a straight man become brave enough to go up to tip a performer: a straight woman almost always has to escort him. Thus, like in the larger culture, straight women can serve as heterosexual props, symbolically attesting to straight men's dominant status and shielding them from what is perceived as a lesser status: the gay men present.

On the evening of the show, I was unable to meet this obligation—an escort and signifier of their heterosexuality—because once the show began I was emceeing and performing. Nevertheless, as reflected in the following scene, I unconsciously fulfilled this presumed duty of sorts for both my students and myself. One of my duties as emcee is to make newcomers feel welcome to participate in the show (give the performers tips). Although Tina had already done this by thanking my students for attending and otherwise making note of their presence on five previous occasions this evening, I took this a step further and brought them up on stage as a form of filler entertainment between performances.

The Students and I

Me: Brad, Brad, come on. Come on Brad, and bring your spouse with you. [*Gesturing for him and then several others to come up on stage.*] Kevin,

you too. Joanne, Arlene, come on and join everyone else on stage. Please
... [*After getting ten students up on stage, I continue, now addressing both
the students and audience.*] I want to know why you all go to a school
where they erect all the buildings. Any answers?

Student: They love to erect things.

Me: They like to erect things, the priests do? Is that what you're telling me?
Because I'd like to know how many of you are going to be around in
1998? Because the building I work and teach in states on the front of it
that it was erected in 1898. So I want to know how many people here
[*gesturing to the audience*] want to help them [*gesturing to the students*]
celebrate a hundred-year-old erection in 1998? [*This statement results in
lots of crowd laughter that becomes even louder as Paige runs up to the
stage.*] Paige, please come up and help them celebrate a hundred-year
erection. [*Paige jumps up to the stage and immediately attaches herself to
the aforementioned Brad, which leads to even louder crowd laughter.*] I
want to thank my students for coming down and supporting me these
past two years. I really do. Please, if you would, give a hand to my
students that celebrate erections and Paige who helps.

Although my bringing my students up to the stage could easily be seen as
an imitative attempt at camp humor on my part, it also physically and
quite visibly demarcated the straight students from the gay and lesbian
audience. While both the female and male students appeared a little nervous about having to get up on a stage, they also seemed to find comfort
in the relational distancing such actions entailed, and all seemed to be
laughing *with* the audience at my joke.

Straight Women

For the most part, and perhaps not that surprising given the androcentric emphasis of the activities, straight women who attended shows with
me were of little concern to the gay men present. They frequently attended shows with their boyfriends or a group of other students, so the
lesbians largely also ignored them. As a result of their seeming invisibility
in this setting, several of them reported to me how much fun it was to go
to a bar and not be hit on/sexually harassed. Because of this, straight
women usually would have to attend several shows before anyone would
even really notice their presence.

Being students, they always dressed casually. And while a few were
quite feminine in appearance, as long as they were not glamorous, they

apparently posed little threat to the gay drag queens who most laid claim to such an image in this setting. Moreover, straight women often would compliment individual gay drag queens on how pretty they were. If anything, being told that they were so fashionably "beautiful" seemed to further reinforce their elevated status in comparison to the lesbians and the "real girls" in the audience, which perhaps added to the gay drag queens' sense of magnificence. Since the straight women frequently tipped well, I would further speculate that both the performers and the audience tacitly accepted them for their monetary contribution to the court. In a sense, tipping is a way of giving participatory approval to the setting and saying, "I think you are okay and I am not here in judgment of you."

On the evening of the show, as previously noted, there were nine straight women in attendance. Other than generically thanking them for coming to the show as "Steve's students" and asking them to "give generously to the cause," the performers made little note of their presence. One exception to this was my spouse, Anna Papageorge. Although the members of the court were resistant to her presence when we initially entered the setting, over time they came to truly appreciate her, and she was frequently sought out as a confidant to discuss matters of fashion and personal relationships. Moreover, she was a constant signifier and visible reminder of my straight status. Thus, during the show Tina thanked her over the microphone for attending the show—apparently so that everyone in the audience could hear her sincere gratitude—and made note of how "gorgeous" her hair was tonight. She came to be accepted and respected for exactly what she was perceived to be—a nonjudgmental, supportive straight individual and good friend to many.

Beyond Gender: Performing Equality

Wanting to look like a man is as big a joke as wanting to look like a woman. It's just another set of rules to play with. Gender's still the game.
— Mathu Anderson, quoted in Catherine Chermayeff, Jonathan David, and Nan Richardson, *Drag Diaries*

What the hell, I'm a drag queen. And we don't always deal in reality. You can say we deal in something kind of realer. We deal in dreams. We're as American as apple pie.
— From the movie *Stonewall* (1997)

Drag settings, such as the ISCS, provide the participant or viewer with a profusion of gendered identities beyond the two—strictly male or female—one would normally expect to find. The inclusion of straight men and women who accompanied me to shows further fractured any remaining vestiges of a dichotomized reality. Veiled behind an array of idealized images and perceived corresponding actions emerges a kaleidoscope of at least six fluid gender identities convincingly being performed by the participants of this setting. Even should a performance seemingly be unsuccessful and breach the intended appearance, as was the case in Paige's lip-sync routine this evening, an image materializes in its place that demonstrates that things often are far more apparent than real, but nevertheless genuinely authentic if the targeted audience accepts it as such.

Paige

Tina: Ladies and gentlemen, please welcome her Serene Highness, Miss Debutante XIX, Paige DeMonet Sapphire Rockafellar. [*Enter Paige, appearing fairly inebriated—her number is one of the last at tonight's show—and still wearing her white jumpsuit. Paige performs in a powerful, high-energy fashion. In an almost aggressive but still feminine manner, she lip-syncs the words to a female recording artist being played in the background.*]

Paige: "If you like loving, kissing, and hugging . . . I think about you, you, you." [*Each time she lip-syncs "you," she gestures to individual audience members in a seductive manner. After receiving tips from over fifteen audience members, she starts to spin in a circle while nodding her head to the increasing tempo of the song. As a result, she loses some of her jewelry and then her wig. From her now seemingly blemished appearance unfolds a new image. With short hair parted carefully to the side, underlined by what appears even more noticeable makeup, a new Paige emerges looking as if she should be appearing with Liza Minnelli in the musical Cabaret. The audience begins to clap and laugh uncontrollably. Always being an excellent performer, Paige plays off her faux pas as an unexpected but acceptable part of her routine. Given the audience's applause, they apparently agree.*]

In a culture like ours, where "image is everything," as the commercial jingle states, perhaps what really counts is that the reality of a situation is undertaken by the culturally appropriate holders and imitators of the desired identity in relation to their desired audience. Otherwise, the corresponding performance is seen as a fraud, a fabrication, a lie, and not at all legitimate or real. Thus, at a drag show, should a gay drag queen lose her hair, no one's offended or unnerved by the image that takes its place. It is just seen as part of the act of doing gender in a context where an array of gendered routines are being performed. When the boundaries associated with the relational states of male or female are seemingly violated, the transgressors are not only frequently forgiven but sometimes applauded (as above) for their actions because of the fluid nature of the gendered identities being performed.

An even wider assortment of gendered identities exists in general society, but apparently most of us fail to see this since we are wearing the lenses of a dichotomous worldview. It always seems easier to observe what we want to see—or have been taught to see—instead of what might or could be there. Through a blatantly imitative, frequently creative and playful manner, members of the court demonstrate that gender, as we presently know it, is in fact a game, and far too often an oppressive one at that. Although their actions are not subversive in intent, and are actually quite conservative in basis, in a setting where kings can be queens and queens can be kings, gender loses its concrete basis. My involvement in this setting has taught me to view gender through a multifaceted lens and demonstrated to me the legitimacy of undertaking seemingly illicit performances to undermine preexisting gender inequalities.

My attempts at trying to live a feminist gender identity, like those of anyone who claims such a stance, are largely performed in relation to others. For me, and similar to the participants of the court, this also means that I must be a gender traitor. No longer positively speaking from (or acting in accordance with) the identities I was cast into at birth, a white heterosexual male from an upper-middle-class background, I have been frequently asked, "So what do you think you are/or want to be? A woman? A person of color? Gay? Poor?" To which I have responded, "Since in present realities all of the above states (identities) of being/ statuses are dichotomously based on domination and subordination, I would rather not be any of these but instead live [perform/do drag] in a manner that is predicated on no one's denial." While some may perceive such a stance to be an absurdity in present realities, I ultimately seek out audiences where in concert we could create and actually live nonoppressive interpersonal identities. Like many drag queens (and kings), I dream of a world full of acceptable possibilities. Such an outlook seems far "realer" than the limitations of preexisting caricatures/social statuses that are based on the farcical rejection of others.

REFERENCES

Baker, Roger. 1994. *Drag: A History of Female Impersonation in the Performing Arts*. New York: New York University Press.

Butler, Judith. 1990. *Gender Trouble: Feminism and Subversion of Identity*. New York: Routledge.

———. 1991. "Imitation and Gender Insubordination." In *Inside/out: Lesbian Theories, Gay Theories*, edited by Diana Fuss, 13–31. New York: Routledge.

Chermayeff, Catherine, Jonathan David, and Nan Richardson. 1995. *Drag Diaries*. San Francisco: Chronicle Books.

Connell, R. W. 1995. *Masculinities*. Berkeley: University of California Press.

Delphy, Christine. 1993. "Rethinking Sex and Gender." *Women's Studies International Forum* 16:1–9.

Fleisher, Julian. 1996. *The Drag Queens of New York: An Illustrated Field Guide*. New York: Riverhead Books.

Garber, Marjorie. 1992. *Vested Interests: Cross-Dressing and Cultural Anxiety*. New York: Routledge.

Haraway, Donna. 1988. "Situated Knowledges: The Science Question in Feminism and the Privilege of Partial Perspective." *Feminist Studies* 14:575–99.

Hawkesworth, M. E. 1989. "Knower, Knowing, Known: Feminist Theory and Claims of Truth." *Signs: Journal of Women in Culture and Society* 14:533–57.

Hekman, S. 1987. "The Feminization of Epistemology: Gender and the Social Sciences." *Women and Politics* 7:65–83.

James, Christine. 1997. "Feminism and Masculinity: Reconceptualising the Dichotomy for Reason and Emotion." *International Journal of Sociology and Social Policy* 17: 129–47.

Lacan, Jacques. 1983. *Feminine Sexuality*. Translated by Jacqueline Rose. New York: Norton.

Lorber, Judith. 1994. *The Paradoxes of Gender*. New Haven: Yale University Press.

Schacht, Steven P. 1996a. "Misogyny on and off the 'Pitch': The Gendered World of Male Rugby Players." *Gender & Society* 10:550–65.

———. 1996b. "*Paris Is Burning*: How Society's Stratification Systems Make Drag Queens of Us All." Paper presented at the annual meeting of the American Sociological Association, New York.

———. 1997. "Female Impersonators and the Social Construction of 'Other': Toward a Situational Understanding of Gender and Power." Paper presented at the annual meeting of the American Sociological Association, Toronto.

Stoltenberg, John. 1996. "How Power Makes Men: The Grammar of Identity." Unpublished manuscript.

Trumbach, Randolph. 1994. "London's Sapphists: From Three Sexes to Four Genders in the Making of Modern Culture." In *Third Sex, Third Gender: Beyond Sexual Dimorphism in Culture and History,* edited by Gilbert Herdt, 111–36. New York: Zone Books.

West, Candace, and Don H. Zimmerman. 1987. "Doing Gender." *Gender & Society* 1:125–51.

NOTES

1. My initial involvement in a drag community was in Springfield, Missouri, with largely professional female impersonators (individuals doing drag to make a living). Here, over nearly a year's time, I became good friends with several of the key performers and served as a judge for a local Miss Gay Missouri Pageant. I have also attended several events sponsored by out-of-town "sister" courts (in Seattle, Washington, and Missoula, Montana), walking as a member of the ISCS, attended several shows by widely known professional performers in Portland, Oregon (Darcel's XV's), and in Chicago (the Baton Club), and was invited to and subsequently attended the Miss Continental Pageant, perhaps the most prominent female impersonator pageant in North America, Labor Day weekend, 1996, in Chicago.

2. Although I am straight and obviously fit another gender category, I largely assumed the identity of drag king both in terms of my relational interaction with the drag queens and to a lesser extent, in my presentation of self.

3. One exception to this conclusion is an annual event called Turnabout, when members of the court are expected to appear as their gendered opposite. Thus, gay queens become gay kings, gay kings become gay queens, lesbian kings become lesbian queens, and lesbian queens become lesbian kings. All of this demonstrates not only the extremely imitative but also the remarkably fluid nature of doing gender.

4. Interestingly, although members of the court (especially drag queens and lesbian drag kings, discussed next) would be considered gender benders to outsiders in the dominant culture, even within this context such individuals have emerged. This is evidenced in the aforementioned preop transsexuals, bisexuals, transvestites, and gay cross-dressers who do not live up to idealized images of female beauty. Through their nonconformity, they bend the rules and implicitly are trying to create and perform new gender identities within the context.

5. Although still few in number, several lesbian drag queens who do not perform, like Donna's girlfriend Lori, frequently do attend shows in apparent support of their lesbian drag king partners.

6. Over the past four years my spouse and I have brought well over two hundred students and other straight and gay friends to an array of drag events in seven different cities, both as a learning experience and as a form of community outreach. Judging from their comments after attending, I would say this has been a positive experience for all but one individual; several accompanied us to numerous shows.

Chapter Thirteen

Gender Politics for Men

R. W. Connell

When I was about ten or eleven years old I played in a school rugby football team for a short time. Rugby is a game in which you clasp a pointed ball to your chest and try to run through a wall of opposing players to put the ball on the ground behind them. They attempt to throw you to the ground, seize the ball, and run through a wall of your players in order to put the ball on the ground behind you. When half the game is over, everyone turns around and runs the other way.

This is the most popular sport in Sydney, my hometown, and rightly so. It is closely related to great art. Each half of the game runs for about the same length of time as Beethoven's Ninth Symphony. The ball weighs about as much as a hardcover edition of Dante's *Inferno*. And at the end of the season, each player's face resembles a portrait by Picasso.

So, as a lover of the arts, I joined the school rugby team. Being a slow runner, I became a forward. This gave me the right and the duty to join in "scrums," where the forwards link up in a phalanx and try to push the other team off the ball by weight and strength. Those at the back of the scrum place their heads among the other players' buttocks to get leverage to push, and cannot see very well (though they can still smell). So I don't know who it was that—in a scrum during my second game—pulled out a tuft of my hair. I hope it was a member of the opposing team.

I changed to soccer the next week. This was a serious decision. In Australia in the 1950s soccer players were known to have limp wrists, and were thought to wear frilly nighties to bed. Even today soccer players in Australia are suspected of dilettantism. Now that my hair is coming out for quite different reasons, forty years later, I still remember the incident and in a sense I am still living with its consequences. It was one of the moments when I began my dissent from hegemonic masculinity.

There is, at present, an international questioning of the kind of masculinity I met on the rugby field and that others meet in the military, in corporate boardrooms, and in most governments in the world. "International" is no overstatement. Some of the best historical research on masculinity has been done in New Zealand, and some of the best sociology in Australia. Some of the best theory has been done in England, some of the best field observation in the United States. Some of the best youth work has been done in Germany, and some of the most important political work in Canada and South Africa.

This questioning has been provoked by an international feminist movement, which brought to light the oppression of women and the patriarchal character of major institutions and dominant forms of culture. It became clear that the questions politicians classify as "women's issues" are also issues about men. Men are gendered too. Once this is acknowledged, hard questions arise about how men become gendered, how masculinity is related to gender inequality, and how men can become part of the solution rather than part of the problem.

Men's Interests

In the days of the attempt to set up a "men's liberation" movement, in the 1970s, it was assumed that feminism was good for men, because men too suffered from rigid sex roles. As women broke out of their sex role, men would be enabled to break out of theirs, and would have fuller, better, and healthier lives as a result.

The failure of any large number to sign on as the men's auxiliary to feminism, in the years since, suggests a flaw in this analysis. Men's dominant position in the gender order has a material payoff, and the discussions of masculinity have constantly underestimated how big it is. In the rich capitalist countries such as the United States, men's average incomes are approximately double the average incomes of women. Men have ten times the political access of women worldwide (measured by representation in parliaments). Men have even greater control of corporate wealth (looking at top management in major corporations). Men control the means of violence, in the form of weapons and armed forces.

I call these advantages the "patriarchal dividend" for men, and this dividend is not withering away. The gender segregation of the workforce in the rich countries has declined little in recent years. Men's representation in parliaments worldwide has risen, not fallen, in recent years. As corporations have gone multinational—under the aegis of corporate hegemonic masculinity—they have increasingly escaped the national-level political structures through which women press for equal opportunity and an end to discrimination. The new international garment manufacturing and microprocessor assembly industries, for instance, are arenas of rampant sexism. Violence against women has not measurably declined.

Yet not all men are corporate executives or mass killers. Though men in general gain the patriarchal dividend, specific groups of men gain very little of it. For instance, working-class youth, economically dispossessed by structural unemployment, may gain no economic advantage at all over the women in their communities. Other groups of men pay part of the price, alongside women, for the maintenance of an unequal gender order. Gay men are systematically made targets of prejudice and violence. Effeminate and wimpish men are constantly put down. Black men, in the United States (as in South Africa) suffer massively higher levels of lethal violence than white men.

There are, then, divisions of interest among men on gender issues. I would also want to emphasize that not all interests are egotistic. Interests are also relational, that is, constituted in the social relations one shares with other people. Most men have relational interests that they share with particular women, for instance, as parents needing child care provision and good health services for children, or as workers, needing improved conditions and security. Gay men share with lesbians an interest in fighting discrimination.

When we look at men's lives concretely, we regularly find dense networks of relationships with women: with mothers, wives, partners, sisters, daughters, aunts, grandmothers, friends, workmates, neighbors. Very few men have a life-world that is blocked off from women, that is genuinely a "separate sphere."

Each of these relationships can be the basis for men's relational interest in reform. For instance, I have an interest in my wife's being free of the threat of intimidation or rape, in her having job security and equal pay, in her having the best possible health care. I have an interest in my daughter's being free of sexual harassment at school, in her having access to any kind of training and all occupations, in her growing up a confident and autonomous person.

Men's interest in gender hierarchy, defined by the patriarchal dividend, is real and large, but it is internally divided, and it is cross-cut by relational interests shared with women. Which of these interests is actually pursued by particular men is a matter of politics—politics in the quite familiar sense of organizing in the pursuit of programs.

Men who try to develop a politics in support of feminism, whether gay or straight, are not in for an easy ride. They are likely to be met with derision from many other men, and from some women. It is almost a journalistic cliché that women despise Sensitive New Age Guys. They will not necessarily get warm support from feminist women, some of whom are deeply distrustful of all men, most of whom are wary of men's power, and all of whom make a political commitment to solidarity with women. Since change in gender requires reconstructing personal relations as well as public life, there are many opportunities for personal hurt, mistaken judgments, and anger.

I do not think men seeking progressive reforms of masculinity can expect to be comfortable, while we live in a world marked by gendered violence and inequality. Masculinity therapy offers personal comfort as a substitute for social change. But this is not the only use for emotional support. As shown by John Rowan's book *The Horned God*, therapeutic methods and emotional exploration can be used to support men, as feminist therapy supports women, in the stresses of a project of social change.[1]

Political Purposes

Given the difficulties of the project, what might motivate men to press on into the flames? We need some conception of where the politics should be headed, a vision of the world we are trying to produce. Other forces certainly are making choices, which children and youth face here and now in a barrage of advertising masquerading as sport, militarism masquerading as entertainment, commercial sex masquerading as personal freedom.

The goal defined by sex role reformers in the 1970s was the abolition of masculinity (and femininity) by a movement toward androgyny, the blending of the two existing sex roles. This grasped the fact that we have to change personal life, but underestimated the complexity of masculinities and femininities, put too much emphasis on attitudes and not enough on material inequalities and issues of power.

We might better think of the goal as "recomposing" the elements of gender: making the full range of gender symbolism and practice available to all people. Though this may sound exotic when formulated as a strategy, bits of it are quite familiar in practice. In schools, for instance, it is quite a common goal to "expand the options" for girls, by trying to make science and technology courses more available to them; and for boys, by encouraging them to learn to cook or to sew.

It has been argued that the most effective form of sex education with teenagers is "learning to be the opposite sex," that is, trying to get girls and boys to think through heterosexual relationships from the point of view of the other party. (Most school sex education is forbidden, however, to go beyond heterosexual thoughts.) Bronwyn Davies, an Australian feminist educator, wryly suggests that children are good poststructuralists, and readily learn to move among different gender positions in culture.[2]

The bodily dimension of gender is often thought to be the absolute limit of change. When I am interviewed about these issues on radio, interviewers often seem to think that bodily difference (either in sport or in reproduction) is a knockout question. But if we understand gender as being about the way bodies are drawn into a historical process, then we can recognize contradictions in existing embodiments and can see enormous possibilities of *re-embodiment* for men. There are different ways of using, feeling, and showing male bodies.

I am charmed to see, in shops selling artistic postcards and posters, a genre showing muscular male bodies cuddling babies. Why not make this a widespread pleasure? Provided, of course, the men are also sharing the other tactile experiences of baby-care—getting the milk in, wringing out the nappies, and wiping up the shit.

But rearranging elements is not enough. As the American feminist Wendy Chapkis argues, playing with the elements of gender can be benign only if we unpack the "package deal" that, for women, links beauty and status, and for men links desirability and power.[3] We can rearrange difference only if we contest dominance. So a recomposing strategy requires a project of social justice.

Gender relations involve different spheres of practice, so there is an unavoidable complexity in gender politics. Theoretical work in social science distinguishes at least three spheres: the relations of power, the relations of production, and the relations of cathexis.[4] In each case we can define directions for a politics of gender justice.

Pursuing justice in power relations means contesting men's predominance in the state, professions, and management, and ending violence against women.

Some groups of men have specifically focused on the issue of men's violence toward women. Generally maintaining a relationship (sometimes tense) with women's groups mobilizing around domestic violence or rape, such groups have worked with violent men to try to reduce the chance of further violence, and have launched wider educational campaigns. The most extensive has been the White Ribbon campaign in Canada, which arose from commemorations of the 1989 massacre of women at the University of Montreal. In this case, mass media and mainstream politicians as well as community groups have been brought into a campaign rejecting violence against women, with considerable impact at a national level.

Pursuing justice in economic relations means equalizing incomes, sharing the burden of household work, and equalizing access to education and training. A key vehicle for such politics is workers' organizations.

While male-controlled unions have often been antagonistic to women, even in totally masculinized industries some unions have taken progressive action. In 1979–80 the United Steelworkers successfully pressed for women to be hired at the Hamilton steelworks in Canada. A serious effort was made to encourage discussion of the issues by the male membership, and a fair level of support for the change was gained. A few years earlier, the Builders Labourers Federation in New South Wales sponsored the entry of women workers on exclusively male building sites. In this case, the women clerks in the union office had challenged the sexism of a left-wing male leadership and persuaded them to change their policy. In another Canadian example, in electrical manufacturing in Westinghouse plants, it was pressure from below that led to the integration of women into formerly all-male shops. Stan Gray, the activist who tells the story, notes that this was only the beginning of the process. A sprawling struggle, in the context of recession and layoffs, nevertheless moved on to campaigns against workplace sexism; some of the men came to see sexism as divisive and against their own interests as workers.[5]

Pursuing justice in the structure of cathexis means ending homophobia, reconstructing heterosexual relations on the basis of reciprocity not hierarchy, and disconnecting masculinity from pressures toward violence. The peace movement is perhaps the longest-established forum where significant numbers of men have been engaged in a critique of an important part of hegemonic masculinity, violence. Quaker traditions, the Gandhian legacy, and the nonviolence civil rights movement in the United States are part of this heritage. Though the peace movement has not generally defined masculinity as its target (that connection being made by feminist groups in actions excluding men, such as the Greenham Common encampment in Britain), it has provided a forum for political action that in fact contests hegemonic masculinity.

Along these lines we can define an agenda for a progressive politics of masculinity, and can find many examples of worthwhile practice. That still leaves open the question of the overall form this politics should take.

A Men's Movement?

It is commonly assumed that a progressive politics of masculinity must take the form of a social movement. The usual model is feminism; many writers imply a close parallel between the women's movement and a men's movement. More remotely, the labor movement and civil rights movements serve as models.

I would argue that these parallels are not close, and may be seriously misleading. The movements just listed are mobilizations of oppressed or exploited groups to end their subordination. They seek the unity of the group and assert the dignity of a previously stigmatized identity.

"Men" as a group, and heterosexual men in particular, are not oppressed or disadvantaged (though that belief is now promoted by right-wing campaigns against affirmative action). As I have noted, men *in general* gain a patriarchal dividend. Hegemonic masculinity is not a stigmatized identity. Quite the opposite: the culture already honors it. Seeking the unity of "men" can only mean emphasizing the experiences and interests men have that separate them from women, rather than the interests they share with women that might lead toward social justice.

This is not an abstract theoretical point. It has happened in practice in the history of some antisexist men's groups, such as the American group MOVE studied by Paul Lichterman.[6] Initially involved both in antiviolence work with batterers and in raising public issues about masculinity, this group gradually moved toward a therapeutic ideology, developed a concern with being "positive" about men, and moved away from public stands and issues about the structure of power. What happened in this specific case also happened much more broadly in the transition from "men's liberation" in the early 1970s to masculinity therapy in the 1980s. The evangelical Christian Promise Keepers and the African American Million Man March of 1995 both follow the model of a social movement and both have been vehicles for promoting patriarchal understandings of masculinity in the context of the pursuit of evangelical religion or racial justice. The idea of a husband as the responsible "head of the family" has proved attractive in mobilizing middle-class men (and has proved attractive to many women, too, where the alternative is abandonment or violence). The definition and the movement are carefully policed against homosexuality (gay men, but not their gayness, are welcome in the Promise Keepers—they are seen as potential converts).

To fight for justice in gender relations often means, paradoxically, doing the opposite of the things that would create a "men's movement." That is, tackling issues that inevitably divide men rather than unite them: issues like homophobia, affirmative action for women, equal pay, sexual harassment, and violence.

This is not for a moment to doubt the importance of solidarity among the men, and the women, involved with these issues. Indeed, I would emphasize this point strongly. Experience has shown that work on these issues is stressful, often painful, and difficult to sustain without support. This points to the importance, for men engaged in such struggles, of networks such as the National Organization for Men Against Sexism in the United States. Journals such as *Changing Men* in the United States, *XY* in Australia, and *Achilles Heel* in Britain are key elements in antisexist networks.

Rather than a grand "men's movement," we should be thinking of a variety of struggles in diverse sites, linked through networking rather than mass mobilization or formal organization. Men are likely to be detached from the defense of patriarchy in small numbers at a time, in a great variety of circumstances. So the likely political pattern is one of unevenness between situations, with differently configured issues and possibilities of action.

The examples discussed in the last section, the White Ribbon movement, the union movement, and the peace movement, illustrate these points. What is involved in all three cases is not a social movement of men focused on masculinity, but some kind of alliance politics. Here the project of social justice depends on the overlapping of interests or commitments between different groups. The overlapping may be temporary, but can be long-term (a perfectly familiar situation in politics). Existing power resources can be used for new ends. We do not have to start from scratch all the time.

It is often assumed that alliance means compromise and therefore containment. The familiar militant gesture of insisting on revolutionary purity is not unknown in men's countersexist politics.[7] The chances of actually changing the world this way are slight.

Pluralism in alliance-making is necessary, but containment is not a necessary result. Given that patriarchy is a historical structure, not a timeless dichotomy of men abusing women, it will be ended by a historical process. The strategic problem is to generate pressures that will culminate in the long run in a transformation of the structure; and any initiative that sets up pressure in that direction is worth having. Lynne Segal, in the best feminist appraisal of issues about masculinity, is cool about the pace of change; her book is called *Slow Motion*. But she is in no doubt about the possibilities of change, through hard work in familiar institutions such as workplaces, unions, and political parties.[8]

In the long run, as Keynes remarked, we are all dead; and while we are still alive, we want to see something more than a rise in the probability of social justice in the distant future. So as well as long-term educational strategies, we also need what British feminists called "prefigurative politics"—at least samples of paradise, at least little bits of justice, here and now.

Again, this is familiar in principle. Progressive education hoped to prefigure the good society in democratic schools; industrial democracy hoped to prefigure a democratically controlled economy in each workplace. In my household (like many others) we hope to prefigure a society in which gender equality and sexual tolerance are routine, a bedrock of civilization.

However, the prefigurative politics of gender and sexuality are not necessarily rock-like. They may, on the contrary, be scandalous, hilarious, or disturbing. Halloween on Haight Street; Cal-PEP, an AIDS prevention program run by prostitutes and former prostitutes; the pleasures and dangers of queer culture; integrated sports. Prefiguration may also be peaceable: fathers taking toddlers and babies in push-chairs for an outing.

Much of the effective work done on masculinity is educational, above all. It involves attempts to reformulate knowledge, to expand understanding, to create new capacities for practice. I think we might value this fact and build on it. It is in education that we have some of the best chances to prefigure new ways of being men and boys. I will end, therefore, with some remarks on the problems of educational strategies.

Education

"Gender" in discussions of schools has mainly signaled issues about girls. The recent debate marks an important recognition that boys are gendered too. The commonest error is to assume that a strategy formulated for one situation must work for the other. Given the patriarchal dividend, which gives boys an interest in claiming the gender privilege open to them, a simple translation will not generally work.

Educational responses to issues about boys must have two sides. They must be concerned with the impact of the advantaged group's actions on the less advantaged group. (Thus, the issue of harassment of girls is rightly a major concern of programs concerned with boys.)

They must also be concerned with the *costs* paid for the situation of advantage. (Thus, the impact of harassment on boys, in the form of bullying among boys, and poisoned relationships with girls, is also a major concern.) The long-term costs to boys and men, though often hard to assess, may well be the most important.

Recent discussions of educational strategies for boys have rightly pointed to the negative impact on boys of narrow models of masculinity and obsolete ideas about men's and women's work. Such stereotypes, if adopted by the boys, severely limit their cultural experiences, their vocational choices, and their expectations about future personal relationships, both with men and with women.

These issues go beyond equity policy in the narrow sense to broad curriculum objectives. Educational policy about boys must concern the range of their experiences and their understanding of life options. Maximizing the range of pupils' knowledge, eliminating barriers to their awareness, interest, and tolerance, and widening the range of their own life choices are general educational goals that have specific applications in the education of boys.

These goals cannot be pursued if gender itself is not made an object of enquiry and learning. This has been an important trend in education for girls and women, both in "mainstream" curriculum areas and in the growth of new fields such as women's studies. Recent research on masculinity has produced a body of knowledge that makes it easier than before to develop a curriculum about gender that is gender-inclusive and plainly relevant to boys.

This may require programs with a different structure from those most familiar in gender equity work. Gender equity work in English-speaking countries has emphasized *gender-specific* programs addressed to girls. The first generation of school-level programs concerned with boys has followed this logic, producing programs specifically *for* boys.

Youth work in Germany has made an important distinction between "gender-specific" and "gender-relevant" programs.[9] Both in welfare and in curriculum, schools may now have a need for more of the *gender-relevant* type of programs. These take gender relations as the object of inquiry, discussion, and learning; and they may be addressed to boys and girls together as well as separately.

Not all education occurs in schools, of course. Some of the most impressive recent antisexist work is educational work in difficult circumstances, such as prisons, and around difficult issues, such as violence. An example is the educational program for young men developed by the Australian group Men Against Sexual Assault.

As David Denborough explains the approach, it is possible to find respectful ways of working with young men without shying away from the hard issues of men's violence. Denborough draws on the new masculinity research to develop the strategy, encouraging young men not only to recognize the main narrative of masculinity in their community, but also to search for the counternarratives, the other possibilities that exist in the same situation. A search for countermeanings also appears in Don Sabo's work in an American prison. Sabo notes how sport and physical training at one level play into the cultivation of masculine hardness, but at another level represent a kind of self-care in a hostile and very unhealthy environment.[10]

Educational work on masculinity is not likely to be easy. People in this field are already aware of a number of problems: resistance by boys and men (including those who may be in most need of new programs), difficulties in defining purposes, skepticism from staff, ethical problems in relation to girls' programs, and shortages of materials and research.

Nevertheless, the expansion of young people's knowledge and capacity for choice and action about an important area of their current and future lives is a coherent and important educational goal. It is an issue where the agenda of justice in gender relations is linked to widely shared social purposes and has immediate practical possibilities.

NOTES

This essay began in presentations to a conference on Reproduction and Change in Masculinity, sponsored by the Hans Bockler Foundation of the German union movement, held at Munich in September 1994. It draws on the essay "The Politics of Changing Men," published in *Socialist Review*, 1995, and on research on "boys and schools" done for the New South Wales Department of School Education (which is of course not responsible for my views on the matter). I am grateful to Heinz Kindler, Gudrun Linne, Van Davy, and Lee Bell for making these projects possible.

1. John Rowan, *The Horned God: Feminism and Men as Wounding and Healing* (London: Routledge and Kegan Paul, 1987).

2. Bronwyn Davies, *Shards of Glass* (Sydney: Allen and Unwin, 1993).

3. Wendy Chapkis, *Beauty Secrets: Women and the Politics of Appearance* (Boston: South End Press, 1986).

4. See R. W. Connell, *Gender and Power*, for a more detailed account of these structures (Cambridge: Polity Press, 1987).

5. June Corman et al., *Recasting Steel Labour*; Meredith Burgmann, "Revolution and Machismo," in Elizabeth Windschuttle, ed., *Women, Class and History* ([Sydney?], Australia: Fontana, 1980); Stan Gray, "Sharing the Shop Floor," in Michael Kaufman, ed., *Beyond Patriarchy: Essays by Men on Pleasure, Power, and Change* (Toronto: Oxford University Press, 1987).

6. Paul Lichterman, "Making the Politics of Masculinity," *Comparative Social Research* 11(1989): 185–208.

7. See, for instance, John Stoltenberg, *Refusing to Be a Man* (London: Fontana, 1990).

8. Lynne Segal, *Slow Motion: Changing Masculinities, Changing Men* (London: Virago, 1990).

9. Heinz Kindler, *Maske(r)ade: Jungen- und Mannarerbeit für die Praxis* (Schwäbisch-Gmünd und Tabingen: Neuling Verlag, 1993).

10. David Denborough, *Step by Step: Developing Respectful Ways of Working with Young Men to Reduce Violence* (Sydney: Men Against Sexual Assault, 1994); Don Sabo, "Doing Time Doing Masculinity: Sports and Prison," in Michael A. Messner and Donald F. Sabo, eds., *Sex, Violence and Power in Sports: Rethinking Masculinity* (Freedom, CA: Crossing Press, 1994).

Chapter Fourteen

Sex, Gender, and Transformation
From Scoring to Caring

Riane Eisler

It is sometimes said that when women say yes to sex, it is because they want love, and when men say they love a woman, it is because they want sex. But like most gender stereotypes, these are vast overgeneralizations.

Women are sexually aroused by men, just as men are by women. And although convention forbids "good" women sex just for pleasure, women can and do enjoy sex out of sheer lust.[1] Moreover, men, like women, also yearn for love. In fact, despite the notion that romantic love was invented in the West, and only a few hundred years ago at that, a 1991 study of 166 cultures by William Jankoviak and Edward Fisher found clear evidence of romantic love in 147 of these cultures.[2] Surveys have shown that both women and men consider caring, trust, respect, and honesty central to satisfying relationships.[3]

Nonetheless, in dominator societies men are supposed to prove their masculinity by not becoming too emotionally involved with women, which is viewed as a loss of control, and instead having sex with as many women as possible. As illustrated by archetypal male heroes such as Odysseus and Don Juan—and flatly contradicting the notion that impersonal, uncaring sex is a modern invention—this sexual "scoring" script for real men is hardly new. What *is* new is that not only women, but also men in larger numbers than ever before are taking a close look at their stereotypical gender scripts and rejecting those aspects that limit and distort not only sexual relations but all our relations.

It is true that many men still brag of their sexual conquests, men like the American basketball star Wilt Chamberlain, who proudly claimed he had sex with twenty-five thousand women, and even "spiritual" gurus such as Sri Rajneesh, who boasted he had sex with more women than any other man in the world. It is also true that many women are still drawn to such men. But both women and men are beginning to recognize that teaching men to see intimacy as effeminate and to keep score of sexual "wins"—at the same time that women are taught to believe their whole lives should revolve around intimate relations with men—is a truly no-win prescription for *both* women and men.

More and more men are also beginning to recognize that teaching men they must always be in control is a prescription for not only emotional dysfunction but also sexual dysfunction. As sexologists tell us, it is the ability to give up control—to let go—that is basic to a full orgasmic sexual experience, as it is to a peak spiritual experience.

Even beyond this, there is a growing consciousness that the traditional male socialization to be contemptuous of "soft" emotions turns men not into real men but into lesser men. It blunts men's capacity for feeling, be it of pleasure or pain, and suppresses in them those very feelings of empathy and caring that make us uniquely human. And because it produces men who will consider it manly to use violence—be it in intimate or in international relations—at this point in our technological and cultural evolution this kind of socialization poses a threat to human survival.

Gender, Ideology, and Society

Women and men are the two halves of humanity. So it is no exaggeration to say that the contemporary questioning of stereotypical gender roles is nothing less than the questioning of what it means to be human, and that if it succeeds it will bring fundamental changes in all aspects of our lives, from sexuality and spirituality to economics and politics.

To fully grasp this, we need to explore the new approach to the study of society, which I termed *cultural transformation theory*, as well as other new scientific theories that take us beyond the old linear cause-and-effect approaches that still pervade much of our thinking. This is why I want to start this chapter by quickly sketching the emerging new understanding of how complex living systems—which is what social systems are—form, maintain themselves, and change.

Especially helpful in this endeavor are the nonlinear dynamics and the chaos theory associated with the Nobel Prize–winner Ilya Prigogine and others.[4] Emerging primarily from physics, chemistry, biology, and systems science, these new theoretical approaches are part of a larger framework sometimes called the new scientific paradigm. Unlike the conventional Aristotelian scientific paradigm, this new scientific paradigm no longer mistakes what *is* for what *must or should be,* as it no longer deals with living systems, be they biological or social, as static or fixed. On the contrary, one of its main contributions is that it shows how during periods of great system disequilibrium—periods such as ours—seemingly small changes can come together to form the nuclei of a fundamentally transformed system.[5]

Accordingly, the cultural transformation theory I have developed over the past two decades views social systems as self-organizing, self-maintaining, and capable at certain bifurcation points of fundamental transformation. But as the social psychologist David Loye points out, when we move from nonhuman to human systems, a whole new set of factors must be considered, including human consciousness, and with it, the question of human agency in both social maintenance and change.[6] Therefore, taking as a departure point Marx's remark that humans make history but not under circumstances of their own choosing,[7] cultural transformation theory aims to construct a conceptual framework that can help us better understand how these circumstances can be changed in ways that promote human development and actualization.

Cultural transformation theory is based on the perception that our cultural evolution has been shaped by the interacting impact of the dominator and partnership models as two basic possibilities for social organization, and that just as there was in prehistory a shift from partnership to domination as the primary social "attractor," we are now trying to shift in the other direction: from domination to partnership.[8] In the construction of this theory I have taken into account environmental, biological, social, economic, technological, and psychological factors, focusing on their interaction and on how they affect, and are in turn affected by, socialization processes. I have particularly focused on gender socialization, since it so profoundly affects human consciousness about all aspects of our lives, from how we view our bodies to the degree to which we feel we have both personal and social choices.

Applying the interactive approach provided by cultural transformation theory to the study of social systems makes it possible to cut through many confusing controversies, such as the futile "which-came-first-the-chicken-or-the-egg" debate as to whether a particular set of beliefs or ideology is the cause or the result of a particular social and economic structure. It makes it possible to see that there is a constant interaction between ideology and social structure, just as physicists are now discovering that matter and energy are in a constantly interactive flux. It also helps explain why the upheavals of shifting from a primarily agrarian to an industrial economy, and now in the West from manufacturing as the economic base to a more information and service-oriented economy, have been accompanied by major changes in consciousness, including the mounting questioning of stereotypical gender roles and sexual relations. And it makes it possible to better understand how these changes in consciousness have in turn led to further changes in economics, politics, the family, and religion—in other words, changes in material conditions, social institutions, and individual (including sexual) behaviors.

However—and this is a point I again want to underscore—whether all this will in the end lead to fundamental changes still hangs in the balance. Just as biological organisms are maintained by their organs, the institutions that form the organs of a social system are also designed to ensure that the larger whole of which they are a part survives. So, like the organs in a biological body, the institutions that form the social body of a dominator society (from the male-dominated family to the military) work together to maintain themselves as part of a larger, interconnected whole. And just as our bodies continuously reproduce or replicate their cells, in social systems this also involves the basic evolutionary process of reproduction or replication.

Except that in social systems, as the work of Vilmos Csanyi highlights, this replicating or copying process involves more than the replication of structures (institutions and organizations, such as governments, schools, and churches). It heavily relies on the replication of ideas, symbols, and images.[9] And it particularly relies on gender socialization to implant these ideas, symbols, and images in the minds of the individuals whose active involvement or agency is needed to maintain these structures.

This is why, through both words and images, dominator institutions replicate the idea that war and the war of the sexes are inevitable, and that men must be victors in both. It is also why there is an urgent need to replicate partnership ideas and images—particularly to replace dominator gender stereotypes—if we are to construct a social system that is not chronically violent. Of course, partnership ideas and images alone, without structural or institutional changes, cannot bring about this shift. But the spread of these ideas and images is an essential part of this process, not only because it raises our consciousness to the possibility of more satisfying and sustainable alternatives, but because it is essential to counter the powerful backward pull of dominator ideas and images that are constantly regenerated by religious and scientific authorities, politicians, educators, and in our time, the mass media.

To illustrate—and bring us directly to this critical matter of how the social construction of sex and gender is inextricably intertwined with all aspects of social and ideological organization—on the surface it would seem to make no sense that stories eroticizing conquest and domination should become particularly frequent in times before or during wars. Nonetheless, as the social psychologist David Winter has documented in his extensive probe of the rise and fall in the number of stories where males prove their manliness through their repetitive sexual conquests of women, this is exactly what happens.[10] Looked at from the perspective I have just sketched, it makes a lot of sense that this happens. Because, as we have seen, the male socialization for sexual conquests plays a major part in the socialization of men for military conquests.

But—and again this can best be understood if from the perspective of cultural transformation theory we look at social systems as self-organizing and self-maintaining—this intensified production and dissemination of what Winter calls Don Juan stories[11] happens not because political and military leaders deliberately conspire with writers, playwrights, and composers to pump out such tales. It happens because of the dynamic interaction between the ideas and images that provide the material for dominator consciousness, the institutions that maintain this type of society, and the gender roles or scripts required for both women and men to fit into the kinds of institutions that maintain it.

Certainly people who hold power in dominator structures both consciously and unconsciously strive to hold on to that power. But the dynamics of social systems maintenance are far more complex. They involve human agency within the demands of institutional structures, and thus, to paraphrase Anthony Giddens, the continuous reproduction of certain forms of social conduct across time and space.[12] Hence they are inextricably intertwined with the socialization of both women and men for the kinds of roles—and with this, the kinds of habits or routines—that must be constantly re-created, and when faltering, reinforced, if despite outward changes in form, social institutions are to maintain their basic or underlying character.

These then are some of the reasons the modern women's and men's movements—still often trivialized and ridiculed in both academia and the mass media—are of such profound social and political significance. They are not the only movements that in our time challenge an institutional infrastructure based on rankings of domination backed up by force and fear of pain. This has been the aim of all modern progressive political movements. But other movements have not specifically addressed the invisible thread of gender that connects the political and the personal, much less such "peripheral" issues as sex and spirituality. Hence the socialization of men to equate their very identity or masculinity with domination and conquest and the relegation to women of stereotypically feminine characteristics such as compassion and caring have not generally been seen as important. Nor have these issues been addressed by most historians and political scientists, even though the challenge to stereotypical gender scripts has actually been a major theme in Western history during the last three hundred years.

Renegotiating Sex and Gender

Many people still view any attempt to change gender and sexual scripts as not only unnatural but unprecedented. However, there have throughout recorded history been such attempts.[13] Particularly during modern Western history (that is, during the three hundred years since the Enlightenment), these attempts have been especially vigorous.

For instance, based on his study of modern English and American history from a gender-sensitive perspective, the sociologist Michael Kimmel documents how during the late seventeenth and early eighteenth centuries in England "a virtual pamphlet war erupted as both men and women attempted to renegotiate the structure of gender relations and develop new definitions of masculinity and femininity."[14] Like both earlier and later attempts, this too was during a time of technological, economic, and social ferment, when many traditional roles—and with this habits and routines—were challenged. It thus brought some weakening of androcratic rule. But at the same time, it also saw the regrouping of dominator elites.

For example, threatened by industrialization, the landed gentry sought to maintain their control through what historians call the enclosure of their lands, depriving the peasants who had been their tenant laborers of all means of livelihood, forcing them to move in droves to cities, thus ironically contributing to even more rapid urbanization, industrialization, and rebellion against the upper classes. In the same way, as men too sought to maintain control (sometimes, as in our time, with the active help of collaborating women), in Kimmel's words, "women were chipping away at the edges of traditional expectations."[15]

Some women, such as the playwright Aphra Behn, openly rejected marriage as a form of sexual slavery. Others, as we read in the 1706 pamphlet *The Duty of a Husband* (written in response to Samuel Johnson's earlier *Duty of a Wife*), wanted to change marriage into a bond of "mutual love," in which a man would "not like a Tyrant rule his Wife, as if she was his Slave for Life." There was also (as in the 1960s and still today) a heated debate about premarital and extramarital sex. Women often accused men of seduction and abandonment. Men wrote eloquent defenses of premarital sex, and so also did some women. However, as Kimmel notes, no sooner did women "attempt to claim sexual agency, to seek sexual gratification actively," than they were restrained "either by traditional morality" or by accusations of "sexual insatiability."[16]

Also during this period, homosexuality became more prevalent (or just more open), and many men adopted more colorful and frillier dress. But when men challenged traditional stereotypes of masculinity, they were accused (sometimes by women) of "pettiness, vanity, and femininity," and of "being French"—thereby, as Kimmel writes, "linking feminization to treason, and traditional masculinity to patriotism."[17]

In the end, although somewhat modified, traditional gender stereotypes—along with the traditional sexual double standard—prevailed. In fact, less than a century later in Victorian England, women were to be rigidly divided into "good" (or asexual women, who endured sex as their duty but did not enjoy it) and "bad" or "fallen" women (with whom men could do as they wished).

Still, the modern struggle over gender roles and sexual relations was far from over. Particularly in the United States, women during the nineteenth century were vigorously challenging the notion that femininity means social and sexual subordination. As they pushed to gain entry into the "men's world" or public sphere of politics and economics, these pioneering feminists profoundly humanized the lives of women. Moreover, as they gained greater entry into areas from which they had traditionally been banned, these women also profoundly humanized the lives of children and men, vividly illustrating how the social construction of gender roles affects all aspects of society and ideology.

They lobbied for the repeal of oppressive family laws and access for women to higher education, but they also worked for more humane treatment of the mentally ill and for public education. They developed whole new service professions, such as social work and nursing, which profoundly impacted health care. Since drunkenness was then (as now) often used as an excuse for violence against women, some feminists also crusaded for temperance, *not* out of prudishness but for the sake of simple self-defense, as the cultural historian Theodore Roszak points out.[18] They actively worked together with men in the antislavery movement. They also worked with men in the development of the modern labor movement, particularly to outlaw child labor and the virtual imprisonment of women workers in unsanitary and unsafe sweatshops, a common practice tragically illustrated by the Triangle Shirtwaist factory fire, where 146 women were burned to death.[19] They brought attention to the exploitation of women and children in the sex trade. And for more than seventy-five years they defied ridicule and even threats of violence to argue that half the population should no longer be denied the most basic of political rights: the right to vote.

Many men, and also women, ridiculed this demand as unnatural and unfeminine. But there were also those who strongly supported it, including men like the famous liberal philosopher John Stuart Mill and the black abolitionist leader Frederick Douglass, who joined in the struggle to have the Thirteenth Amendment to the U.S. Constitution giving freed male slaves the vote also include black *and* white women.[20]

Finally, half a century after the Thirteenth Amendment was adopted, American women pushed through the Twenty-first Amendment to the U.S. Constitution to make the phrase "universal suffrage" a reality. But then, in part because school and university textbooks and curricula as well as religion and the media—in other words, what was replicated and disseminated as knowledge and truth—were still overwhelmingly controlled by male elites, the movement to renegotiate gender roles and sexual relations again dwindled. There were of course still attempts by individual women to broaden their life options. However, organized feminism as a mass movement was a thing of the past—or so women were told, as they are again sometimes told today.

In reality feminism only lay dormant. When it once again resurged as the women's liberation movement during the 1960s, it was with a force never before seen in recorded history. Never before had so many women all over the globe demanded a renegotiation of gender scripts in both the private and public spheres. Never before had so many men been drawn, sometimes willingly and even eagerly, other times reluctantly and recalcitrantly, into this renegotiation. Most important, never before, not even during the height of the nineteenth-century feminist movement, had these renegotiations about sex and gender been at such a deep and all-pervasive level.

In family relations, the contemporary renegotiation of gender scripts lies at the heart of the movement to shift from a dysfunctional family based on control (that is, a family structured around male domination and abusive child rearing) to a partnership family based on mutual trust and respect. In business, organizational development experts cite findings that more "feminine" or nurturing leadership styles make for greater worker productivity and creativity, and that sexual harassment has detrimental effects on productivity and morale. At the same time, women are beginning to break through the gendered "glass ceiling" barring them from top management. In politics, women are also challenging the stereotypical definition of leadership as male, with the result that unprecedented numbers of women have been elected to office in many countries, from the United States, India, and Japan (where they still have approximately only one-twentieth representation in national legislatures) to the Scandinavian nations (where approximately one-third of national legislators are female).[21] Even in religion, gender roles and relations are being renegotiated. Women are challenging their exclusion from spiritual leadership and are being ordained in mainstream congregations. Some of these congregations are even changing the Judeo-Christian script requiring that the divine be only a Father, Lord, or King by again including Mother in the appellation of deity. Outside mainstream congregations, women and men are beginning to explore a new Goddess spirituality as a more nature and pleasure-affirming faith. Even the view that spirituality precludes women and men from fully enjoying our unique human capacity for erotic pleasure is being challenged, along with the notion that women are less (or alternately, more) lustful than men.

Just as critically, men are today in larger numbers than ever before questioning their stereotypical scripts for masculinity. This too is on a much deeper level than ever before. For individual men, this questioning holds the promise of far greater freedom to explore and express their full humanity. For both women and men it holds the promise of far more satisfying intimate relations. And for society at large, in a world where what has been considered normal for men has been the standard by which all our institutions (from the workplace and the family to religion and politics) have been constructed,[22] it holds the promise of fundamental changes in all aspects of human relations, from international relations to our most intimate sexual relations.

From Masculinity to Masculinities

Just as many women are today challenging the notion of an immutable, unalterable femininity, men during the 1970s began to question the notion of a single "normal" masculinity. Much of this questioning stemmed from the growing recognition by many men that both women and men are capable of both what are stereotypically described as masculine and feminine feelings and behaviors. But much of it has also stemmed from the growing awareness by some men of the enormous costs to them of constructing social institutions so that men are expected to live, and all too often die, in accordance with roles that constantly place them in situations where they have to experience fear and pain, at the same time that they are taught that the most shameful thing for a man is, like a woman, to express fear and pain. Or, to borrow the words of the sociologist Rob Koegel, much of it is directed at "healing the wounds of masculinity," wounds that, as he brings out, stem from a social construction of masculinity appropriate for a dominator rather than a partnership social and ideological organization.[23]

Thus, as Mathew Callahan writes in *Sex, Death, and the Angry Young Man,* men are becoming aware that even when they reach the top of a particular dominator pyramid, they must still be wary (that is, afraid) of other men trying to dislodge them from their positions of control.[24] And all too often they must even be afraid for their lives, as grimly attested to by the endless wars of recorded history, in which men have been wounded, crippled, maimed, killed, and sometimes left behind to slowly die (as during the Napoleonic Wars, when in one battle alone fifty thousand dead and wounded men were abandoned on the blood-soaked field of Wagram).[25] Then there is the violence and pain of boys' fistfights and their often deadly gang fights, as in the drive-by shootings in American inner-city ghettos today, where the leading cause of death among young black men is murder by another young man. Not only that, but the "real" masculinity today in some circles termed the "deep masculine" is, as Tim Beneke writes, ideally approached through "aggressive initiation where boys endure physical pain and injury in the presence of older men" in preparation for a manhood "one proves through taking distress like a man," that is, without any verbal or other expression of one's feelings.[26]

Of course, there are many factors behind male violence, such as poverty, drugs, and, particularly in the United States, lack of adequate gun control laws. But the fact is that in the United States, as in most other parts of the world, it is women—not men—who are the bulk of the poor and the poorest of the poor,[27] and they too have access to drugs and guns. So when we look at the statistic that almost 90 percent of violent crimes in the United States are crimes by men, often against other men,[28] we again come back to the stereotypical male socialization for domination and violence, socialization today magnified a thousandfold by an entertainment industry that presents violence not only as manly and heroic but also as great fun.

The heartening thing is that, despite all this socialization pressure, so many men have failed to conform to this ideal of a tough, violent, and unfeeling "macho" masculinity, or do so only in part.[29] But even for these men, the costs of this type of socialization are high. To begin with, if their failure to conform is too apparent, they suffer great humiliation. Moreover, whether they fully or only partly conform, since this male socialization is part and parcel of the dominator war of the sexes in which someone has to dominate and someone has to be dominated, they too have to pay some of the emotional costs of this war, as attested to by all the songs and romantic literature written by men that focus less on the joys than on the agonies of love.

But here again, ironically, men's stereotypical socialization for conquest and control itself creates part of their pain. According to the "macho" script, only men are supposed to have power. So any show of power by women (which of course includes the power to reject men or otherwise hurt them) is not only painful in itself; it is also painful in the sense of being perceived as a loss of manhood. On top of all this, because distress is something men are not supposed to feel, these feelings themselves (natural when one is hurt) become the source of even more pain from not living up to internalized cultural expectations.

Small wonder then that as more men become conscious of all this, they are undertaking nothing less than what in his book *The Making of Masculinities* Harry Brod calls the "deconstruction and reconstruction of masculinity."[30] For instance, in an essay in Brod's book, the psychologist Joseph Pleck challenges the long-accepted assumption that psychological maturity requires that men and women acquire male or female "sex-role identity"—in other words, that, as psychology students are still taught, learning the traditional gender scripts is the road to human maturity and full development.[31] Similarly, in a recent issue of *Masculinities* (the official publication of the Men's Studies Association) Ken Clatterbaugh points to the current revivals of "essentialist" gender roles through fundamental-ism, neoconservatism, sociobiology, and some neo-Jungian mythopoetic writings as attempts to make something that is socially constructed appear instinctual or biological.[32] Another scholar, Michael Messner, calls for a whole new definition of success for men: one that through a more equal involvement of men in parenting will not only give more satisfaction to men's lives, but have far-reaching humanizing effects on society.[33] Along the same lines, the sociologist Scott Coltrane reports that his research on couples in which men actively participate in parenting shows that this improved and enriched their relationship with their children as well as with their wives. Moreover, based on his cross-cultural study of ninety nonindustrial societies, Coltrane reports that societies in which there is high paternal involvement in child rearing are "characterized by egalitar-ian beliefs and generally similar gender roles" as well as by relative non-violence in all areas of life.[34]

But it is not only in the new academic field of men's studies that dominator stereotypes of masculinity are today being challenged. As Col-trane's work documents, men are beginning to reject these stereotypes in real life. Younger men in particular are beginning to discard stereotypical definitions of fatherhood as a distant disciplinarian-provider role, instead becoming more involved in the intimate caretaking still generally classi-fied as "mothering."[35] For example, shortly before he was assassinated John Lennon publicly announced, "I like it to be known that, yes, I looked after the baby and I made bread and I was a househusband and I am proud of it."[36]

More and more men are also asking themselves the questions John Lennon asked: "Isn't it time we destroyed the macho ethic? . . . Where has it gotten us all these thousands of years?"[37] For instance, in *The Male Predicament*, James Dittes writes about how both women and men have been crippled by stereotypical gender roles and relations.[38] And Michael McGill's *McGill Report on Male Intimacy*, reporting research on men's problems with intimacy (and findings that men have far fewer close rela-tionships than women), probes the many reasons "men aren't more lov-ing and why they need to be." He concludes that rather than having "more power and control by withholding themselves from relationships," men are limited by their fear of intimacy in their ability to act powerfully in relations, and that men need to learn that masculinity and intimacy are not inimical.[39]

Another subject men write about is how traditional stereotypes of masculinity have inhibited their capacity for sexual pleasure. For example, in *Delivering the Male*, Clayton Barbeau concludes that "the male mystique" is a major obstacle to healthy sex. "Healthy sexuality," he writes, "finds expression as a free gift, not as a compulsion, and arises out of the desire to give and receive pleasure in union with the beloved." Speaking more personally, he continues, "I cannot express tenderness in my love relationship if I am—because of my miseducation in the male mystique—afraid of showing tenderness. My sexual love-making cannot be a total communication of myself, if I am unwilling to give myself away in intimate sharing."[40]

Nonetheless, as we have seen, this intimate sharing is precisely what men are forbidden in their stereotypical "scoring" script for sexuality. For here, as in the legend of Don Juan and Casanova's *Memoirs*[41] (a work sometimes touted as a minor classic), control and power over women, not giving and receiving pleasure—much less union with the beloved— is the prime motivation.

Sex, Winners, and Losers

Actually, Casanova's autobiographical writings (which also tell of his fraudulent lotteries, petty thefts, and observations of the prominent figures of his time) are not all that well written. In fact, in their repetitive boasts of his "victories" over women, they are boring. But they do provide an early record of the sexual malfunction psychologists today call sexual compulsivity.

Sexual compulsivity can take many forms, and not only men but also women can be afflicted by it. But while most women and a certain number of men are primarily driven by the "feminine" need to please others (that is, to give pleasure as a way of gaining acceptance and love), for men conditioned to equate masculinity with conquest (as for Casanova and Don Juan), the issue is not love—or even sex. Rather, it is the domination of the female "adversary" and/or the frequency of "performance."

Indeed, as we saw earlier, for some of the men with this compulsion, the aim is to give pain instead of pleasure, which the sex torture killer takes to its logical brutal extreme. But for most men with this compulsion the "pleasure" of humiliating the conquered woman (or in homosexual relations, the man who takes the woman's place) suffices. Thus, in recounting his maneuvers to get the women he compulsively pursues to "surrender," Casanova makes it clear that what excites him is not sex but overcoming women's resistance and imposing on them his will. Hence, once he has psychologically or physically overpowered a woman, and once this victory has been duly recorded in his memoirs, he sets out to find another body to add to his tally of sexual conquests.

Of course, this "sexual conquest" mentality is not exclusive to men. Women too are sometimes infected by it, though they may not count their conquests by how many men they have sex with but by how many men's hearts they have broken. But whereas women have traditionally been censured for this, men's conquests of women have generally been admired, even prescribed by the dominator script for real masculinity.

One effect of this script has been that for many men sexual love has tended to become extreme possessiveness. Again, this is not unique to men. But it is in men that it has most often assumed its most violent expression, as in the all-too-familiar fictional and real-life stories in which a man shows his "love" for a woman by beating or even killing her when he suspects that her body is not his exclusive possession.

Another effect has been a drastically reduced possibility for men to experience emotional (rather than only physical) intimacy with a woman. Still another effect has been an impairment in male sexual functioning. As Mosher and Tomkins write, the hypermasculine script's equation of "relaxed enjoyment" with the "inferior" feminine role would tend to make sex (no matter how often a man "scores" or even how often he comes) a limited sexual, not to speak of emotional, experience. Moreover, as Wilhelm Reich observed, male ejaculation is not the same as a full orgasmic experience.[42]

I want to here emphasize that all this is a matter not of absolutes but of the degree to which men have internalized rigid masculine and feminine role definitions. For instance, the psychologist Else Frenkel-Brunswick found that men who defined human relations in terms of rigid masculine-superior and feminine-inferior roles often described sex as merely a "hygienic release of tension." It is significant, as she also reported in the classic work on this subject, *The Authoritarian Personality*, that these were the same men who scored high on the F (for fascist) psychological measurements: men characterized by extreme prejudice and intolerance toward Jews, blacks, and other "inferior" and/or "dangerous" out-groups.[43]

Similarly, a 1971 study of German political extremists from both the Right and Left (including members of the leftist terrorist Baader-Meinhof gang) found that these men generally suffered from problems of sexual dysfunction, including the inability to achieve orgasm.[44] Again, these were characteristically men who defined their masculine identity in terms of control, violence, and the suppression of empathy. Many of these men had sadistic or masochistic fantasies in which they felt pleasure in torturing or wounding someone or in being punished by others. They frequently reported unpleasant sensations during any kind of sexual activity. However—and not surprisingly, since what is sexually exciting to such men is not giving and receiving pleasure but rather a sense of power over another human being—members of the Baader-Meinhof gang frequently reported erotic excitation during political discussions and demonstrations.[45]

So not only is the hypermasculine script for sex generally devoid of caring, ultimately it is also devoid of pleasure, except, as Mosher and Tomkins keenly observed, the "pleasure" of imposing one's will on another through fear and force.

Of course, not all men buy into this script. But that it has impaired the way many men perceive and experience sex is dramatically brought out by Don Sabo's remarkable article "The Myth of the Sexual Athlete," published a few years ago in the men's journal *Changing Men.*

Sabo, who played organized sports for fifteen years, begins by describing his inner conflict as a boy between a socialization for "masculine control" and his need for "feminine intimacy." "Inside," he writes, "most of the boys, like myself, needed to love and be loved." Yet "the message that got imparted was to 'catch feels,' be cool." He then relates how when he went to college and became part of the "jock" subculture, at Sunday breakfasts the topic was often the "sexual exploits of the night before," including "laughing reports of 'gang bangs.' " So after a while, for him and for most of his buddies, dating became a "sport" where sex was basically a game in which "winners" and "losers" vied for domination and women were viewed as "opponents."[46]

Not surprisingly, as Sabo points out, this "man-as-hunter/woman-as-prey" sexual script made it hard for men to form loving relationships. And in the end it became an obstacle to sexual functioning since, again in Sabo's words, it led young men to "organize their energies and perceptions around a performance ethic," which turned them into sexual "achievement machines." The more obsessively these "sexual athletes" fixated on "masculine" frequency of performance rather than "feminine feelings," the more driven they were to "score" and to have and maintain erections. However, the more preoccupied they became with "erectile potency and performance," the less able they were to enjoy sex and avoid the "unmanly" sexual dysfunction of impotence they so feared.[47]

As Sabo also notes, not only "jocks" but many other men have internalized this "eroticism without intimacy" script: men in fraternities, motorcycle gangs, the armed forces, and urban gangs.[48] In fact, what Mosher and Tomkins call "the callous sex scene" is often in such groups part of the initiation into manhood.[49] And of course this impersonal, scoring-type sex is today mass marketed through both hard- and soft-core pornography, as well as through much of corporate advertising.

But even with all this, more and more men like Sabo—men who only a short time ago bought into dominator sexuality—are becoming conscious that even when men are "winners" in this adversarial kind of sex, they too are losers. Just as important, more and more men are also becoming conscious, in Sabo's words, that "until equality between the sexes becomes more of a social reality, no new model of a more humane sexuality will take hold."[50]

The Many Faces of the Men's Movement

Clearly not all the men who are today taking a new look at masculinity and sexuality share such views. As Susan Faludi notes in *Backlash,* among the thousands of books and articles on the "masculinity question" are also quite a few fiercely woman-hating, hypermasculine tracts.[51] And still more contain a mix of dominator and partnership ideas.

Just as there are many different factions in the women's movement, there are also different—sometimes totally opposed—factions in what the media generally lump together as "the men's movement."[52] Those men who are working for gender equity, to reduce male violence, and to change their own thinking and behavior so they can have more satisfying love relations are clearly on the partnership side of the line. Clearly on the other side of the line are those men openly working against equality for women, either denying there is inequality or claiming that women should be, and want to be, dominated by men. Where it gets less simple is in groups such as Robert Bly's "Wild Man" workshops and other groups that still urge men to identify with dominator archetypes such as the warrior and the king, while at the same time often talking about equal partnership between women and men and a more generally just and equitable society.

Certainly the impulse behind many of the men's groups that have been given so much press, where men meet in sweat lodges, drum in the woods, and tell stories about warriors and kings, is toward a less limited masculinity. This is particularly true for the white-collar and professional men (who can afford these workshops) looking for a new masculine script in which men are not so constrained by stiff codes of basically adversarial interaction with other men, and in which, as leaders of these groups put it, men can "bond."

But although it is touted as new, the script for men offered by some of these groups is actually not all that different from the old macho script except that it is dressed up in New Age clothes. As in the old macho all-male peer groups, once again male identity is defined in negative terms, as *not* being like a woman. As in the old macho script of contempt for the "feminine," Bly berates his followers for being "too soft" or "feminine" and thus "unmanly"—expressing horror of being "controlled" by women, from whom, according to him, men must at all costs be independent.[53] To this end, men must even distance themselves from their own mothers lest they be contaminated, in Bly's words, by "too much feminine energy."[54]

One of the most ironic things about Bly is that he originally preached that men should embrace their "feminine principle," which, as he said in a Great Mother conference he conducted in the 1970s, is essential for world peace. But of course the contemporary struggle between the dominator and partnership models is not only between different groups; it also takes place within the same organization and within the same individual.

Still, I cannot help but think that men like Bly would think and act very differently if all of us were taught a history that tells us about gender relations. For example, we would then all be familiar with the hypermasculinity revival of the nineteenth century, when also in reaction to feminism, men wrote of their "horror" of a nation losing "its manhood"; defined manhood in ways that, as Theodore Roszak writes, "cheapen compassion and tenderness" and "ennoble violence and suffering";[55] and in the end created the "macho" cultural climate that set the stage for the bloodbath of World War I. In short, we would know, and be warned, that all this talk of a New Age masculinity of "real" manhood is not merely empty rhetoric; that no matter how it is packaged, exhorting men to again emulate the old dominator archetypes of king and warrior is dangerous— not only to women, for whom it presages a return to the "good old days" of open, unashamed male dominance, but to men and to children of both genders.[56]

Moreover, if we were taught psychology from a gender perspective, we would all also be aware that one of the ways this destructive type of masculinity is maintained in dominator societies is precisely through the long-accepted and totally arbitrary notion (as Pleck writes in critiquing it) that for a man to develop normally he must learn *not* to identify with his mother—that the mark of masculinity is a man's separation from, and rejection of, any "feminine" identity.[57] For we would then be aware, as the psychologist Knoll Evans points out, that the prohibition against identifying and thus empathizing with his mother is a way of teaching a man not to feel "soft" or "feminine" emotions and thus not to empathize with any woman,[58] not even, in Roszak's words, the "woman most des- perately in need of liberation," the " 'woman' every man has locked up in the dungeons of his own psyche."[59] And we would further know that it is precisely in those societies and families where women are most rigidly dominated by men that mothers are the most controlling of their sons— the males on whom they can most effectively vent their pent-up anger and frustration.[60]

In sum, we would know that to the extent that men's groups today buy into the old macho scripts, they are reinforcing precisely the kind of society and family where men and women (and this obviously includes mothers and sons) both consciously and unconsciously hurt one another in all the ways that men (and women) complain they have been hurt. We would know that myths such as Freud's Oedipus complex, which sets up the angry sons to take over from the equally angry fathers and in the process "possess" as many women as possible (including in fantasy even their own mothers), and Jungian-type archetypes that still idealize "he- roic" male violence do *not* reflect the human psyche, but rather the dom- inator psyche: the same psyche that today threatens all life on this planet.

And we would immediately see the difference between, on the one hand, encouraging men to feel self-pity and continuing to blame women for their problems and, on the other, helping men to feel empathy for both women and men, including themselves. Finally, we would recognize something that is actually quite obvious: that men, like women, need close loving bonds with *both* women and men, including *both* mothers and fathers.

Having said this, I want to also say that I think the contention of Bly and other New Age writers that men (and I must add, women) need new initiation rites into adulthood is valid. In fact, I hope this recognition will eventually lead to truly new rites of passage for men—rites, however, very different from those in *Iron John,* from macho-script "callous sex" scenes, and from all the other ways of inculcating in men contempt for women and the "feminine."[61]

I also want to say that I think the recognition that men need new role models is very important, and that a key issue, implicit in some of men's fears of becoming too "feminine," is the need for men to find new role models for assertiveness. The point is not for men to now take the submissive stance traditionally associated with femininity, but for both women and men to learn to express their needs and desires in a strong and assertive manner without intimidation or violence.

Finally, I want to say that the recognition by Jungian and New Age men's groups that there has to be a spiritual dimension to the "new masculinity" is very important. But it is my hope that what this will eventually lead this segment of the men's movement to deal with are the core spiritual questions raised by sages throughout history, questions about the need for men to adopt in their behavior values such as empathy and nonviolence, and questions dealing with fundamental issues of equality and justice.

Women, Men, and Partnership

To me, the most encouraging aspect of the contemporary men's movement is how many men are in fact probing precisely these core spiritual and social issues. It has been my good fortune to live with one of these men, my partner and husband, the social psychologist David Loye, and to see how his research and writing have increasingly focused on gender, first in *The Partnership Way*[62] (which we wrote together) and then in the books he is now completing on the relationship between social structure, gender, and what he calls moral sensitivity. I am particularly excited about this new work, as it not only provides the first unified scientific perspective on morality but also traces moral development through biological and cultural evolution.

Another man who has passionately written about these core spiritual and moral issues from a gender perspective is John Stoltenberg, whose book *Refusing to Be a Man* is unprecedented in its outright rejection of dominator masculinity (also unprecented is the fact that a book with such a title got published at all). A collection of thirteen essays that, as Stoltenberg writes in his introduction, "might provoke some people to outrage," it expresses Stoltenberg's outrage at the profound injustice of traditional gender and sexual relations, and particularly at the erotization of male supremacy, which as Stoltenberg notes "makes inequality feel like sex."[63]

In the essay "Pornography and Male Supremacy" Stoltenberg writes, "Once you have sexualized inequality, once it is a learned and internalized prerequisite for sexual arousal and sexual gratification," sexual freedom becomes a license for men to more effectively hunt and subdue women. "Pornography," he continues, "institutionalizes male supremacy the way segregation institutionalizes white supremacy." Stoltenberg has even had the courage to criticize some of the pornography of gay men, an act vociferously condemned by some political liberals. Only, as Stoltenberg points out, the problem is hardly one of gay men or of erotic images; it is that all too often "the values in the sex depicted in gay made sex films" are "very much the values that male supremacists tend to have: taking, using, estranging, dominating—essentially power mongering."[64]

But unfortunately, rather than publicizing the work of men like Stoltenberg, who have the courage to join hands with other men and with women to heal a distorted male sexuality that has helped maintain a dominator society, the media still tend to give greatest publicity to those men's groups that see women, and particularly feminism, as a threat to their masculinity, just as they tend to focus on the more separatist (or as they inflammatorily put it, "man-hating") factions of feminism, thus again presenting feminists as men's enemies. Tragically, in so doing they are pointing the very men searching for new ways of relating to themselves and to women in precisely the direction that *cannot* help them develop the new models of masculinity they say they want and need, instead of giving them information about the ideas and groups that can.

For example, there are today men's groups such as Men Against Rape, Men Against Domestic Violence, and Men to Stop Battering. There are organizations such as the National Organization of Men Against Sexism, national conferences with themes such as "Building Bridges for a Multi-cultural Men's Community,"[65] and publications such as *Changing Men* and *Masculinities*. Recognizing that women and men share essentially the same human goals, such organizations, conferences, and publications are important and unprecedented signposts on the road to partnership. To-gether with national women's organizations such as the National Organ-ization for Women (NOW), the National Women's Political Caucus (NWPC), and the Older Women's League (OWL), international confer-ences such as the WEDO (Women's Environment and Development Or-ganization) 1994 conference "Women and Power," national conferences such as "Empowering Women: Achieving Human Rights in the Twenty-first Century,"[66] and publications such as *Ms., Woman of Power,* and *Women's International News,* they provide the nuclei for the gradual con-solidation of the women's and men's movements into an overarching partnership movement: an integrated movement for progressive change that places both sexual and gender relations at the center rather than the periphery of the political agenda.

I say gradual because, particularly for women who have for so long been conditioned to defer to and please men, separate women's and men's groups are essential. Although the partnership movement is the logical melding of the women's and men's movements with the environ-mental, human rights, and other progressive movements, this is not to say that the women's and men's movements will soon be unnecessary. Quite the contrary, both will be essential for a long time, since some of the strongest threads in the cultural warp and woof that hold repressive institutions together are dominator stereotypes of sex and gender.

Moreover, to recognize that there are aspects of "traditional" mascu-linity that idealize the very behaviors that today endanger human survival is not to say that everything stereotypically taught men as masculine needs to be left behind. In the same way that there are traits stereotypically labeled feminine, such as empathy and caring, that men can (and if per-mitted, do) share—traits that do *not* make a human being less of a man, but rather more so—there are traits stereotypically labeled masculine that are excellent human traits for both men and women. These too are traits that both women and men can (and if permitted, do) share, for example, stating what one wants rather than feeling one has to manipulate or placate, as socially disempowered people are taught they must do.

In short, the point of all this is not that everything now taught men as masculine is dysfunctional or that everything taught women as feminine is superior—much less that women are superior to men. Nor is the deconstruction and reconstruction of gender stereotypes and sexual relations about moving to a "unisex" society where women and men become the same. On the contrary, what the women's, men's, and partnership movements are about is the creation of a far more interesting and exciting society, one where diversity—be it based on gender, race, religion, or ethnic origin—can be truly valued.

Certainly these movements are not about constructing a bland, passionless sexuality. On the contrary, they are about constructing a far more intense and passionate sexuality. Nor are they about moving to a world in which there will no longer be any fighting or conflict. Rather, they are about constructing a world where both men's and women's life scripts contain many different types of behaviors, including the today urgently needed creative conflict resolution skills that in both interpersonal and international relations can successfully be applied to the inevitable clashes of human needs and desires that are all too often still dealt with through violence. And it is to construct this far safer, more satisfying, and more interesting world that, after millennia of the dominator war of the sexes, women and men all over the world are today coming together not as adversaries, but as partners in a jointly beneficial enterprise.

REFERENCES

Abraham, Ralph, and Christopher Shaw. 1984. *Dynamics: The Geometry of Behavior*. Santa Cruz: Aerial Press.

Adorno, T. W., Else Frenkel-Brunswick, Daniel Levinson, and R. Nevitt Stanford. 1964. *The Authoritarian Personality*. New York: Wiley.

Barbeau, Clayton. 1982. *Delivering the Male*. San Francisco: Harper and Row.

Beneke, Tim. 1993. "Deep Masculinity as Social Control: Foucault, Bly and Masculinity." *masculinities* 1:13–19.

Bly, Robert. 1991. "The Need for Male Initiation." In *To Be a Man*, edited by Keith Thompson. Los Angeles: Tarcher.

Brod, Harry. 1987. *The Making of Masculinities: The New Men's Studies*. Boston: Allen and Unwin.

Callahan, Mathew. 1993. *Sex, Death, and the Angry Young Man: Conversations with Riane Eisler and David Loye*. Ojai, CA: Times Change Press.

Capra, Fritjof. 1982. *The Turning Point*. New York: Bantam Books.

Caputi, Jane, and Gordene O. MacKenzie. 1992. "Pumping Iron John." In *Women*

Respond to the Men's Movement, edited by Kay Leigh Hagan. San Francisco: HarperSanFrancisco.

Castelot, Andre. 1971. *Napoleon*. New York: Harper and Row.

Clatterbaugh, Kenneth. 1989. "Masculinist Perspectives." *Changing Men* 20:4–6.

———. 1993. "The Mythopoetic Foundations of New-Age Patriarchy." *Masculinities* 1:2–12.

Coltrane, Scott. 1988. "Father-Child Relationships and the Status of Women." *American Journal of Sociology* 93:1060–95.

Csanyi, Vilmos. 1989. *Evolutionary Systems and Society: A General Theory*. Durham, NC: Duke University Press.

Davis, Angela. 1983. *Women, Race, and Class*. New York: Vintage Books.

Dittes, James E. 1985. *The Male Predicament*. San Francisco: Harper and Row.

Eisler, Riane. 1987a. *The Chalice and the Blade: Our History, Our Future*. San Francisco: Harper and Row.

———. 1987b. "Woman, Man and the Evolution of Social Structure." *World Futures: The Journal of General Evolution* 23:79–92.

———. 1987c. "Human Rights: Toward an Integrated Theory for Action." *Human Rights Quarterly* 9:287–308.

———. 1991. "Cultural Evolution: Social Shifts and Phase Changes." In *The New Evolutionary Paradigm*, edited by Ervin Laszlo, 179–200. New York: Gordon and Breach.

———. 1993a. "Technology, Gender, and History: Toward a Nonlinear Model of Social Evolution." In *The Evolution of Cognitive Maps: New Paradigms for the Twenty-first Century*, edited by Ervin Laszlo, Ignazio Masulli, Robert Artigiani, and Vilmos Csanyi, 181–203. New York: Gordon and Breach.

———. 1993b. "From Domination to Partnership: The Foundations of Global Peace." In *Communication and Culture in War and Peace*, edited by Colleen Roach, 145–174. Newbury Park, CA: Sage.

———. 1993c. "The Challenge of Human Rights for All: What We Can Do." In *Creating the Twenty-first Century: Rights, Responsibilities and Remedies*, edited by Bertram Gross and Peter Juviler. Armonk, NY: M. E. Sharpe.

———. 1993d. "The Rights of Women, Children, and Men." In *Creating the Twenty-first Century: Rights, Responsibilities and Remedies*, edited by Bertram Gross and Peter Juviler. Armonk, NY: M. E. Sharpe.

Eisler, Riane, and David Loye. 1990. *The Partnership Way*. San Francisco: HarperSanFrancisco.

Faludi, Susan. 1991. *Backlash: The Undeclared War against American Women*. New York: Crown.

Gerzon, Mark. 1982. *A Choice of Heroes*. Boston: Houghton Mifflin.

Giddens, Anthony. 1984. *The Constitution of Society*. Berkeley: University of California Press.

Hagan, Kay Leigh, ed. 1992. *Women Respond to the Men's Movement*. San Francisco: HarperSanFrancisco.

Kerber, Linda, and Jane DeHart Mathews, eds. 1982. *Women's America*. New York: Oxford University Press.

Kimmel, Michael S. 1987. "The Contemporary Crisis of Masculinity in Historical Perspective." In *The Making of Masculinities*, edited by Harry Brod. Boston: Allen and Unwin.

Kimmel, Michael S., and Thomas E. Mosmiller, eds. 1992. *Against the Tide: Pro-Feminist Men in the United States, 1776–1990*. Boston: Beacon Press.

Koegel, Rob. 1994. "Healing the Wounds of Masculinity: A Crucial Role for Educators." *Holistic Education Review 7*.

Livermore, Beth. 1993. "The Lessons of Love." *Psychology Today*, March–April.

Loye, David. 1995. "The Psychology of Prediction in Chaotic States." In *The Proceedings of the Society of Chaos Theory in Psychology*, edited by Robin Rebertson and Allan Combs. Hillsdale, NJ: Erlbaum.

Loye, David, and Riane Eisler. 1987. "Chaos and Transformation: Implications of Non-equilibrium Theory for Social Science and Society." *Behavioral Science* 32:53–65.

Marx, Karl, and Friedrich Engels. 1960. *Werke*, Vol. 8. Berlin: Dietz Verlag.

Maturana, Humberto, and Francisco Varela. 1980. *Autopoeisis and Cognition*. Boston: Reidel.

McClelland, David. 1980. *Power*. New York: Irvington.

McGill, Michael E. 1985. *The McGill Report on Male Intimacy*. New York: Harper and Row.

Miedzian, Myriam. 1991. *Boys Will Be Boys*. New York: Anchor Books.

Monet, Joseph, ed. 1948. *Casanova's Memoirs*, by Giovanni Casanova. Abridged ed. New York: Hillman Periodicals.

Mosher, Donald L., and Silvan S. Tomkins. 1988. "Scripting the Macho Man." *Journal of Sex Research* 25:60–84.

Prigogine, Ilya, and Isabel Stengers. 1984. *Order Out of Chaos*. New York: Bantam.

Roszak, Theodore. 1969. "The Hard and the Soft." In *Masculine/Feminine*, edited by Betty Roszak and Theodore Roszak, 92–93. New York: Harper Colophon Books.

Sabo, Don. 1989. "The Myth of the Sexual Athlete." *Changing Men* 20:38–39.

Stephenson, June. 1991. *Men Are Not Cost-Effective*. Napa, CA: Diemer, Smith.

Stoltenberg, John. 1990. *Refusing to Be a Man*. New York: Penguin.

———. 1993. *The End of Manhood*. New York: Penguin.

Winter, David. 1973. *The Power Motive*. New York: Free Press.

Wright, Karen. 1992. "Evolution of the Big O." *Discovery*, June.

NOTES

1. It is hard to tell to what extent young women who today talk of male bodies in the same graphic sexual language once reserved for men are doing what women have always wanted to do, and to what extent it is a matter of imitating behaviors associated with male power and male prerogatives, but clearly for women sex purely for pleasure can be just as exciting and enjoyable as for men.

2. William Jankoviak and Edward Fisher study quoted in Livermore 1993, 33. Jankoviak and Fisher even speculate that in those few cultures where they did not find such evidence, it was mainly because the anthropologists did not broach the subject.

3. 1988 study by Beverly Fehr, quoted in Livermore 1993, 34.

4. Prigogine and Stengers 1984. This is the same approach that informs the work of scientists such as Ralph Abraham, Fritjof Capra, Vilmos Csanyi, David Loye, and Humberto Maturana. See, for example, Abraham and Shaw 1984; Capra 1982; Csanyi 1989; Loye 1995; and Maturana and Varela 1980.

5. See introduction and chap. 10 in *The Chalice and the Blade*. See also Loye and Eisler 1987.

6. Loye 1995.

7. Marx and Engels 1960, 115.

8. Eisler 1987a, 1987b, 1991, 1993a, 1993b.

9. Csanyi 1989.

10. For details, see Winter 1973 and *The Chalice and the Blade*, chap. 10.

11. Winter calls these stories Don Juan stories after the legendary hero of folk tales, celebrated literary works such as Goethe's *Faust*, and even one of the world's most beloved operas, Mozart's *Don Giovanni*. Don Juan is a man who compulsively seduces (or, as in Don Giovanni's case, rapes) women. In some versions he is punished; in *Faust*, by the loss of his immortal soul. But by and large the tenor of Don Juan stories is one of admiration for his manly exploits.

12. Giddens 1984, xxi. Giddens's theory of structuration focuses on the interactive processes through which this happens.

13. This is explored in extensive detail in *The Chalice and the Blade*.

14. Kimmel 1987, 127.

15. Ibid., 126–27.

16. Ibid., 128–33. As in the 1691 pamphlet *Restored Maidenhead*, to counter any real female sexual independence, some men (like some men today) argued that it is well known that women want to be raped (ibid., 133).

17. Ibid., 135–36.

18. Roszak 1969, 96.

19. Kerber and Mathews 1982, 222–25. This high toll in lives was due to the fact that the women were locked in so they could not go outside, even to go to

the bathroom, except at designated times. Unfortunately such practices are still found in some regions of the world today—for example, in some of the "maqui-ladora" sweatshops in Mexico, the Philippines, and other regions where cheap female labor is exploited. It also sometimes still leads to tragedies, like the fire at the Kader Industrial Company plant outside Bangkok reported in the interna-tional press, in which many women's lives were again lost. (See *Ms.* July/August 1993, 15, for a report of how more than two hundred workers, almost all women, were crushed behind locked doors and under collapsed stairwells at this plant, where doors were always kept locked from the outside.)

20. Unfortunately, as often happens in dominator politics, in the struggle for the vote, two traditionally disempowered groups—black men and white women—were pitted against each other. Some suffragist leaders wrote resentfully of the unfairness of giving uneducated black men the vote while denying it to educated women. Their invocation of racial stereotypes in turn led to resentment, leading to a still-lingering rift. For an account of this, see Davis 1983.

21. See, for example, *Human Development Report, 1991* (New York: Oxford University Press, 1991), 179.

22. Brod 1987, 40. As Brod writes, "The overgeneralization from male to ge-neric human experience not only distorts our understanding of what, if anything, is truly generic to humanity but also precludes the study of masculinity as a *specific male* experience, rather than a universal paradigm for *human* experience" (ibid.). This is one reason Brod argues that although de facto most of what we are taught about the human condition has been "men's studies"—that is, written by men about men—there is a need for a discipline that "raises new questions and demonstrates the inadequacy of established frameworks in answering old ones" (ibid., 41).

23. Koegel 1994. Reprints of "Healing the Wounds of Masculinity" can be obtained from the Center of Partnership Studies, P.O. Box 51936, Pacific Grove, CA 93950.

24. Callahan 1993.

25. Castelot 1971, 377.

26. Beneke 1993.

27. See chap. 12, *The Chalice and the Blade.*

28. Stephenson 1991; see also Miedzian 1991.

29. See, for example, Kimmel and Mosmiller 1992.

30. Brod 1987, 1.

31. Brod 1987.

32. Clatterbaugh 1993, 6.

33. Brod 1987, 209.

34. Coltrane 1988, 1073.

35. Even the legendary Dr. Benjamin Spock, who for many decades wrote books on parenting in which fathers barely figured, finally changed his position.

In the 1976 edition of his classic *Baby and Child Care,* he wrote that a father needs to more equally participate in child care because by so doing he "will do best by his children, his wife *and himself"* (quoted in Gerzon 1982, 196).

36. Quoted in Gerzon 1982, 207.

37. Brod 1987, 121.

38. Dittes writes that "a lot of the crippling that has come to light is the crippling done by men" who "are taught and induced to do it so compellingly that it often becomes automatic and unthinking" (1985, 113).

39. McGill 1985, xvii, 225.

40. Barbeau 1982, 121.

41. Monet 1948. Casanova wrote of the period in France during the reigns of Louis XV and Louis XVI, but his autobiography did not appear until the early nineteenth century.

42. For example, as Karen Wright notes, "Paralysis victims bereft of feeling below the waist often get erections and ejaculate without having a climax and prepubescent boys can achieve orgasm, even multiple ones, without ejaculating" (Wright 1992, 56).

43. Adorno, Frenkel-Brunswick, et al. 1964.

44. A study of 336 students in 1971 at Heidelberg University (then a center of radical activity) by Ronald Grosarth-Maticek, originally reported in the German journal *Sexualmedizin,* described in "Revolution Yes, Orgasm No," *Cambio 16* (Madrid), October 22, 1978, and in *Atlas World Press Review,* February 1979, 12.

45. Ibid.

46. Sabo 1989, 38.

47. Ibid.

48. Ibid.

49. " 'The specific callous sexual act that is to count as manly varies,' they write. It can be 'You're not a real man until you catch the clap,' or 'You're not a real man until you've scored ten times,' or 'You're not a real man unless you take what you need' " (Mosher and Tomkins 1988, 72). But the sex is not for the man himself but for his peers. As they put it, "Sol Gordon's joke has it that neither party enjoys their initial experience with sexual intercourse, the boy gets his orgasm the next day when he tells his friends" (ibid.).

50. Sabo 1989, 39.

51. Faludi 1991.

52. For an analysis of these various perspectives, see Clatterbaugh 1989; Kimmel 1987.

53. Quoted in Faludi 1991, 308–12.

54. Bly 1991, 38–42. The third and fourth issues of *Masculinities* were devoted to the subject of profeminist men responding to the men's movement, and featured a number of incisive critiques of Bly and others in the so-called mythopoetic men's movement. There have also been important critiques by women of

Bly. One of the most interesting and funny ones is "Pumping Iron John" by Jane
Caputi and Gordene o. MacKenzie (1992).

55. Roszak 1969, 92–93.

56. A number of studies show that the cultural movement to a masculinity of
male supremacy presages violence and repression. Thus, Roszak writes of the
dominator backlash that eventually led to World War I, "Compulsive masculinity
is written all over the political style of the period." Just as violence, particularly
sexual violence, is often the outcome of all-male drinking sessions, Roszak writes
of those years as "one long drunken stag party where boys from every walk of life
and every ideological persuasion goad one another on to ever more bizarre professions of toughness, daring, and counter-phobic mania—until at last the boast-
ing turns suicidal and these would-be supermen plunge the whole of Western
society into the bloodbath of world war" (Roszak 1969, 92). See also David
McClelland's study of times when the emphasis in popular culture is to down-
grade "affiliation" (more "feminine" peaceful and compassionate values) and
reidealize "power" (more "masculine" or "hard" values) and David Winter's
study of times when Don Juan "lady-killer" type fiction proliferates (McClelland
1980; Winter 1973).

57. Pleck in Brod 1987. See also Hagan, *Women Respond to the Men's Movement* (1992).

58. Knoll Evans, personal correspondence and work in progress.

59. Roszak 1969, 101.

60. Winter 1973; personal communication with Knoll Evans; personal correspondence with a psychiatrist who lived and worked with women in Saudi Arabia.

61. For some alternative scripts of masculinity and femininity, see Loye and
Eisler 1987, especially the section on dominator and partnership heroes and her-
oines.

62. Ibid. See also Callahan 1993, which contains conversations with Loye and
Eisler.

63. Stoltenberg 1990, 129. See also Stoltenberg 1993.

64. Stoltenberg 1990, 110, 129, 130.

65. This was the eighteenth National Conference on Men and Masculinity,
held in 1991 and sponsored by the National Organization of Men Against Sexism,
54 Mint Street, Suite 300, San Francisco, CA 94103.

66. This 1993 conference, which I helped organize, was held in Coeur d'Alene,
Idaho, and used the new integrated model for human rights proposed in Eisler
1987c, 1993c, 1993d.

Chapter Fifteen

Men
Comrades in Struggle

bell hooks

Feminism defined as a movement to end sexist oppression enables women and men, girls and boys to participate equally in revolutionary struggle. So far, contemporary feminist movement has been primarily generated by the efforts of women; men have rarely participated. This lack of partici- pation is not solely a consequence of antifeminism. By making women's liberation synonymous with women gaining social equality with men, liberal feminists effectively created a situation in which they, not men, designated feminist movement "women's work." Even as they were at- tacking sex role divisions of labor, the institutionalized sexism that assigns unpaid, devalued, "dirty" work to women, they were assigning to women yet another sex role task: making feminist revolution. Women's libera- tionists called on all women to join feminist movement, but they did not continually stress that men should assume responsibility for actively struggling to end sexist oppression. Men, they argued, were all-powerful, misogynist, oppressor—the enemy. Women were the oppressed—the victims. Such rhetoric reinforced sexist ideology by positing in an inverted form the notion of a basic conflict between the sexes, the implication being that the empowerment of women would necessarily be at the ex- pense of men.

As with other issues, the insistence on a "woman-only" feminist move- ment and a virulent antimale stance reflected the race and class back- ground of participants. Bourgeois white women, especially radical femi- nists, were envious and angry at privileged white men for denying them an equal share in class privilege. In part, feminism provided them with a public forum for the expression of their anger as well as a political platform they could use to call attention to issues of social equality, demand change, and promote specific reforms. They were not eager to call attention to the fact that men do not share a common social status; that patriarchy does not negate the existence of class and race privilege or exploitation; that all men do not benefit equally from sexism. They did not want to acknowledge that bourgeois white women, though often victimized by sexism, have more power and privilege, are less likely to be exploited or oppressed, than poor, uneducated, nonwhite males. At the time, many white women's liberationists did not care about the fate of oppressed groups of men. In keeping with the exercise of race and/or class privilege, they deemed the life experiences of these men unworthy of their attention, dismissed them, and simultaneously deflected attention away from their support of continued exploitation and oppression. Assertions like "all men are the enemy" and "all men hate women" lumped all groups of men in one category, thereby suggesting that they share equally in all forms of male privilege. One of the first written statements that endeavored to make an antimale stance a central feminist position was "The Redstocking Manifesto." Clause 3 of the manifesto reads,

> We identify the agents of our oppression as men. Male supremacy is the oldest, most basic form of domination. All other forms of exploitation and oppression (racism, capitalism, imperialism, etc.) are extensions of male supremacy: men dominate women, a few men dominate the rest. All power situations throughout history have been male-dominated and male-oriented. Men have controlled all political, economic, and cultural institutions and backed up this control with physical force. They have used their power to keep women in an inferior position. All men receive economic, sexual, and psychological benefits from male supremacy. All men have oppressed women.

Antimale sentiments alienated many poor and working-class women, particularly nonwhite women, from feminist movement. Their life experiences had shown them that they have more in common with men of their race and/or class group than with bourgeois white women. They know the sufferings and hardships women face in their communities; they also know the sufferings and hardships men face and they have compassion for them. They have had the experience of struggling with them for a better life. This has been especially true for black women. Throughout our history in the United States, black women have shared equal responsibility in all struggles to resist racist oppression. Despite sexism, black women have continually contributed equally to antiracist struggle, and frequently, before contemporary black liberation effort, black men recognized this contribution. There is a special tie binding people together who struggle collectively for liberation. Black women and men have been united by such ties. They have known the experience of political solidarity. It is the experience of shared resistance struggle that led black women to reject the antimale stance of some feminist activists. This does not mean that black women were not willing to acknowledge the reality of black male sexism. It does mean that many of us do not believe we will combat sexism or woman-hating by attacking black men or responding to them in kind.

Bourgeois white women cannot conceptualize the bonds that develop between women and men in liberation struggle and have not had as many positive experiences working with men politically. Patriarchal white male rule has usually devalued female political input. Despite the prevalence of sexism in black communities, the role black women play in social institutions, whether primary or secondary, is recognized by everyone as significant and valuable. In an interview with Claudia Tate, black woman writer Maya Angelou explains her sense of the different roles black and white women play in their communities:

> Black women and white women are in strange positions in our separate communities. In the social gatherings of black people, black women have always been predominant. That is to say, in the church it's always Sister Hudson, Sister Thomas, and Sister Wetheringay who keep the church alive. In lay gatherings it's always Lottie who cooks, and Mary who's going to Bonita's where there is a good party going on. Also, black women are the nurturers of children in our community. White women are in a different position in their social institutions. White men, who are in effect their fathers, husbands, brothers, their sons, nephews, and uncles say to white women or imply in any case: "I don't really need you to run my institutions. I need you in certain places and in those places you must be kept— in the bedroom, in the kitchen, in the nursery, and on the pedestal." Black women have never been told this.

Without the material input of black women, as participants and leaders, many male-dominated institutions in black communities would cease to exist; this is not the case in all-white communities.

Many black women refused participation in feminist movement because they felt that an antimale stance was not a sound basis for action. They were convinced that virulent expressions of these sentiments intensify sexism by adding to the antagonism that already exists between women and men. For years black women (and some black men) had been struggling to overcome the tensions and antagonisms between black females and males that are generated by internalized racism (i.e., when the white patriarchy suggests that one group has caused the oppression of the other). Black women were saying to black men, "we are not one another's enemy," "we must resist the socialization that teaches us to hate ourselves and one another." This affirmation of bonding between black women and men was part of antiracist struggle. It could have been a part of feminist struggle had white women's liberationists stressed the need for women and men to resist the sexist socialization that teaches us to hate and fear one another. They chose instead to emphasize hate, especially male woman-hating, suggesting that it could not be changed. Therefore no viable political solidarity could exist between women and men. Women of color, from various ethnic backgrounds, as well as women who were active in the gay movement, not only experienced the development of solidarity between women and men in resistance struggle, but recognized its value. They were not willing to devalue this bonding by allying themselves with antimale, bourgeois white women. Encouraging political bonding between women and men to radically resist sexist oppression would have called attention to the transformative potential of feminism. The antimale stance was a reactionary perspective that made feminism appear to be a movement that would enable white women to usurp white male power, replacing white male supremacist rule with white female supremacist rule.

Within feminist organizations, the issue of female separatism was initially separated from the antimale stance; it was only as the movement progressed that the two perspectives merged. Many all-female, sex-segregated groups were formed because women recognized that separatist organizing could hasten female consciousness-raising, lay the groundwork for the development of solidarity between women, and generally advance the movement. It was believed that mixed groups would get bogged down by male power trips. Separatist groups were seen as a necessary strategy, not as a way to attack men. Ultimately the purpose of such groups was integration with equality. The positive implications of separatist organizing were diminished when radical feminists, like Ti Grace Atkinson, proposed sexual separatism as an ultimate goal of feminist movement. Reactionary separatism is rooted in the conviction that male supremacy is an absolute aspect of our culture, that women have only two alternatives: accepting it or withdrawing from it to create subcultures. This position eliminates any need for revolutionary struggle and it is in no way a threat to the status quo. In the essay "Separate to Integrate," Barbara Leon stresses that male supremacists would rather feminist movement remain "separate and unequal." She gives the example of orchestra conductor Antonia Brico's efforts to shift from an all-women orchestra to a mixed orchestra, only to find she could not get support for the latter:

> Antonia Brico's efforts were acceptable as long as she confined herself to proving that women were qualified musicians. She had no trouble finding 100 women who could play in an orchestra or getting financial backing for them to do so. But finding the backing for men and women to play together in a truly integrated orchestra proved to be impossible. Fighting for integration proved to be more of a threat to male supremacy and, therefore, harder to achieve.
>
> The women's movement is at the same point now. We can take the easier way of accepting segregation, but that would mean losing the very goals for which the movement was formed. Reactionary separatism has been a way of halting the push of feminism.

During the course of contemporary feminist movement, reactionary separatism has led many women to abandon feminist struggle, yet it remains an accepted pattern for feminist organizing, for example, among autonomous women's groups within the peace movement. As a policy, it has helped to marginalize feminist struggle, to make it seem more a personal solution to individual problems, especially problems with men, than a political movement that aims to transform society as a whole. To return to an emphasis on feminism as revolutionary struggle, women can no longer allow feminism to be another arena for the continued expression of antagonism between the sexes. The time has come for women active in feminist movement to develop new strategies for including men in the struggle against sexism.

All men support and perpetuate sexism and sexist oppression in one form or another. It is crucial that feminist activists not get bogged down in intensifying our awareness of this fact to the extent that we do not stress the more unemphasized point, which is that men can lead life-affirming, meaningful lives without exploiting and oppressing women. Like women, men have been socialized to passively accept sexist ideology. While they need not blame themselves for accepting sexism, they must assume responsibility for eliminating it. It angers women activists who push separatism as a goal of feminist movement to hear emphasis placed on men being victimized by sexism; they cling to the "all men are the enemy" version of reality. Men are not exploited or oppressed by sexism, but there are ways in which they suffer as a result of it. This suffering should not be ignored. While it in no way diminishes the seriousness of male abuse and oppression of women, or negates male responsibility for exploitative actions, the pain men experience can serve as a catalyst calling attention to the need for change. Recognition of the painful consequences of sexism in their lives led some men to establish consciousness-raising groups to examine this. Paul Hornacek explains the purpose of these gatherings in his essay "Anti-Sexist Consciousness-Raising Groups for Men":

> Men have reported a variety of different reasons for deciding to seek a C-R group, all of which have an underlying link to the feminist movement. Most are experiencing emotional pain as a result of their male sex role and are dissatisfied with it. Some have had confrontations with radical feminists in public or private encounters and have been repeatedly criticized for being sexist. Some come as a result of their commitment to social change and their recognition that sexism and patriarchy are elements of an intolerable social system that needs to be altered.

Men in the consciousness-raising groups Hornacek describes acknowledge that they benefit from patriarchy and yet are also hurt by it. Men's groups, like women's support groups, run the risk of overemphasizing personal change at the expense of political analysis and struggle.

Separatist ideology encourages women to ignore the negative impact of sexism on male personhood. It stresses polarization between the sexes. According to Joy Justice, separatists believe that there are "two basic perspectives" on the issue of naming the victims of sexism: "There is the perspective that men oppress women. And there is the perspective that people are people, and we are all hurt by rigid sex roles." Many separatists feel that the latter perspective is a sign of co-optation, representing women's refusal to confront the fact that men are the enemy; they insist on the primacy of the first perspective. Both perspectives accurately describe our predicament. Men *do* oppress women. People *are* hurt by rigid sex role patterns. These two realities coexist. Male oppression of women cannot be excused by the recognition that there are ways men are hurt by rigid sex roles. Feminist activists should acknowledge that hurt—it exists. It does not erase or lessen male responsibility for supporting and perpetuating their power under patriarchy to exploit and oppress women in a manner far more grievous than the psychological stress or emotional pain caused by male conformity to rigid sex role patterns.

Women active in feminist movement have not wanted to focus in any way on male pain so as not to deflect attention away from the focus on male privilege. Separatist feminist rhetoric suggested that all men shared equally in male privilege, that all men reap positive benefits from sexism. Yet the poor or working-class man who has been socialized via sexist ideology to believe that there are privileges and powers he should possess solely because he is male often finds that few if any of these benefits are automatically bestowed him in life. More than any other male group in the United States, he is constantly concerned about the contradiction between the notion of masculinity he was taught and his inability to live up to that notion. He is usually "hurt," emotionally scarred because he does not have the privilege or power society has taught him "real men" should possess. Alienated, frustrated, pissed off, he may attack, abuse, and oppress an individual woman or women, but he is not reaping positive benefits from his support and perpetuation of sexist ideology. When he beats or rapes women, he is not exercising privilege or reaping positive rewards; he may feel satisfied in exercising the only form of domination allowed him. The ruling class male power structure that promotes his sexist abuse of women reaps the real material benefits and privileges from his actions. As long as he is attacking women and not sexism or capitalism, he helps to maintain a system that allows him few, if any, benefits or privileges. He is an oppressor. He is an enemy to women. He is also an enemy to himself. He is also oppressed. His abuse of women is not justifiable. Even though he has been socialized to act as he does, there are existing social movements that would enable him to struggle for self-recovery and liberation. By ignoring these movements, he chooses to remain both oppressor and oppressed. If feminist movement ignores his predicament, dismisses his hurt, or writes him off as just another male enemy, then we are passively condoning his actions.

The process by which men act as oppressors and are oppressed is particularly visible in black communities, where men are working-class and poor. In her essay "Notes for Yet Another Paper on Black Feminism, or Will the Real Enemy Please Stand Up?" black feminist activist Barbara Smith suggests that black women are unwilling to confront the problem of sexist oppression in black communities:

> By naming sexist oppression as a problem it would appear that we would have to identify as threatening a group we have heretofore assumed to be our allies—Black men. This seems to be one of the major stumbling blocks to beginning to analyze the sexual relationships/sexual politics of our lives.

The phrase "men are not the enemy" dismisses feminism and the reality of patriarchy in one breath and also overlooks some major realities. If we cannot entertain the idea that some men are the enemy, especially white men and in a different sense Black men too, then we will never be able to figure out all the reasons why, for example, we are beaten up every day, why we are sterilized against our wills, why we are being raped by our neighbors, why we are pregnant at age twelve, and why we are at home on welfare with more children than we can support or care for. Acknowledging the sexism of Black men does not mean that we become "manhaters" or necessarily eliminates them from our lives. What it does mean is that we must struggle for a different basis of interaction with them.

Women in black communities have been reluctant to publicly discuss sexist oppression, but they have always known it exists. We too have been socialized to accept sexist ideology, and many black women feel that black male abuse of women is a reflection of frustrated masculinity. Such thoughts lead them to see that this abuse is understandable, even justified. The vast majority of black women think that just publicly stating that these men are the enemy or identifying them as oppressors would do little to change the situation; they fear that it could simply lead to greater victimization. Naming oppressive realities, in and of itself, has not brought about the kinds of changes for oppressed groups that it can for more privileged groups, who command a different quality of attention. The public naming of sexism has generally not resulted in the institutionalized violence that characterized, for example, the response to black civil rights struggles. (Private naming, however, is often met with violent oppression.) Black women have not joined feminist movement not because they cannot face the reality of sexist oppression; they face it daily. They do not join feminist movement because they do not see in feminist theory and practice, especially those writings made available to masses of people, potential solutions.

So far, feminist rhetoric identifying men as the enemy has had few positive implications. Had feminist activists called attention to the relationship between ruling-class men and the vast majority of men, who are socialized to perpetuate and maintain sexism and sexist oppression even as they reap no life-affirming benefits, these men might have been motivated to examine the impact of sexism in their lives. Often feminist activists talk about male abuse of women as if it is an exercise of privilege rather than an expression of moral bankruptcy, insanity, and dehumanization. For example, in Barbara Smith's essay, she identifies white males as "the primary oppressor group in American society" and discusses the nature of their domination of others. At the end of the passage in which this statement is made she comments, "It is not just rich and powerful capitalists who inhibit and destroy life. Rapists, murderers, lynchers, and ordinary bigots do too and exercise very real and violent power because of this white male privilege." Implicit in this statement is the assumption that the act of committing violent crimes against women is either a gesture or an affirmation of privilege. Sexist ideology brainwashes men to believe that their violent abuse of women is beneficial when it is not. Yet feminist activists affirm this logic when we should be constantly naming these acts as expressions of perverted power relations, general lack of control over one's actions, emotional powerlessness, extreme irrationality, and in many cases, outright insanity. Passive male absorption of sexist ideology enables them to interpret this disturbed behavior positively. As long as men are brainwashed to equate violent abuse of women with privilege, they will have no understanding of the damage done to themselves or to others, and no motivation to change.

Individuals committed to feminist revolution must address ways that men can unlearn sexism. Women were never encouraged in contemporary feminist movement to point out to men their responsibility. Some feminist rhetoric "put down" women who related to men at all. Most women's liberationists were saying, "women have nurtured, helped, and supported others for too long—now we must fend for ourselves." Having helped and supported men for centuries by acting in complicity with sexism, women were suddenly encouraged to withdraw their support when it came to the issue of "liberation." The insistence on a concentrated focus on individualism, on the primacy of self, deemed "liberatory" by women's liberationists, was not a visionary, radical concept of freedom. It did provide individual solutions for women, however. It was the same idea of independence perpetuated by the imperial patriarchal state, which equates independence with narcissism and lack of concern with triumph over others. In this way, women active in feminist movement were simply inverting the dominant ideology of the culture; they were not attacking it. They were not presenting practical alternatives to the status quo. In fact, even the statement "men are the enemy" was basically an inversion of the male supremacist doctrine that "women are the enemy"— the old Adam and Eve version of reality.

In retrospect, it is evident that the emphasis on "man as enemy" deflected attention away from improving relationships between women and men, ways for men and women to work together to unlearn sexism. Bourgeois women active in feminist movement exploited the notion of a natural polarization between the sexes to draw attention to equal rights effort. They had an enormous investment in depicting the male as enemy and the female as victim. They were the group of women who could dismiss their ties with men once they had an equal share in class privilege. They were ultimately more concerned with obtaining an equal share in class privilege than with the struggle to eliminate sexism and sexist oppression. Their insistence on separating from men heightened the sense that they, as women without men, needed equality of opportunity. Most women do not have the freedom to separate from men because of economic interdependence. The separatist notion that women could resist sexism by withdrawing from contact with men reflected a bourgeois class perspective. In Cathy McCandless's essay "Some Thoughts about Racism, Classism, and Separatism," she makes the point that separatism is in many ways a false issue because "in this capitalist economy, none of us are truly separate." However, she adds,

> Socially, it's another matter entirely. The richer you are, the less you generally have to acknowledge those you depend upon. Money can buy you a great deal of distance. Given enough of it, it is even possible never to lay eyes upon a man. It's a wonderful luxury, having control over who you lay eyes on, but let's face it: most women's daily survival still involves face-to-face contact with men whether they like it or not. It seems to me that for this reason alone, criticizing women who associate with men not only tends to be counterproductive; it borders on blaming the victim. Particularly if the women taking it upon themselves to set the standards are white and upper or middle class (as has often been the case in my experience) and those to whom they apply these rules are not.

Devaluing the real necessities of life that compel many women to remain in contact with men, as well as not respecting the desire of women to keep contact with men, created an unnecessary conflict of interest for those women who might have been very interested in feminism but felt they could not live up to the politically correct standards.

Feminist writings did not say enough about ways women could directly engage in feminist struggle in subtle, day-to-day contacts with men, although they have addressed crises. Feminism is politically relevant to the masses of women who daily interact with men both publicly and privately, if it addresses ways that interaction, which usually has negative components because sexism is so all-pervasive, can be changed. Women who have daily contact with men need useful strategies that will enable them to integrate feminist movement into their daily life. By inadequately addressing or failing to address the difficult issues, contemporary feminist movement located itself on the periphery of society rather than at the center. Many women and men think feminism is happening, or happened, "out there." Television tells them the "liberated" woman is an exception, that she is primarily a careerist. Commercials like the one that shows a white career woman shifting from work attire to flimsy clothing exposing flesh, singing all the while, "I can bring home the bacon, fry it up in the pan, and never let you forget you're a man" reaffirm that her careerism will not prevent her from assuming the stereotyped sex object role assigned women in male supremacist society.

Often men who claim to support women's liberation do so because they believe they will benefit by no longer having to assume specific, rigid sex roles they find negative or restrictive. The role they are most willing and eager to change is that of economic provider. Commercials like the one described above assure men that women can be breadwinners or even "the" breadwinner, but still allow men to dominate them. Carol Hanisch's essay "Men's Liberation" explores the attempt by these men to exploit women's issues to their own advantage, particularly those issues related to work:

> Another major issue is the attempt by men to drop out of the work force and put their women to work supporting them. Men don't like their jobs, don't like the rat race, and don't like having a boss. That's what all the whining about being a "success symbol" or "success object" is really all about. Well, women don't like those things either, especially since they get paid 40% less than men for working, generally have more boring jobs, and rarely are even allowed to be "successful." But for women working is usually the only way to achieve some equality and power in the family, in their relationship with men, some independence. A man can quit work and pretty much still remain the master of the household, gaining for himself a lot of free time since the work he does doesn't come close to what his wife or lover does. In most cases, she's still doing more than her share of the housework in addition to wife work and her job. Instead of fighting to make his job better, to end the rat race, and to get rid of bosses, he sends his woman to work—not much different from the old practice of buying a substitute for the draft, or even pimping. And all in the name of breaking down "role stereotypes" or some such nonsense.

Such a "men's liberation movement" could only be formed in reaction to women's liberation in an attempt to make feminist movement serve the opportunistic interests of individual men. These men identified themselves as victims of sexism, working to liberate men. They identified rigid sex roles as the primary source of their victimization, and though they wanted to change the notion of masculinity, they were not particularly concerned with their sexist exploitation and oppression of women. Narcissism and general self-pity characterized men's liberation groups. Hanisch concludes her essay with the statement,

> Women don't want to pretend to be weak and passive. And we don't want phony, weak, passive acting men any more than we want phony supermen full of bravado and little else. What women want is for men to be honest. Women want men to be bold—boldly honest, aggressive in their human pursuits. Boldly passionate, sexual and sensual. And women want this for themselves. It's time men became boldly radical. Daring to go to the root of their own exploitation and seeing that it is not women or "sex roles" or "society" causing their unhappiness, but capitalists and capitalism. It's time men dare to name and fight these, their real exploiters.

Men who have dared to be honest about sexism and sexist oppression, who have chosen to assume responsibility for opposing and resisting it, often find themselves isolated. Their politics are disdained by antifeminist men and women, and are often ignored by women active in feminist movement. Writing about his efforts to publicly support feminism in a local newspaper in Santa Cruz, Morris Conerly explains,

> Talking with a group of men, the subject of Women's Liberation inevitably comes up. A few laughs, snickers, angry mutterings, and denunciations follow. There is a group consensus that men are in an embattled position and must close ranks against the assaults of misguided females. Without fail, someone will solicit me for my view, which is that I am 100% for Women's Liberation. That throws them for a loop and they start staring at me as if my eyebrows were crawling with lice.
> They're thinking, "What kind of man is he?" I am a black man who understands that women are not my enemy. If I were a white man with a position of power, one could understand the reason for defending the status quo. Even then, the defense of a morally bankrupt doctrine that exploits and oppresses others would be inexcusable.

Conerly stresses that it was not easy for him to publicly support feminist movement, that it took time:

Why did it take me some time? Because I was scared of the negative reaction I knew would come my way by supporting Women's Liberation. In my mind I could hear it from the brothers and sisters. "What kind of man are you?" "Who's wearing the pants?" "Why are you in that white shit?" And on and on. Sure enough the attacks came as I had foreseen but by that time my belief was firm enough to withstand public scorn.

With growth there is pain . . . and that truism certainly applied in my case.

Men who actively struggle against sexism have a place in feminist movement. They are our comrades. Feminists have recognized and supported the work of men who take responsibility for sexist oppression—men's work with batterers, for example. Those women's liberationists who see no value in this participation must rethink and reexamine the process by which revolutionary struggle is advanced. Individual men tend to become involved in feminist movement because of the pain generated in relationships with women. Usually a woman friend or companion has called attention to their support of male supremacy. Jon Snodgrass introduces the book he edited, *For Men against Sexism*, by telling readers,

> While there were aspects of women's liberation which appealed to men, on the whole my reaction was typical of men. I was threatened by the movement and responded with anger and ridicule. I believed that men and women were oppressed by capitalism, but not that women were oppressed by men. I argued that "men are oppressed too" and that it's workers who need liberation! I was unable to recognize a hierarchy of inequality between men and women (in the working class) nor to attribute it to male domination. My blindness to patriarchy I now think, was a function of my male privilege. As a member of the male gender case, I either ignored or suppressed women's liberation.
>
> My full introduction to the women's movement came through a personal relationship. . . . As our relationship developed, I began to receive repeated criticism for being sexist. At first I responded, as part of the male backlash, with anger and denial. In time, however, I began to recognize the validity of the accusation, and eventually even to acknowledge the sexism in my denial of the accusations.

Snodgrass participated in the men's consciousness-raising groups and edited the book of readings in 1977. Toward the end of the 1970s, interest in male antisexist groups declined. Even though more men than ever before support the idea of social equality for women, like women they do not see this support as synonymous with efforts to end sexist oppression, with feminist movement that would radically transform society. Men who advocate feminism as a movement to end sexist oppression must become more vocal and public in their opposition to sexism and sexist oppression. Until men share equal responsibility for struggling to end sexism, feminist movement will reflect the very sexist contradiction we wish to eradicate.

 Separatist ideology encourages us to believe that women alone can make feminist revolution—we cannot. Since men are the primary agents maintaining and supporting sexism and sexist oppression, they can be successfully eradicated only if men are compelled to assume responsibility for transforming their consciousness and the consciousness of society as a whole. After hundreds of years of antiracist struggle, more than ever before nonwhite people are currently calling attention to the primary role white people must play in antiracist struggle. The same is true of the struggle to eradicate sexism: men have a primary role to play. This does not mean that they are better equipped to lead feminist movement; it does mean that they should share equally in resistance struggle. In particular, men have a tremendous contribution to make to feminist struggle in the area of exposing, confronting, opposing, and transforming the sexism of their male peers. When men show a willingness to assume equal responsibility in feminist struggle, performing whatever tasks are necessary, women should affirm their revolutionary work by acknowledging them as comrades in struggle.

REFERENCES

Angelou, Maya. 1983. Interview. In *Black Women Writers at Work*, edited by Claudia Tate. New York: Continuum.

Hanisch, Carol. 1975. "Men's Liberation." In *Feminist Revolution*, 60–63. New Paltz, NY: Redstockings.

Hornacek, Paul. 1977. "Anti-Sexist Consciousness-Raising Groups for Men." In *A Book of Readings for Men against Sexism*, edited by Jon Snodgrass. Albion: Times Change Press.

Leon, Barbara. 1975. "Separate to Integrate." In *Feminist Revolution*, 139–44. New Paltz, NY: Redstockings.

McCandless, Cathy. 1979. "Some Thoughts about Racism, Classism, and Separatism." In *Top Ranking*, edited by Joan Gibbs and Sara Bennett, 105–15. New York: February Third Press.

"Redstocking Manifesto." 1970. In *Voices from Women's Liberation*, edited by
Leslie B. Tanner, 109. New York: Signet, NAL.

Smith, Barbara. 1979. "Notes for Yet Another Paper on Black Feminism, Or Will
the Real Enemy Please Stand Up." *Conditions: Five* 2 (2): 123–27.

Snodgrass, Jon, ed. 1977. *For Men against Sexism*. Albion: Times Change Press.

Part IV

Profeminist Men's Groups Working toward Meaningful Change

The American culture is at its base racist, classist, sexist, and homophobic. It teaches that competition, aggressiveness, and even violence are acceptable ways to get what one wants. These messages are especially targeted at young men, who are taught at an early age to objectify "things"—the weak, women, and even nature—so that they can be exploited and used in the pursuit of personal gratification and material success. To justify such a superior status, ideological tools are always necessary to view others as lesser, subordinate, and not as worthy. More and more people today are beginning to realize that these attitudes and patterns of behavior are incompatible with a just society and in all probability the survival of our planet.

If men wish to break this pattern of oppression, exploitation, and violence against others and the planet itself, they must first examine their own attitudes, values, and behaviors in both their private and public lives that sustain such outcomes. While a man can understand sexism by reading and study, this goal is perhaps more effectively achieved by joining one of many men's discussion groups. It is important that men assume responsibility for their own role in perpetuating the preexisting system of oppression and violence, and make a commitment to alter their own behaviors that help make such patterns possible. Focusing discussions on how men are also oppressed by the system, while true, does not lead to significant social change.

Consciousness raising without corresponding social action does little to remedy injustice and oppression. New knowledge or awareness devoid of innovative action is one of the worst forms of complicity. Moreover, this means not only changing one's own behaviors but also questioning the actions of other men and holding them accountable when others are harmed by them. Men must break the silence; they must speak out against the oppression and violence that result from institutionalized sexism. Often this begins at the personal level: speaking to coworkers about sexual harassment, talking with one's son about alternatives to objectification and violence, or pointing out sexist advertising to a local business.

Many men fear being labeled "wimpy," weak, or a loser if they fail to act like "real men." Having empathy, expressing an emotional commitment to those seen as lesser, and demonstrating a willingness to act in ways not predicated on others' denial do make one vulnerable. But to adopt such positions an individual must be quite strong and passionately brave; ultimately he would be a "winner" in a system no longer based on oppression. Men of all ages need role models who demonstrate alternative ways of being in the world not based on aggression and exploitation. Adult men, in both their words and actions, can serve as mentors to teens, teaching them affirming, involved parenting skills and nonviolent ways of resolving family problems. Men can talk to other men about the tremendous harm done by rape, sexual harassment, prostitution, and pornography (pictorials that socialize and support such destructive behaviors). Men who wish to no longer be part of the problem must learn that the only way to be part of the solution is by adopting new, nonoppressive ways of acting and speaking out to other men.

The men's groups described below are only a small sample of the many organized efforts men are undertaking to reduce sexism and violence toward women in their local communities. These groups differ in size, objectives, and funding, but each is guided by feminist principles and is primarily involved in working with other men. Some are established agencies working with male perpetrators of violence against women, while others focus primarily on individual consciousness raising and increasing community awareness. Each, however, in its own way is vitally important to the construction of larger feminist realities. We offer the following as a list of potential resources for those wishing to establish similar groups or programs in their community. Let's begin the work together. Let's make the necessary changes happen for the benefit of everyone.

The National Organization for Men Against Sexism

Robert Brannon and Michael Kimmel

The National Organization for Men Against Sexism (NOMAS) is a national organization with an unusually broad range of goals and values devoted to achieving a gender-just society. The organization grew out of a series of feminist-inspired writings and conferences in the early 1970s exploring men's relationships to feminism, and has developed a coherent set of principles about gender and inequality. Today, NOMAS sponsors a wide variety of activities, from publications and conferences to demonstrations and organizations.

A Brief History

Men's support of women's struggle for equality has a long, if little-known, history. With the beginning of the second wave of American feminism, explicitly antisexist men's groups and writings began to appear around 1970. The first National Conference on Men and Masculinity (M&M) was held in Knoxville, Tennessee, organized by male graduate students who had met in a women's studies class. The next year, Robert Lewis issued a call for the second conference with these themes: "To explore basic assumptions about power, to see the political as personal; to confront basic cultural phobias about race, sex, and class; to get in touch with the strength and beauty of our sexuality; to ask for and receive nurturance from other men; to experience brotherhood." This idealism was met head-on by the realities of sexual politics. Less than a week before the conference was to begin, it was banished from the university campus when an administrator noticed a workshop on "homophobia" included in the program. The conference was moved to a nearby hotel.

National M&M conferences have been held annually since 1975, and NOMAS has also supported numerous regional and local conferences. In 1982 the antisexist men's movement was formalized as the National Organization for Men. This name was later changed to the National Organization for Changing Men; in 1990 the organization took its current name.

In part, these changes of name encapsulate the efforts on the part of "profeminist" men to clearly define their politics with regard to women's liberation, men's issues, and gay and lesbian issues. The organization's original name was abandoned because a group supporting "men's rights" had already begun to use it to promote antifeminist ideas. NOCM differentiated the organization from "all" men, and stressed that its members were involved in the process of change and promoting change. But still the direction of change was unclear. NOMAS makes clear the organization's commitment to women's equality and its principled stance against sexism.

Principles

NOMAS stands for three coequal principles:

1. full and active support for the feminist movement and women's full equality in all areas;
2. opposition to heterosexism and homophobia, and support for full equality for gay men and lesbians; and
3. support and brotherhood with men who are challenging the rigid definitions of masculinity and seeking to live richer and more fully expressive emotional lives.

NOMAS is also opposed to discrimination based on race, religion, size, appearance, physical ability, and other human variations; we see these unjust distinctions as linked to the inequality that is intrinsic to patriarchy.

Membership

Although NOMAS is an organization for men against sexism, it is not exclusively an organization *of* men. NOMAS has always welcomed women members, and has always included feminist women in its national leadership. There are currently three women in the NOMAS National Leadership Collective, including one of the organization's cochairs. There are also provisions that encourage the representation of minority members; there are currently four people of color in the Leadership Collective.

For further information, contact:
Michael Kimmel
Department of Sociology
State University of New York at Stony Brook
Stony Brook, NY 11794

The University of New Hampshire's Men's Discussion Group on Stopping Rape

John R. Kraft

The Men's Discussion Group on Stopping Rape at the University of New Hampshire comprises several men who come together to share everything they have learned about sexual assault and ways to reduce the prevalence of sexual assault. The Men's Discussion Group on Stopping Rape is sponsored by the Sexual Harassment and Rape Prevention Program (SHARPP) at the University of New Hampshire. Because SHARPP is a campus organization and we are under the auspices of SHARPP, we are permitted to hold meetings in the Student Union and advertise in the student newspaper. SHARPP also has one of their staff cofacilitate the meeting and supplies some basic resources (e.g., announcement fliers). Although the current cofacilitators of the group have had specialized training in the feminist understanding of sexual assault, this is by coincidence only. All the group members, including the cofacilitators, view this group as a grassroots organization, and everyone volunteers their time and energy to make it work. Meetings are held once every three weeks and are open to men only. Because we want to receive essential feedback from women and ensure that our discussion is consistent with women's experiences, every third meeting is open to both women and men. Each member of the group has the responsibility to facilitate a discussion and choose a topic that will help us contribute to a rape-free society. Examples of topics discussed this year are consent in sexual relations; objectification of women by men; things feminists say that sound extreme but are not; causes of rape; and pornography.

Mission Statement

We, the men involved with the Men's Discussion Group on Stopping Rape, view our group as a catalyst for action on both the individual and group level. As a group we may find it necessary to act as a whole to promote awareness and create social change, and as individuals we are to speak and act in ways consistent with stopping rape. Our primary focus is to combat sexual assault and other forms of violence against women. In order to achieve clarity on sexual assault we will need to address all forms of male sexism. Sexual assault does not happen in isolation from other forms of sexism and sexual violence. Sexual assault is one behavior on a continuum of behaviors by which men dominate women. Our goals are to cooperate with women (especially feminists) who are already working toward a rape-free society. As men, we realize that much has already been said and done by women (especially feminists) and that we need to be consistent with their efforts. We as men realize that certain ways of being male perpetuate a rape-prone society and that we need to confront our own behaviors as well as other men's behaviors. Just because we discuss issues surrounding sexual assault, we are not immune from being complicit in rape. We examine how we have become complicit in a rape-prone society and how we will contribute actively to a rape-free society. By concentrating on men raping women, we do not mean to discount the experiences of men who have been raped by men or women or women who have been raped by women. But because men raping women is by far the most frequent occurrence we are dedicated to taking action on this form of rape. We hope that anything learned in preventing men from raping women is helpful and useful to prevent rapes involving other perpetrators and victims.

Meetings of the Men's Discussion Group on Stopping Rape are to run according to the following guiding principles:

1. We come together with a common goal—to discuss and learn how to counter sexual assault and other forms of male sexism.
2. All views in support of the common goal are welcome and deserve to be expressed in our discussions.
3. Most of what we discuss will be emotional, and these emotions deserve to be expressed in our discussion.
4. Our best thoughts and feelings will promote vigorous discussion and not divisiveness. Every effort should be made to push arguments past ideological differences to attain the common goal.
5. Many topics of the discussion will be challenging at a personal as well as a political level. When faced with an ideological challenge, discussion members should be assisted in overcoming impediments to confronting their own sexism. None of the members of this group should be made to feel unwelcome because they are not as far along in their antisexism development as others.
6. No one is believed to have arrived at the paramount of antisexism. It is a lifelong pursuit of personal learning and action.
7. On a regular basis the Men's Discussion Group on Stopping Rape should be open to both men and women. Regular open meetings with women in attendance will insure that our discussions are consistent with and supportive of women's experiences.

The Men's Discussion Group on Stopping Rape is shaped by what feminists have had to say about sexual assault and the sexism that supports a rape-prone society. One of the basic assumptions of our group is that rape is the result of men's behavior and if rape is to become less frequent or eradicated, it must be men who change. We, the men of the group, accept that it is our responsibility to stop sexual assault. Moreover, we realize that it is not enough for the men in this group to just talk among ourselves about stopping rape. If our discussions do not affect how we discuss sexual assault and our other behaviors outside the confines of the meeting, then the discussion is useless. The goal of the discussion is not just a prowomen understanding of sexual assault, but more important, action in the form of speaking out and acting out against cultural practices that support rape. We realize that first, we must change our own behaviors because we too are products of a rape-prone society, and second, change the pro-rape behaviors of other men by speaking out.

For further information, contact:
John R. Kraft
UNH Men's Discussion Group on Stopping Rape
Graduate Student
Durham, NH 03824

RAVEN (Rape And Violence End Now)

Founded nearly twenty years ago as an organization to address men's violence toward women, the agency began as a male collective to offer support for men wishing to change their behavior. The RAVEN Program is administered by SLOCM (St. Louis Organization for Changing Men).

RAVEN's mission is to provide educational programs that help men become nonviolent, assume personal responsibility, and behave respectfully.

The following are RAVEN's core beliefs, which were approved and adopted by SLOCM board resolution on November 21, 1995: we are committed to ending societal violence; we are committed to ending men's violence, abuse, and battering; we believe that everyone has a right to personal and bodily integrity; we are committed to respecting each person's experience; we believe that people are responsible for their behaviors and that they are capable of changing them; and we advocate gender justice and peaceful masculinity.

Five years ago women became part of the volunteer force and today are a presence in every area of the RAVEN workforce, from the volunteer educators to the supervisor of direct services (who also directs a shelter for battered women in Rolla, MO) and members of the board. It is our belief that men need to see respectful interaction between men and women modeled in classes and group. It is important that we practice what we preach.

All educators whether they are working with men on site or giving prevention education talks in the community are volunteers who are battered women's advocates, former program members, and professionals from the social helping agencies.

Volunteers attend eleven hours of a joint training sponsored by the MCADV (Missouri Coalition Against Domestic Violence). There is a further RAVEN-specific training of approximately thirty hours, which includes fifteen hours of auditing the educational sessions and participating in post-session debriefings.

Fees for services are on a sliding scale. Support for our nonprofit agency comes from state grants from the Department of Family Services and public donations. Regular contact is maintained with probation and parole, the courts, and other services advocating on behalf of battered women.

The specific service offered by RAVEN is nonviolence education offered weekly to our clients as well as formal presentations and informal talks about domestic violence prevention to schools, religious institutions, chemical dependency programs, and penal institutions. The on-site educational program is fifty-two units, each one and a half hours long; the program is composed of twelve units of class and forty units of group. The basis for the class lectures is the RAVEN class material, which studies gender, oppression, definitions of violence and abuse (which include the experience of the survivors or victims), family of origin, feelings, nonviolence awareness, nonviolent parenting or modeling of peaceful masculinity, assertiveness, and self-esteem.

The basis for the group work is the Duluth curriculum from Duluth, Minnesota, which provides videos and written materials to stimulate reflection, role playing, and group discussion.

In beginning a program for men who are abusive, organizers must get a sense of the local community's determination to deal with domestic violence. This knowledge should be incorporated in the planning of a new program. For programs already in existence, movement toward coordination of community resources is extremely important for ensuring the program's effectiveness.

Program effectiveness has traditionally been difficult to monitor out of concern for partner safety as well as insufficient staffing. The men with whom the educational intervention appears to leave lasting effects are the ones who remain involved in the work in some service capacity. RAVEN has begun to assist Provident Counseling, a local mental health provider, with monthly groups for Hispanic men. RAVEN also hopes to be able to offer groups for gay men who batter.

For further information, contact:
Mark Moloney and Mary Sue Guenther
RAVEN (Rape And Violence End Now)
7314 Manchester, 2nd Floor
St. Louis, MO 63143
(573)364-6579

Men Against Pornography

We want to help create sexual justice, and we believe that pornography stands in the way of it. We see pornography as a key element in the oppression of women. And we see that one way pornography works is by manipulating men's sexuality.

Many men have learned a lot from pornography about what sex is supposed to be, what women are supposed to be, and what we're supposed to be as men. Pornography gives men false ideas and expectations about women's sexual nature; it implies that women want men to possess and dominate them. Pornography also encourages us to "get off" by putting women down, so it gives us a false notion of our own natures as well.

We know that lies can be very difficult to face if they also turn you on. But we know that sexual equality will never exist until men develop the skills and courage to challenge the lies that pornography makes us believe.

We want to help men confront what pornography really is and what it really does. We want to encourage men to examine their sexual relationship to pornography. We want to enable and encourage men to become involved in the struggle to end sexual oppression.

Our group was founded in New York City in 1984. Originally we conducted a workshop with groups consisting primarily of men. Inspired by a viewing of a Women Against Pornography slide show ("Try to imagine men in these poses," it says at one point), cofounder John Stoltenberg devised a guided, experiential exercise in which several men are selected at random out of the group and each given a magazine such as *Penthouse, Playboy,* or *Hustler;* then they are told to "do the pose" in a designated photograph. While these men are struggling into their assigned poses, the rest of the workshop participants (which may include women) are invited to go from pose to pose comparing each one to the picture it was based on and to call out comments about how to get the pose more accurate in terms of body position and facial expression. After this is done at each of the poses, the group reassembles in small groups to talk about how it felt to do the pose or how it felt to be a spectator.

Our purpose was to reach men, to help them see the real situation of women in the pictures in men's magazines, in order to understand viscerally that what's "sexy" in pornography has a lot to do with the subordination of women. Once men experience for themselves how thoroughly inauthentic those images in the men's magazines are—how they have nothing to do with any honest kind of eroticism—men seemed a little more ready to deal with pornography in their lives; they seemed more able to hear and understand what women have been saying about the lies pornography tells.

After the Men Against Pornography "pose workshop" was written up in *Ms.* magazine, we were featured on several local and national television shows. John Stoltenberg wrote a complete description of how the workshop works, including a how-to guide for facilitating it, in a book called *What Makes Pornography "Sexy"?* (Minneapolis: Milkweed Editions, 1994).

For many years we have protested the annual *Sports Illustrated* "swimsuit issue" because we believe that for male consumers, there is a connection between this publication and the values in pornography, a connection with negative consequences for women's civil equality. Often joined by members of Women Against Pornography and the New York City chapter of the National Organization for Women, we have mounted demonstrations outside the headquarters of the publisher, Time Warner, on the day the "swimsuit issue" goes on sale. We wrote and circulated widely a list called "The Top 10 Ways Sports Illustrated Disrespects Women" (available on the Web at http://www.talkintrash.com/ sports-illustrated/SportsIll10.html), and in 1996 we initiated a boycott against Time Warner, described at a Web site titled "America Says No to the Sports Illustrated 'Swimsuit Issue' " (http://members.aol.com/fair sport/si/).

From our beginnings, we have been inspired by, and have endeavored to maintain formal and informal lines of communication with, those feminists who are accountable to people who are harmed in and through pornography and prostitution. From what we have learned in this process, we drafted and circulated a general principle of accountability for profeminist men's activism against pornography and prostitution (available at http://www. geocities.com/CapitotHill/5863/poa.html).

Our most recent project is *Quitting Pornography: Men Speak Out about How They Did It—And Why,* an online anthology of first-person stories from a wide range of contributors. (It is available on the Men Against Pornography Web site, http://www.geocities.com/CapitolHill/1139). Other actions over the years have included an *amicus* brief we joined in support of the Dworkin-MacKinnon antipornography civil rights ordinance; street demonstrations against a local Playboy Club, a Playboy press party, and a local sports-themed strip club; a workshop devised by cofounder Dexter Guerrieri titled "Speakout on Masturbation"; and a protest against American Express, which had authorized use of its credit card for phone sex, brothels, and escort services.

We have remained a small, dedicated group, meeting regularly to discuss and plan our various actions and projects. We are aware that many of the ideas we have initiated have been picked up and put to creative use by other activists. We are proud to have played a part in helping to make visible, from a feminist worldview, the political and personal effects that pornography has on its target consumers, men. We have been pleased to hear of other action-oriented groups that have formed, calling themselves some version of Men Against Pornography, and we hope that by our example we can continue to encourage others to confront the pornography industry's role in maintaining and eroticizing male supremacy.

For further information, contact:
Men Against Pornography
P.O. Box 150786
Brooklyn, NY 11215-0786
home page: http://www.geocities.com/CapitolHill/1139
email: map-usa@geocities.com

The Mentors in Violence Prevention (MVP) Program

Jackson Katz

In 1972 Miller Brewing Company bought the rights to Meister Brau Light, a beer that the small Chicago brewery had been attempting to market to women as a diet beer. Not surprisingly, the effort had failed. Still, Miller's market research had shown that beer drinkers would welcome a beer that didn't fill them up, but men didn't want to drink a beer that could be seen as "feminine."

So Miller had a problem, because in 1972, much more so than in the late 1990s, concern with calories was seen as a decidedly "feminine" preoccupation, and in the early seventies men comprised an overwhelming percentage of the beer market. Their solution was to initiate an ad campaign that featured a series of macho football players and other sports icons, with Dick Butkus and Bubba Smith among the first cohort. They placed these football stars in a crowded bar, surrounded them with their buddies, and put a Lite beer in their hands. (They also made sure there were hegemonically attractive women walking by, for any number of reasons.)

The message: Dick Butkus and Bubba Smith can drink light beer, and no one is going to accuse them of being wimps; you can, too. The result was that the Miller Lite television commercials became the most celebrated ads in TV history, winning Clio awards for advertising excellence nearly annually in the 1970s. Today, Miller Lite is the official beer of the National Football League.

This stunning shift came about because some savvy marketers nearly three decades ago figured that men would change their gendered behavior if given "permission" to do so by men with more status in the masculine hierarchy. In other words, if men in positions of cultural leadership would take risks and model new ways of being male, large numbers of men were likely to respond in turn by changing their attitudes and attendant behaviors (albeit, in this case, consumer behaviors).

The idea that men with traditionally "masculine" credibility can help revise the very definition of what it means to be masculine is directly related to the rationale behind the Mentors in Violence Prevention (MVP) Program, which was founded in 1993 at Northeastern University's Center for the Study of Sport in Society. The multiracial MVP Program is the first nationwide attempt to enlist male high school and college student-athletes in the fight against rape, battering, sexual harassment, and all forms of men's violence against women.

This leadership model of gender violence prevention derives from the idea, developed over the past generation by theorists and activists in the feminist anti-rape and anti-battering movements, that cultural attitudes that support rape and battering serve both to encourage men's violence against women and to disregard and even blame women victimized by assaultive males. A key premise of MVP is that male student-athletes can help delegitimize rape-supportive and battering-supportive attitudes by publicly repudiating the sexist, domination-oriented definitions of masculinity that reinforce them. Because male athletes, particularly those who are successful in the sports of football, basketball, hockey, lacrosse, wrestling, and baseball, are exemplars of manly success for many young males, others' perceptions of these athletes' attitudes toward women help to produce and shape the norms of male behavior.

The key teaching tool utilized in MVP sessions is the *Playbook,* which consists of a series of school-based, party, and residence hall scenarios involving actual and potential assaults against women. The subject matter in these scenarios ranges from sexist comments overheard in the locker room to verbal threats of physical harm, to date rape and gang rape. MVP workshop leaders make it clear that all of these are related; we also discuss the relationship between sexism and heterosexism. *Playbook* scenarios include a potential gay-bashing incident and the harassment of a lesbian couple.

MVP sessions are held, when possible, with single-sex groups, including teams and fraternities, although we have worked in high schools and middle schools with mostly mixed-gender classes and student organizations. The sessions themselves are highly interactive, with trainers encouraging young men and women to share experiences they've had, in high school or college, that are similar to the ones included in the *Playbook.* The *Playbook* scenarios are designed to be as realistic as possible.

The *Playbook* and its various scenarios lead to highly interactive discussions about real-life situations that most men have experienced, or at least known about, in their families, circles of friends, teams, home, or campus communities. MVP staff share stories from our own lives, and encourage the young men to do likewise. We don't argue that encouraging superhero behavior at the point of attack is the way to prevent gender violence. Rather, we use the scenarios as a stepping off point for a larger discussion, allowing us to ask provocative questions and raise relevant issues. For example, why do men hit women? Can a man establish his manhood by physically controlling a woman? What, then, does it mean to be a man? If men who are not abusive don't confront men who are, is their silence part of the problem?

For further information, contact:
    Jackson Katz
    Northwestern University
    Sport In Society
    716 Columbus Avenue
    Rm 161
    Boston, MA 02180

End Violence Now: An Educational Program for Men

EVN is a nonprofit organization of primarily men working with men toward the safety of battered women in all forms. EVN operates from the principles of the battered women's movement. We believe that everyone deserves a violence-free life, and that violence, stalking, and the sexual abuse of women and children are crimes.

EVN was created as a collective to work toward the elimination of all forms of abuse against women and children and to work toward ensuring the safety of battered women and their children. We recognize the many forms that this violence and abuse takes, including sexism, racism, homophobia, ableism, classism, and ageism (to name a few). We strive to both critique and change the existing systems of oppression, while modeling an alternative within our collective.

EVN is directly accountable to the local battered women's shelter in Atlanta, and we call on national leadership in particular when necessary. Our funding comes from (1) fee for service for batterers in our intervention work, (2) private contributions, (3) members of EVN, who work at other jobs and contribute what they can.

We work primarily in three ways: (1) public education with community groups (at the local, national, and international levels) such as churches, schools, and so forth; (2) in-service training and work with other professionals who come in contact with battered women and children (i.e., medical personnel, lawyers, and social service agencies); and (3) direct service to men who admit they have a problem with violence and/or abuse, and who want to change. We serve on various state and local task forces, in collaboration with local shelters, police, prosecutors, and community groups. Our most recent community awareness project was being the state representative to the Silent Witness Initiative.

We do not believe in couples counseling. When one party in a relationship has used violence or abuse to get their way, it is not safe for the victim. Our experience tells us that she can either lie in couples counseling (in which case the counseling is ineffective), or she can tell the truth (in which case she is liable to "pay" for it later). After a man acknowledges his violence and has had a period of nonabusiveness, then couples counseling may be useful.

We believe that men can stop being abusive and violent. In twenty-four weeks, men are given the tools for change. A man's willingness to change and his commitment to doing so are usually what make the difference. We measure effectiveness of this change by a woman's feelings of safety.

To this end, we do what we call "safety checks" during the program and we ask the given woman about the man's behavior. This information is important, but voluntary on her part. The leader will ask her if she feels safe about having the information shared with the group. If she does not feel safe, it will not be shared.

His learning to hear her reality is central to his changing. Ultimately, the question is not whether he has changed, but how the woman feels about him. The central intent of the program is her safety and peace of mind.

We believe that men can be abusive without ever hitting, and that men will often use whatever is necessary to get what they want in a relationship. Men will often try other things first, and use physical abuse only when all else fails. In other words, a man can yell, scream, be silent, isolate his partner, use economics, and so on to get what he wants.

Each member of EVN has been through over eight years of training. The program director is a licenced clinical psychologist, and the group's leaders have B.A.'s, some with graduate training. All members have been through the program as participants. We offer internships that run approximately six months to men wanting to learn how to replicate our work. All members are required to make a commitment to women's safety and to live nonviolently.

For further information, contact:
John Hokanson
End Violence Now
P.O. Box 3321
Lilburn, GA 30226-3321
(770)717-9447

manalive Education and Research Institute (MERI)

MERI is a nonprofit organization working to end men's violence against women. Established by *manalive*, a network of community-based batterer intervention programs organized by men for men, it conducts training, education, and research beyond the scope of the local batterer intervention programs. The *manalive* system of batterer interventions was developed by community organizer and educational consultant Hamish Sinclair in 1980 for Marin Abused Women's Services (MAWS), San Rafael, California, in response to women's experience of violence and their urgent need for it to stop. *manalive* programs are a unique combination of peer-based reeducation and community advocacy based on a profeminist sociocultural analysis of men's violence.

During the last sixteen years, over twelve thousand men have attended *manalive* classes. In 1993 *manalive* provided the model for the standards for batterer intervention programs advocated by the California Alliance Against Domestic Violence adopted by the California legislature. Today, local *manalive* programs offer over thirty classes in Northern California, including Spanish-language classes. In addition, there are classes in San Francisco City Sheriff's Department jails and the California State Prison at San Quentin. Numerous intervention programs across the country and in Canada, Scotland, England, Mexico, and Australia have incorporated *manalive* theory and methods into their programs.

Theory

Throughout history men have been violent to their spouses or intimate partners with impunity. Women's advocates propose that such violence is part of the cultural heritage that privileges men over women. From this perspective, men's violence against their intimate partners is the tradition-

ally accepted enforcement of these commonly held beliefs of male superiority. In *manalive* programs this set of assumptions is called the Male-
Role Belief System.

In *manalive* classes men's socialization to view themselves as superior
and obligated by tradition to control and coerce their intimate partners is
directly addressed. The Male-Role Belief System provides an analytical
framework for men to understand the historical nature and dynamics of
relationships between women and men. By focusing attention on socially
conditioned and institutionally supported stereotypes of women and men
and their appropriate roles, it helps men understand how both women
and men measure themselves by these images.

manalive has developed the Theory of Control and Coercion to describe the facets of every violent incident. The controlling attitude meas-
ures everyone and everything against their established role. The coercive
behaviors force others to conform to these roles. Men escalate their coercive behavior from emotional to verbal abuse to physical violence to
achieve their expected level of control. Controlling attitudes and coercive
behaviors are characteristic of many men's relationships outside the
home. When the affirmation of one's superiority is the goal, control and
coercion shape relationships whether they are characterized by gender,
class, race, cultural, or national differences.

Methodology

manalive's basic intervention strategy is group socioeducational classes
in the context of community advocacy programs dedicated to social
change. Because men learn how to be men from other men—fathers,
brothers, teachers, priests, sports figures, friends—and have been shaped
by male-dominated institutions created by men, *manalive* programs are
for men only and are facilitated by men. *manalive's* peer advocacy model
is a very dynamic process in which the ideal of "each one teach one" is
rigorously practiced. All *manalive* staff and volunteers are formerly abusive men who have been through the program and undertaken a rigorous
second-year training program to become facilitators and community advocates.

While women justly fear that men-only programs will collude with a
world that allows men to deny their violence, minimize its impact,
and blame their victims for it, supervised peer groups, similar to this

model, have been shown to be very effective means of changing behavior. As a matter of accountability, *manalive* programs build alliances with local women's shelters or domestic violence coalitions in their communities.

manalive Education and Research Institute

Based on *manalive* theory and methodology, the institute conducts training programs, public education, research, and advocacy projects. MERI trains batterer intervention program staff, violence prevention advocates, and government and social service professionals in the nature and dynamics of male-role violence, the social sources of men's violence, and individual and community intervention methods that address beliefs that continue to sanction the subordination of women.

The goals of the institute are to

- Advocate the importance of a gendered analysis of men's violence based on the experience of women.
- Support a social change approach to ending men's violence, especially violence against women, by engaging men in establishing community intervention and advocacy programs.
- Promote the reeducation, peer-based intervention methods, and community advocacy techniques pioneered by *manalive.*
- Contribute to research on intervention methods that address male-role socialization as a critical factor in men's violence against women.
- Advance a social action research agenda that deepens our understanding of the importance of sociocultural factors in the process of individual and social change.

For further information, contact:
Hamish Sinclair, Executive Director
or JoAnn McAllister, Research Director
manalive Education and Research Institute (MERI)
345 Johnstone Drive
San Rafael, CA 94903
(415)499-1500

Men As Peacemakers

The Men As Peacemakers project is a partnership between the *News-Tribune*, WDSE-TV, and a group of concerned male community leaders. The project grew out of Violence Free Duluth, a community movement begun in the aftermath of a string of brutal murders that hit Duluth in 1993 and 1994.

With an initial $54,000 grant from the Pew Charitable Trust, the partners are encouraging men to get off the sidelines and get involved in reducing violence in their communities. While men are responsible for the majority of violence in their communities, traditionally few men have done much to stop it. Society teaches young people, particularly young males, that violence is acceptable. This group seeks ways to change these messages and reduce the violence in our communities. This program seeks out other men to join in the effort to make our communities safer places to live.

Most Men As Peacemakers members don't have careers related to violence issues. We come from a broad range of beliefs and experiences, willing to work in common to reduce violence. We respect and support the work that has gone before us and we respond as community volunteers out of a deep belief that violence can no longer play such a dominant role in our culture. We have learned that it doesn't take a lot of time to make a difference. We believe men have a special responsibility to help end violence, and Men As Peacemakers supports these efforts.

We link individual men with community organizations that need volunteer help—help mentoring children, comforting victims of violence, teaching nonviolence. We teach other men about the link between men and violence, while discovering ways to live as men without violence. Through education and advocacy, we raise community consciousness about violence and how to end it. We challenge and support each other as we try to live every part of our lives firmly committed to the principles of Men As Peacemakers.

Peacemaking men stand up and say that there is an alternative to violence, and that violence is no longer acceptable. They help children develop the assets they need—positive values, family structure, and role models—to grow up healthy. Peacemaking men resist the sense of powerlessness that violence brings to our community. They know they can't do it alone.

Men As Peacemakers holds regular community meetings to talk about men's role in violence and what men can do about it. We have signed up men to volunteer for organizations as diverse as the YMCA's Friendship Between the Ages, the Boy Scouts, schools, juvenile centers, and Program Aid Victims of Sexual Assault. We are getting hundreds of men publicly committed to Men As Peacemakers' principles; dedicating volunteer hours to community organizations that foster the prevention of violence; and helping one another with education, awareness, and individual support.

In 1996 we worked with the *Duluth News-Tribune* on a groundbreaking series of feature reports on the link between men and violence in our community. WDSE-Public Television and Men As Peacemakers produced a televised town meeting, video documentary, and companion Teacher's Guide on Men and Violence. Men As Peacemakers sponsors an annual Men's March for Peace and lends its support to many other community violence-prevention efforts.

Our vision for the future? By getting men involved, we join with others to reverse the erosion of community that accompanies the rising tide of violence. We will raise much-needed funds for violence-prevention organizations to accompany our volunteer commitments. With our help, the incidence of violence in our community will be reduced in significant and measurable ways.

Community issues that are of concern to Men As Peacemakers include

- Making the streets safe from violent crime.
- Ending child abuse, battering, and domestic violence.
- Providing positive male role models for children and teens.
- Teaching fathers good parenting skills.
- Combating gang activities and negative youth peer pressure.
- Addressing media violence and violence in the popular culture.
- Establishing alcohol treatment programs.
- Addressing the link between playing sports and aggressive behavior.
- Combating hate crimes such as racism, sexism, and homophobia.
- Addressing the underlying causes of violence such as poverty, hopelessness, and despair.

For further information, contact:
Men As Peacemakers
320 West 2nd St., Room 503

Duluth, MN 55802
(218)726-2067

Men's Network for Change (MNC)

The Men's Network for Change was founded by men who had participated in the Grindstone and Kingston Men's Conferences or men's support groups, to create a clear space for profeminism. The first MNC
gathering was in Orangeville in the spring of 1989. There are now MNC
members all over Canada.

Mission Statement

In a society dominated by men, a patriarchal society, men have dispro-
portionate economic, political, and social power over women. But the
very things that give us power exact a price. We are not born patriarchs.
The process that leads us to accept the current norms of masculinity and
the domination of some men over others leaves us all brutalized, limited,
and angry. We usually do not acknowledge our isolation, fear, frustration,
and alienation. Women, children, the planet, and indeed we ourselves
suffer the consequences.

We are men committed to working against sexism and patriarchy, in
support of freedom of sexual orientation, and deeply opposed to the
many forms of violence in the world. We support those social movements
that challenge us to rethink our lives as men and reevaluate our society.
These include the feminist women's movement, the gay, lesbian, and
bisexual movement; antiracist struggles; native people's, peace, ecology,
and labor movements.

We see our actions as part of a struggle against the many forces, institutions, and structures that limit the potential of all human beings. The
equality of women is a crucial step in the creation of a society that embodies human liberation. For us, political action touches all aspects of life:
our actions at home and in the streets, in school, at work, in relationships,
and in the institutions of local and national decision making. The changes
we want in society as a whole are changes we strive to make ourselves.

Our goal is to reach out to other men, to invite them to join us to
create a society where men no longer dominate women; where all humans

can reclaim their full potential; and where men will celebrate our passion, our strength, and our capacity to nurture, to love and be loved. Our goal is to provide a public and collective voice of men in support of women's liberation. Our goal is to continue to support the many movements for progressive change. Our goal is to contribute to changing the lives of men, women, and children and the state of our planet.

Specific MNC Positions

1. Ending men's violence against women, children, and ourselves. Men are not innately violent. Violent behavior is learned, and thus alternatives to violence must be taught and demonstrated. "Men's silence is the oxygen that fuels men's violence" (Ray Jones).
2. Reproductive choice as a woman's right. We want a world in which gender relations are based on equality. We are opposed to any law or practice that gives men control over women's bodies. We fully support women's right to all reproductive choices.
3. Men and children. We, as men, have a responsibility to enhance the nurturing and parenting of our children. Where there are conflicts in parenting arrangements, this responsibility will not be accomplished by legislation imposing mandatory access, mediation, and joint custody. Although it is still necessary, we recognize the limitations of the existing sole custody system for everyone, and strive to find alternative services and solutions that are just and that support children, women, and men.
4. Sexual orientation. Lesbians, gay men, and bisexuals have the right to full participation in our society without discrimination at work, in the home, or in the community. We encourage members to challenge homophobia, and we invite all people to examine their attitudes and behavior concerning sexual orientation and to build relations based on mutual respect.
5. We strongly support funding for programs for violent men that link men's violence to men's domination of women and to the workings of male-dominated societies. To be effective, these programs must aim to enhance men's lives by understanding that the dominant definitions of masculinity are harmful not only to women and children but also men themselves.

For further information, contact:
Ken Fisher
133 avenue des Plages
Pontiac (Luskville) Quebec, JOX 2GO, Canada
(819)455-9295

Contributors

R. W. Connell is a professor of education at the University of Sydney and the author or coauthor of fifteen books, including *Class Structure in Australian History; Making the Difference; Gender and Power; Schools and Social Justice;* and *Masculinities.* He is a past president of the Sociological Association of Australia and New Zealand and a frequent contributor to research journals in sociology, education, political science, gender studies, and related fields.

Riane Eisler is the author of *The Chalice and the Blade: Our History, Our Future*, a fundamental reexamination of Western culture translated into fifteen languages, including Russian, Spanish, Japanese, German, French, and Chinese. Eisler is cofounder of the Center for Partnership Studies (P.O. Box 51936, Pacific Grove, CA 93950, http://www.partnershipway.org), has taught at UCLA and Immaculate Heart College, and is a founding member of the General Evolution Research Group. Her other books include *Sacred Pleasure: Sex, Myth, and the Politics of the Body; The Partnership Way; Women, Men, and the Global Quality of Life; Dissolution,* and *The Equal Rights Handbook.* She has contributed to many anthologies and journals ranging from *Political Psychology*, the *Human Rights Quarterly*, and *Humanities in Society* to the *International Journal of Women's Studies, Futures,* and *Behavioral Science.*

Doris W. Ewing is an associate professor of sociology at Southwest Missouri State University. Her primary areas of research and teaching interest are in race, class, gender, and disability. For many years she has been actively involved with disability and women's nonprofit organizations to bring about positive social change in the community. Her recent scholarship has focused on the issue of feminism and men.

Kay Leigh Hagan is a writer, speaker, activist, and unrepentant feminist. She is the author of *Fugitive Information: Essays from a Feminist Hot-*

head; *Internal Affairs: A Journalkeeping Workbook for Self-Intimacy*; and *Prayers to the Moon: Exercises in Self-Reflection*; and the editor of *Women Respond to the Men's Movement: A Feminist Collection*. Traveling widely to present workshops on self-determination, gender justice, and feminism, she focuses on the politics of personal change with a special concern for understanding how we internalize both oppression and privilege.

bell hooks is Distinguished Professor of English at the City University of New York. She is the author of many books, including *Ain't I a Woman*; *Black Looks*; *Outlaw Culture*; *Teaching to Transgress*; and *Reel to Real*. Her most recent books are *Killing Rage* and *Bone Black*. She writes frequently for such magazines as *Spin*, *Interview*, *Essence*, and *Z*.

Christine A. James is one of the first four Ph.D. candidates in philosophy at the University of South Carolina, where she teaches courses in logic and ethics. She has published articles on feminism, philosophy of masculinity, and irrationality in *disClosure: A Journal of Social Theory* and *Kinesis*.

Robert Jensen is an assistant professor at the University of Texas at Austin, where he teaches journalism and media courses. His research interests include feminist and lesbian/gay issues in media, law, and ethics. He is coeditor of *Freeing the First Amendment: Critical Perspectives on Freedom of Expression* and coauthor of a forthcoming book on pornography.

Michael S. Kimmel is a professor of sociology at State University of New York at Stony Brook. His books include *Changing Men*; *Men's Lives*; *Men Confront Pornography*; *Against the Tide: Profeminist Men in the United States, 1776–1990*; and *Manhood in America: A Cultural History*. He is a spokesperson for the National Organization for Men Against Sexism (NOMAS) and editor for book series on men and masculinity at the University of California Press and Sage. He lectures extensively on campuses here and abroad.

Gary Lemons is an associate professor at the New School for Social Research, where he teaches courses on African American literature and feminist studies. Most recent publications include "Teaching (Bi)racial Space That Has No Name: Reflections of a Black Male Feminist Teacher"; "Young Men, Tell Our Stories of How We Made It Over:

Beyond the Politics of Identity"; "A New Response to Angry Black (Male Anti-) Feminists: Reclaiming Feminist Forefathers, Becoming Womanist Sons"; and " 'When and Where *We* Enter': Reclaiming the Legacy of Black (Male) Feminism: W. E. B. Du Bois and My Search for a *Womanist* Forefather."

Michael A. Messner is an associate professor of sociology and gender studies at the University of Southern California, where he teaches courses on sex and gender, men and masculinity, sexuality, and gender and sport. He is coeditor of *Men's Lives; Sport, Men, and the Gender Order: Critical Feminist Perspectives;* and *Through the Prism of Difference: Readings on Sex and Gender.* He has authored *Power Play: Sports and the Problem of Masculinity; Politics of Masculinities: Men in Movements;* and coauthored *Sex, Violence, and Power in Sports: Rethinking Masculinity.*

Steven P. Schacht is a visiting assistant professor of sociology at Plattsburg State University of New York. His primary areas of research and teaching interest are race, class, gender, and sexuality. In addition to his interests in exploring constructive relationships between men and feminism, he has recently written a statistics textbook (*Social Statistics: A User-Friendly Approach*) and several articles based on his ethnographic experiences with rugby players and female impersonators.

Matthew Shepherd is a postgraduate student who recently completed his Ph.D. dissertation, entitled "Rethinking Masculinity: Discourses of Gender and Power in Two Workplaces." Using Freudian and feminist theories, he found continuity in discourses of masculinity between the academic and manufacturing workplaces studied.

John Stoltenberg, a frequent speaker and workshop leader at colleges and conferences, is the author of *Refusing to Be a Man: Essays on Sex and Justice; The End of Manhood: A Book of Men of Conscience;* and *What Makes Pornography "Sexy"?* He is currently writing a book about the culture of sexual orientation.

Permissions

Chapter 2 reprinted from the *International Journal of Sociology and Social Policy* 17 (1–2) 1997. Copyright © 1996 by Michael S. Kimmel. All rights reserved.

Chapter 3 is a revised version of an article originally appearing in the *International Journal of Sociology and Social Policy* 17 (1–2) 1997. Used by permission of the author.

Chapter 4 is a revised version of a chapter that originally appeared in Michael A. Messner, *Politics of Masculinities: Men in Movements* (1997). Reprinted by permission of Sage Publications, Inc.

Chapter 5 reprinted from the *International Journal of Sociology and Social Policy* 17 (1–2) 1997. Copyright © 1995 by John Stoltenberg. Reprinted by permission.

Chapter 6 reprinted from the *International Journal of Sociology and Social Policy* 17 (1–2) 1997. Used by permission of the author.

Chapter 7 reprinted from the *Journal of Gender Studies* 6(2) 1997. Used by permission of the authors.

Chapter 8 copyright © 1996, 1997 by John Stoltenberg. Used by permission of the author.

Chapter 9 reprinted from the *International Journal of Sociology and Social Policy* 17 (1–2) 1997. Copyright © 1998 by Kay Leigh Hagan. Reprinted by permission.

Chapter 10 reprinted from the *International Journal of Sociology and Social Policy* 17 (1–2) 1997. Used by permission of the author.

Chapter 11 reprinted from the *International Journal of Sociology and Social Policy* 17 (1–2) 1997. Used by permission of the author.